"To control the future, you must cont[rol?] observed. The church's failure to under[stand?] the experiences of women cripples [both?] Christianity. *The Making of Biblical* Womanhood is a p[rofound?] historical examination of patriarchy's impact from the perspective of Christian women. Without this book, we cannot fully know ourselves or our faith."

—**Mimi Haddad**, president of CBE International

"*The Making of Biblical Womanhood* will send shock waves through conservative evangelical Christianity. Powerful personal testimony, a solid handle on the theology and biblical issues at stake in the debate over the role of women in the church, and a historian's understanding of how the past can speak to the present inform Barr's convincing challenge to patriarchy and complementarianism. This book is a game changer."

—**John Fea**, professor, Messiah University

"In this timely, valuable volume—written with pluck and aplomb—Barr shows that 'biblical womanhood' is more a socio-historical construct than a scriptural prescription. I trust this deeply personal and purposely provocative book will be widely and carefully read, especially by those in patriarchal, Protestant evangelical circles who will be tempted to dismiss it out of hand."

—**Todd D. Still**, professor, Baylor University, Truett Seminary

"*The Making of Biblical Womanhood* is an exceptionally thoughtful and valuable contribution to debates in contemporary American religion. Barr combines an autobiographical approach to her topic with exemplary textual and historical scholarship, all presented in admirably lucid writing. The resulting book is at once convincing and moving."

—**Philip Jenkins**, author of *Fertility and Faith: The Demographic Revolution and the Transformation of World Religions*

"I have never lived in the world of complementarianism, but I have seen its damage up close in many students and their churches. Barr's searing report of her own journey makes her account of the bankruptcy of complementarian interpretations of the Bible and church history urgent and compelling. To borrow her conclusion: it's time for this travesty to stop!"

—**Beverly Roberts Gaventa**, professor, Baylor University

"Barr shakes our shallow historical foundations by revealing how much of so-called 'biblical' womanhood reflects the culture rather than Christ. By taking us through her own heartbreaking journey of exclusion from her faith community, she demonstrates the temerity that we need to live the simple, yet disruptive truth that all women and men are created in the image of God."

—Jemar Tisby, CEO of The Witness Inc.; *New York Times* bestselling author of *The Color of Compromise*

"This is a book unlike anything I've read before. Drawing on her extensive research into the history of Christianity, Barr upends everything you thought you knew about Christianity and gender."

—**Kristin Kobes Du Mez**, professor, Calvin University; author of *Jesus and John Wayne*

"*The Making of Biblical Womanhood* has done in one volume what many other books in recent years have done in part: it demonstrates that so-called biblical womanhood is not actually biblical. Though Barr explores and analyzes church history and theology in this well-researched book, it is no boring academic tome. She weaves together personal narrative to remind readers of the humanity of this issue too. I have waited my entire adult life for a book like this, and I am excited that it has finally arrived."

—**Jonathan Merritt**, contributing writer for *The Atlantic*; author of *Learning to Speak God from Scratch*

"I love how Barr's expertise in medieval church history contributes to the discussion of women in the church. While I may not align completely with Barr's argument, I affirm with her the need to acknowledge the different ways women have led in church history and should now. I affirm with her that Christ calls women in his church to teach. And I affirm with her that so-called complementarianism isn't the only option, or even a good one, for those who uphold the authority of Scripture. I'm glad she wrote it."

—**Aimee Byrd**, author of *Recovering from Biblical Manhood and Womanhood* and *No Little Women*

"*The Making of Biblical Womanhood* is a journey into the sometimes pained, sometimes joyous heart of Barr's own story but also into the secret rooms of a conservative Christian doctrine of 'biblical womanhood' that is no more biblical than choir robes or three-point sermons, or Christian nationalism. The number of mistaken theological interpretations present in evangelical complementarianism Barr exposes are too many to count. I could not put this book down."

—**Scot McKnight**, professor, Northern Seminary

The Making of

Biblical

Womanhood

How the Subjugation of Women
Became Gospel Truth

BETH ALLISON BARR

Brazos Press
a division of Baker Publishing Group
Grand Rapids, Michigan

Published by Brazos Press
a division of Baker Publishing Group
PO Box 6287, Grand Rapids, MI 49516-6287
www.brazospress.com

Printed in the United States of America

Library of Congress Cataloging-in-Publication Data
Names: Barr, Beth Allison, 1975– author.
Title: The making of biblical womanhood : how the subjugation of women became gospel truth / Beth Allison Barr.
Description: Grand Rapids, Michigan : Brazos Press, a division of Baker Publishing Group, [2021] | Includes bibliographical references.
Identifiers: LCCN 2020037130 | ISBN 9781587434709 (paperback) | ISBN 9781587435348 (casebound)
Subjects: LCSH: Women—Religious aspects—Christianity—History of doctrines. | Sex role—Religious aspects—Christianity—History of doctrines. | Women—Biblical teaching. | Sex role—Biblical teaching.
Classification: LCC BT704 .B375 2021 | DDC 220.8/30542—dc23
LC record available at https://lccn.loc.gov/2020037130

Unless otherwise indicated, Scripture quotations are from the New Revised Standard Version of the Bible, copyright © 1989 National Council of the Churches of Christ in the United States of America. Used by permission. All rights reserved.

Scripture quotations labeled ESV are from The Holy Bible, English Standard Version® (ESV®), copyright © 2001 by Crossway, a publishing ministry of Good News Publishers. Used by permission. All rights reserved. ESV Text Edition: 2016

Scripture quotations labeled KJV are from the King James Version of the Bible.

Scripture quotations labeled NIV are from THE HOLY BIBLE, NEW INTERNATIONAL VERSION®, NIV® Copyright © 1973, 1978, 1984, 2011 by Biblica, Inc.® Used by permission. All rights reserved worldwide.

Scripture quotations labeled RSV are from the Revised Standard Version of the Bible, copyright 1946, 1952 [2nd edition, 1971] National Council of the Churches of Christ in the United States of America. Used by permission. All rights reserved worldwide.

Excerpts from Beth Allison Barr, "'He Is Bothyn Modyr, Broþyr, & Syster vn-to Me': Women and the Bible in Late Medieval and Early Modern English Sermons," *Church History and Religious Culture* 94, no. 3 (Summer 2014): 297–315, are used by permission.

Excerpts from Beth Allison Barr, "Paul, Medieval Women, and Fifty Years of the CFH: New Perspectives," *Fides et Historia* 51, no. 1 (Winter/Spring 2019): 1–17, are used by permission.

Excerpts from Beth Allison Barr, "Women in Early Baptist Sermons: A Late Medieval Perspective," *Perspectives in Religious Studies* 41, no. 1 (2014): 13–29, are used by permission.

Baker Publishing Group publications use paper produced from sustainable forestry practices and post-consumer waste whenever possible.

22 23 24 25 26 27 28   11 10 9 8 7 6 5

For the women I have taught
For the women I have mentored
For the evangelical women and men ready to listen
This is for you

But, mostly, this is for my children,
Elena and Stephen
May you be free to be all
that God has called you to be

Contents

Acknowledgments

THE PEOPLE IN MY LIFE made this book possible.

I am so grateful for my editors and the team at Brazos Press. Katelyn Beaty believed in this project, guiding me when I needed it most. Melisa Blok showed me where I should say more and helped me know when I had said enough. This book is infinitely better because of you both. Brazos Press has been a joy to work with, from beginning to end. Thank you.

I could not have completed this project without the support of my Baylor colleagues. Larry Lyon, dean of the Baylor Graduate School, gave me space to write even though I was a newly minted associate dean. Barry Hankins, chair of the Baylor history department, gave me freedom to focus on this book ahead of other projects. He understood the importance, and he stood with me. Thank you, Barry. And, of course, my writing group colleagues, Kara Poe Alexander, Leslie Hahner, and Theresa Kennedy, honed the skills I needed to write this book. For ten years you have written with me. For ten years you have made me better. Leslie, thank you for the concept of shape-shifting.

For the past twenty years, I have relied on the assistance of archivists throughout the UK. For several of the manuscripts referenced in these pages, I am especially grateful for the assistance and patience of the reading room staff at the British Library in London, the Weston Library in Oxford, and the library and archives staff at Longleat House in Warminster. I am also grateful to the Louisville Institute and their financial support for this project.

It was my friends Kim and Brandon, Karol and Mike, Jennifer and Chris, Donna and Todd, and my Baylor colleague David, who walked with me through some of the most difficult days of 2016 and 2017. You helped me heal and gain perspective without growing bitter. The Conference on Faith and History gave me a rich community when I had lost the community of my church. It has been such a privilege to serve as your president. Although I do not know her personally, Sarah Bessey's *Out of Sorts* brought comfort to my soul at exactly the right moment.

This book would simply not exist without my Anxious Bench community. Christopher Gehrz, Kristin Kobes Du Mez, Philip Jenkins, David Swartz, and Andrea Turpin gave me the confidence—professionally, personally, and spiritually—that I needed to write the blog posts that grew into this book. John Turner, it was you who gave me the idea for the title. I am thankful also to Patheos for granting me, as with all their authors, the intellectual rights to my articles.

This book is for all my students. But it is especially for Lynneth, Liz, and Anna. You were with me on that terrible weekend in 2016. You gave me the courage I needed to be braver than I ever knew I could be. And Tay, you started this journey with me. I am so glad I can show you how it ends. Thanks also to Katherine and Liz for all your editorial assistance.

This book is also for the professor who gave me a chance in 1997. Judith, you gave me eyes to see from a different vantage point and the tools to do something about it. I aspire to be the mentor for my students that you have always been for me.

Last but not least, this book is for my family, who has walked with me every step of the way. For my parents, Kathy and Crawford Allison, who have always fought for me. Their steadfast faith and love strengthen me. For my husband, Jeb, who has always fought alongside me. If only more pastors had the integrity and faith of my husband, the church would be a vastly different place. And for my children, Stephen and Elena: you are the reason I keep fighting for a better Christian world. You fill me with joy and, every day, you renew my hope.

I NEVER MEANT to be an activist.

My Southern Baptist world of small-town Texas preached the divinely ordained roles of women. In everything from sermons to Sunday school lessons to advice from well-meaning teachers, women were called to secondary roles in church and family, with an emphasis on marriage and children. Once, I remember hearing a woman speak from behind our church pulpit. She was single, a missionary, and—an adult explained to me—only describing her experiences. This rationalization just reinforced her strangeness. A single woman behind the pulpit was aberrant; married women behind their husbands were the norm.

James Dobson was everywhere, filling even the airwaves with his regular radio broadcast. As a teenager, I remember flipping through his book *Love for a Lifetime*. I learned that biology predetermined my physical weakness and emotional instability, drawing me to my divinely created masculine complement. Dobson wrote to strengthen marriages, offering help to spouses, who are pulled apart by their natural differences: "Show me a quiet, reserved husband and I'll show you a frustrated wife," he wrote. "She wants to know what he's thinking and what happened at his office and how he sees the children, and especially, how he feels about her. The husband, by contrast, finds some things better left unsaid. It is a classic struggle."[1] In just a few sentences, Dobson impressed upon me the shape of the normal Christian household—a father returning from his office job to the home front managed by his wife and children.

1

Select biblical passages, undergirded by the notes in my study Bible, were woven through sermons, Bible studies, and devotionals, creating a seamless picture of scriptural support for female subordination. Women were made to desire their husbands and let them rule (Genesis); women were to trust God and wait for their perfect husband (Ruth); men's voices were public, while women's voices were private (1 Corinthians; 1 Timothy); when women did take charge, it was either sinful (Eve) or because men had failed to do their jobs (Deborah). A woman's position was supportive and secondary, unless she had to temporarily step into leadership when men could not.

This was my understanding of biblical womanhood: God designed women primarily to be submissive wives, virtuous mothers, and joyful homemakers. God designed men to lead in the home as husbands and fathers, as well as in church as pastors, elders, and deacons. I believed that this gender hierarchy was divinely ordained. Elisabeth Elliot famously wrote that femininity receives. Women surrender, help, and respond while husbands provide, protect, and initiate. A biblical woman is a submissive woman.[2]

This was my world for more than forty years.

Until, one day, it wasn't.

On that day, I left church because I couldn't take it anymore. More than three months prior, on September 19, 2016—the same hour my first doctoral student was orally defending her qualifying exams and dissertation prospectus—my husband was fired from his job as a youth pastor. He had served in the role for more than twenty years, fourteen in this church alone. Suddenly, quietly, painfully, he was told to walk away with a month of severance pay. Some friends, to whom we will forever be grateful, learned what happened and fought for us. They were able to delay the job loss for three months, enough for us to prepare the youth and transition the ministry; they also secured us an additional five months of severance pay. They gave us space to breathe.

The day I walked out of church, a Sunday in December almost three months later, the enormity of what was happening to us had finally become real.

I stood in front of a table someone had set up in the foyer. It had a picture of my family, with a little box on one side and a framed statement on the other. I don't remember what the framed statement said—maybe a Scripture verse or something about the church being grateful for our ministry. Markers lay beside a stack of paper. People could write notes of farewell and tuck them inside the box.

I know the majority of people who wrote us notes were sincere. Most were genuinely sorry to see us go, bewildered by the circumstances. Some were upset and angry. Some were shaken by the church's lack of transparency. Some were sadly anticipating the loss of our close friendship. For the words left by these people, sincere in their goodbyes, I am thankful.

But I don't think the spirit behind the box, the reason the table was set up, was just for these people. It was about keeping up appearances. The carefully constructed table controlled the narrative about my husband's and my departure. It helped convey that our leaving was a good decision made by shepherds caring for their flock. After all, providing a public forum to say goodbye was what you did when pastors left. When they left for new jobs or to go back to school or to become missionaries.

Yet what was happening to us was none of those things. My husband was fired after he challenged church leadership over the issue of women in ministry.

Images crowded into my head. The text I received from my husband on September 19: "The meeting did not go well." The brokenness and confusion of our youth workers, who were pushed out of serving in youth ministry because of their friendship with us. The faces of the youth that awful night, when we were forced to tell them we were leaving without telling them the full truth. The shadows of the elders standing guard around the room, watching as we told the youth we were leaving. The gut-wrenching tears of my son when he learned that he would never be in his father's youth group. The dark garden in Virginia where I walked around and around and around one night, barely suppressing anxiety while my role as conference organizer left my husband alone in Texas to face one of his hardest weeks ever.

I could feel the raw edges of grief, anger, and righteous indignation rising inside me.

So I left. I walked straight out the church doors. Past the people standing in the foyer, including those who had been talking to me next to that table. Past one of the elders who tried to speak to me. I walked out the church doors and straight to my car. I left behind that table and its carefully constructed story. I left behind the narrative, propagated by my mostly upper-middle-class, white church, that all was well and that all would be well because God had ordained it so. I drove straight home.

Then I opened my laptop and started writing.

The words just flowed.

Different pieces of my life snapping together, sharpening into focus.

For all my adult life, I had served in ministry with my husband, remaining in complementarian churches even as I grew

4

more and more skeptical that "biblical womanhood" as we had been taught matched what the Bible taught. I kept telling myself that maybe things would change—that I, as a woman who taught and had a career, was setting a positive example. I kept telling myself that complementarianism (the theological view that women are divinely created as helpers and men are divinely created as leaders) wasn't at its root misogynistic. I kept telling myself that no church was perfect and that the best way to change a system was by working from within it. So I stayed in the system, and I stayed silent.

I stayed silent when a woman who worked at a Southern Baptist church and attended seminary alongside my husband was paid less by that church because she wasn't ordained. Ironically, the reason she wasn't ordained was because the church was Southern Baptist.

I stayed silent when a newly married woman whose job carried the family insurance quit that job after attending a retreat with women from our church—a retreat that featured a hardline complementarian speaker who convinced this woman that her proper place was in the home. Her decision, from what I heard, caused tension within the family, including financial. She stopped coming to church. I have no idea what happened to her.

I stayed silent when, after our pastor preached a sermon on gender roles, a married couple gave their testimony. The wife encouraged women to verbally agree to what their husbands suggested, even if they really disagreed. God would honor their submission.

I stayed silent when I wasn't allowed to teach youth Sunday school because the class included teenage boys. I led discussions with special permission when no one else was available.

I stayed silent.

It wasn't until that Sunday, three months after the worst had happened, that I realized the hard truth. By staying silent, I had become part of the problem. Instead of making a difference, I had become complicit in a system that used the name of Jesus to oppress and harm women.

And the hardest truth of all was that I bore greater responsibility than most in our church because I had known that complementarian theology was wrong.

Staring at that little table, I realized that most people in our church knew only the theological views that the leaders were telling them. Just like I heard only one narrative of biblical womanhood in church, many evangelicals in complementarian churches know only what they are told—what they are taught in seminary, what they read in the notes of their English Bible translations, what they learn in Sunday school about church history from history books written by pastors, not historians.

My anguish that morning stemmed from my shame as much as from my grief.

You see, I knew that complementarian theology—biblical womanhood—was wrong. I knew that it was based on a handful of verses read apart from their historical context and used as a lens to interpret the rest of the Bible. The tail wags the dog, as Ben Witherington once commented—meaning that cultural assumptions and practices regarding womanhood are read into the biblical text, rather than the biblical text being read within its own historical and cultural context.[3] So much textual and historical evidence counters the complementarian model of biblical womanhood and the theology behind it. Sometimes I am dumbfounded that this is a battle we are still fighting.

As a historian, I also knew that women have been fighting against oppression from the beginning of civilization. I knew that biblical womanhood, rather than looking like the freedom offered by Jesus and proclaimed by Paul, looks much more like the non-Christian systems of female oppression that I teach my students about when we discuss the ancient worlds of Mesopotamia and Greece. As Christians we are called to be different from the world. Yet in our treatment of women, we often look just like everyone else. Ironically, complementarian theology claims it is defending a plain and natural interpretation of the Bible while really defending an interpretation that has been corrupted by our sinful human drive to dominate others and build hierarchies of power and oppression. I can't think of anything less Christlike than hierarchies like these.

As I looked at my laptop screen, grappling with why that table in the foyer had upset me so much, I realized the hard truth about why I had stayed in complementarian churches for so long.

Because I was comfortable.

Because I really thought I could make a difference.

Because I feared my husband would lose his job.

Because I feared disrupting the lives of my children.

Because I loved the life of youth ministry.

Because I loved my friends.

So for the sake of the youth we served; for the sake of the difference my husband made in his job; for the sake of financial security; for the sake of our friends whom we had loved, laughed, and lived life with; and for the sake of our comfort, I chose to stay and to stay silent.

I had good reasons. But I was wrong.

I had become like those who knew about former seminary president Paige Patterson's counsel to an alleged rape survivor, telling her to not report the crime and to forgive her rapist. Instead of speaking out, they stayed silent and allowed him to remain in power.[4] I had become like those in Rachael Denhollander's church who resisted her advocacy. Instead of defending her when she alleged cover-up of sexual abuse by Sovereign Grace Churches, a ministry group that her church was affiliated with, her church family turned away from her. As she said in her impact statement, "My advocacy for sexual assault victims, something I cherished, cost me my church and our closest friends."[5] I had become like the members of Andy Savage's church who, in response to his confession of sexual assault as a former youth pastor, gave him a standing ovation.[6] I had become like the members of Mark Driscoll's church who listened, Sunday after Sunday, as he preached misogyny and toxic masculinity from the pulpit.[7] I had become like so many well-meaning church members who have counseled women to forgive their rapists while simultaneously teaching female culpability in rape.[8] While the blame for abuse lies primarily with the abuser, those who stand by and do nothing share in the blame too. Silent Christians like me have allowed both misogyny and abuse to run rampant in the church. We have allowed teachings to remain intact that oppress women and stand contrary to everything Jesus did and taught.

My husband, while preaching a sermon on integrity, drew an example from the 1994 movie *Quiz Show*. The main character, Charles Van Doren, allows himself to be corrupted by fame and success. He cheats to win the quiz show, week after week. When his deception is finally exposed and he has to confess to his father what he has done, his father, a respected professor at Columbia University, confronts him with these powerful words: "Your name is mine!" By allowing himself to be complicit in a corrupt system, Charles Van Doren had shamed not only himself but also his father.

"Your name is mine!"

Because I am a Christian, because I carry the name of Christ, his name is my name. Christians like Paige Patterson are guilty for what they have done. But because Patterson did it in the name of Jesus, and because fellow Christians stayed silent, his guilt is our guilt too. I knew this.

And that morning my tears confessed my guilt before God.

I made a decision, there in front of my laptop screen. Because my hope is in Jesus, I wasn't going to give up on his church. I walked out of my church that day, but I wasn't walking away from the church itself.

I wasn't giving up.

This meant I could no longer keep what I knew to myself.

This book is my story.

It is the truth I have gleaned from my study of the Bible, from my experiences as a pastor's wife, and from my training as a historian whose research focuses on women in medieval and early modern church history.

This book is for the people in my evangelical world.[9] The women and men I still know and love. It is to you I am speaking. And it is you who I am asking to listen.

Listen not just to my experiences but also to the evidence I present as a historian. I am a historian who believes in the birth, death, and resurrection of Jesus. A historian who still identifies with the evangelical tradition—as a Baptist.

I confess it was experiences in my life, my personal exposure to the ugliness and trauma inflicted by complementarian systems in the name of Jesus, that tipped me over the edge. I can no longer watch silently as gender hierarchies oppress and damage both women and men in the name of Jesus. But what brought me to this edge was not experience; it was historical evidence. It was historical evidence that showed me how biblical womanhood was constructed—brick by brick, century by century.

This is what changed my mind.

Maybe it will change yours too.

IN MAY 2019, Owen Strachan, former president of the Council on Biblical Manhood and Womanhood, wrote an essay titled "Divine Order in a Chaotic Age: On Women Preaching." He got straight to the point, quoting Genesis 1:1: "In the beginning, God made the heavens and the earth." Strachan's argument followed with confidence: God created a divine order in which husbands rule over their wives, and this order was established at the beginning of creation.

> The man is created first in the Old Testament, and possesses what the New Testament will call *headship* over his wife. Adam is constituted the leader of his home; he is given authority in it, authority that is shaped in a Christlike way as the biblical story unfolds. . . . On the basis of a man's domestic leadership, men are called to provide spiritual leadership and protection of the church (1 Timothy 2:9–15). Elders preach, teach, and shepherd the flock of God; only men are called to the office of elder, and only men who excel as heads of their wives and children are to be considered as possible candidates for eldership (1 Timothy 3:1–7; Titus 1:5–9).[1]

Men lead. Women follow. The Bible tells us so.

For a time, I believed this too. It echoed all around during my teenage and young adult years. I heard it attending a Bill Gothard conference, which some people in my small-town Southern Baptist church invited me to. I heard it from my Bible study leaders in college. I heard it from the hosts of Christian radio stations. I heard it from the notes in my study Bible. I heard it at almost every wedding ceremony I attended, spoken loud and clear as each preacher read Ephesians 5. Male headship was a familiar hum in the background of my life: women were called to support their husbands, and men were called to lead their wives. It was unequivocal truth ordained by the inerrant Word of God.

But this was *too familiar* a story.

Even from my early years training as a historian, Christian arguments about male headship troubled me. You see, Christians were not the only ones to argue that women's subordination is the divine order. Christians are, historically speaking, pretty late to the patriarchy game. We may claim that the gendered patterns of our lives are different from those assumed in mainstream culture, but history tells a different tale. Let me show you, from the world history sources I have been teaching for more than two decades, how much Christian patriarchy mimics the patriarchy of the non-Christian world.

What Is Patriarchy?

First, let's talk about patriarchy.

Not long ago, evangelicals were talking a lot about patriarchy. Russell Moore, currently the president of the Ethics and Religious Liberty Commission of the Southern Baptist Convention, declared *patriarchy* a better word for the conservative Christian gender hierarchy than *complementarianism*. He told Mark Dever, pastor of Capitol Hill Baptist Church in Washington, DC, that, despite his support for complementarianism, he hates the word itself. "I prefer the word 'patriarchy,'" Moore said.[2] Moore made a similar argument in an earlier journal article, warning that evangelical abandonment of the word *patriarchy* was capitulation to secular peer pressure. For Moore, this wasn't a good reason to give up the word. As he writes, "We must remember that 'evangelical' is also a negative term in many contexts. We must allow the patriarchs and apostles themselves, not the editors of *Playboy* or *Ms.* magazine, to define the grammar of our faith."[3] Because the word *patriarchy* itself is biblical, biblical Christians should be proud to use it.

I first learned of the evangelical conversation about the word *patriarchy* from a 2012 blog post written by Rachel Held Evans, the well-known author of *A Year of Biblical Womanhood*.[4] She noted that Owen Strachan used the word *patriarchy* too. Of course I looked up the reference. I remember smiling when I read Strachan's words. His straightforward approach provided a compromise between evangelicals who prefer the word *patriarchy*, like Moore, and those who would rather use the word *complementarian* (like Denny Burk, the current president of the Council on Biblical Manhood and Womanhood).[5] "For millennia," Strachan explains, "followers of God have practiced what used to be called patriarchy and is now called complementarianism."[6] Complementarianism is patriarchy. Owen Strachan is right (at least about this).

So, what *is* patriarchy? Historian Judith Bennett explains *patriarchy* as having three main meanings in English:

1. Male ecclesiastical leaders, such as the patriarch (archbishop of Constantinople) in Greek Orthodoxy
2. Legal power of male household heads (fathers/husbands)
3. A society that promotes male authority and female submission

It is this third meaning on which, like Bennett, we will focus. As Bennett writes, "When feminists at rallies chant, 'Hey, Hey, Ho, Ho, Patriarchy's Got to Go,' we are not talking about the ecclesiastical structures of Greek Orthodoxy or about a specific form of fatherly domination within families, but instead about a general system through which women have been and are subordinated to men."[7] This third meaning of patriarchy encompasses the first two. Both the tradition of male church leaders and the authority of male household heads function within cultures that generally promote male authority and female submission.

American evangelicalism provides a case in point. A 2017 Barna study, focused on the perception of women and power in American society, drew evidence from three polls to compare attitudes toward women across several demographics—including gender, age, political preference, and religious identity (evangelical, Protestant, Catholic, and practicing Christian). The study found that evangelicals are the "most hesitant" group in supporting women's work outside the home: only 52 percent "are comfortable with the future possibility of more women than men in the workforce" (a percentage more than 20 points below that of the general American population). Evangelicals also express the most discomfort with a female CEO. The study also found that evangelicals are the least comfortable with women as pastors (39 percent). For evangelicals these attitudes are connected: limiting women's spiritual authority goes hand in hand with limiting women's economic power. As the study puts it, these results are "perhaps due to a more traditional interpretation of women's roles as primary care-givers in the home."[8] Evangelical teachings that subordinate women within the home and inside the walls of the church influence attitudes about women in the workplace.[9] Or, considered within Bennett's framework, male ecclesiastical authority and male household authority exist within broader cultural practices that subordinate women to men. Patriarchy doesn't stay confined to one sphere.

Let's consider an even more specific example of how patriarchal attitudes manifest in evangelical culture. Several years ago, when my husband was serving as a youth pastor, our church was looking for a new secretary. He suggested a friend of ours for the position. The friend really needed some additional work and had the advantage of already being a church member. But the friend was a man. And my husband was suggesting him for church secretary. The response from one of the other pastors was telling. Would this man, the pastor asked, really want to answer the phone? It was okay to hire a woman to answer the phone, but the job would be demeaning to a man. So demeaning, in fact, that the pastor preferred not to hire him, despite our friend's financial need. The job, suitable for a woman to do, was beneath the dignity of a man.

This example of a man being deemed above the work suitable for a woman fits into a larger social pattern in which men's work is more highly valued than women's. Women outnumber men in my hometown of Waco, Texas, and women outnumber men at two of the three local institutions for higher education (more women attend Baylor University and McLennan Community College, while more men attend Texas State Technical College). Yet women in Waco average close to $20,000 less in yearly income than men. The largest wage gap between men and women is at the managerial and higher-administration level, where men earn almost $120,000 per year while women earn only $78,000.[10] Women's work, quite literally, is worth less than men's.

This pattern of devaluing women's work—whether the type of work or the monetary value of the work—is an example of patriarchy: a general system that values men and their contributions more than it values women and their contributions. Russell Moore maintains that this general system of patriarchy is not the same as the complementarian gender hierarchy. Christian patriarchy isn't "pagan patriarchy," as he has called it.[11] Moore warns against a "predatory patriarchy" that harms women, but he also continues to support a system that promotes male authority and female submission. He argues that an orderly family structure in which wives submit only "to their own husbands" and fathers serve as a "visible sign of responsibility" makes life better for everyone.[12]

So is he right? Is Christian patriarchy different?

Christian Patriarchy Is Just Patriarchy

"But you only work part time?"

"So how many hours does that take you away from home during the week?"

"Oh, you breastfeed? I figured you didn't do that since you worked."

"Is your husband okay with you making more money than him?"

These are just a sampling of the questions I have been asked over the past twenty years. A pastor's wife who continued to pursue my own career even while I had children perplexed many in my evangelical community—including some of my college students. One student was particularly vocal. He was theologically conservative and expressed concern about my choice to continue teaching as a wife and mother (especially as a pastor's wife). He challenged me so often in the classroom that I took to rewriting lecture material, trying to minimize his disruptions. I wasn't successful. Once the student suggested that I clear my teaching material with my husband before presenting it to my classroom. This both angered and unnerved me. It angered me that he thought it appropriate to suggest that I submit my teaching materials to the authority of my husband. It unnerved me because every semester I worried about how my vocation as a female professor clashed with conservative Christian expectations about female submission.

When I read Russell Moore's attempt to distinguish "Christian patriarchy" from "pagan patriarchy," the experience I had with this student came to mind. According to Moore, "pagan patriarchy" encourages women to submit to all men, while "Christian patriarchy" only concerns wives submitting to their husbands.[13] Moore has softened his discussion of patriarchy over the years, emphasizing in his 2018 book that, in creation, men and women "are never given dominion over one another." Yet he still clings to male headship. While he writes that "Scripture demolishes the idea that women, in general, are to be submissive to men, in general," he explains wifely submission as cultivating "a voluntary attitude of recognition toward godly leadership."[14] Thus his general attitude remains unchanged: women should not submit to men in general (pagan patriarchy), but wives should submit to their husbands (Christian patriarchy).

Nice try, I thought. Tell that to my conservative male student. Because that student considered me to be under the authority of my husband, he was less willing to accept my authority over him in a university classroom. No matter how much Moore wants to separate "pagan patriarchy" from "Christian patriarchy," he can't. Both systems place power in the hands of men and take power away from women. Both systems teach men that women rank lower than they do. Both systems teach women that their voices are worth less than the voices of men. Moore may claim that women only owe submission "to their own husbands," not to men "in general," but he undermines this claim by excluding women as pastors and elders.[15] If men (simply because of their sex) have the potential to preach and exercise spiritual authority over a church congregation but women (simply because of their sex) do not, then that gives men "in general" authority over women "in general." My conservative male student considered me under the authority of both my husband and my pastor, and he treated me accordingly.

Christian patriarchy does not remain confined within the walls of our homes. It does not stay behind our pulpits. It cannot be peeled off suit coats like a name tag as evangelical men move from denying women's leadership at church to accepting the authority of women at work or women in the classroom. My church secretary example shows how Christian patriarchy spills over into our everyday attitudes and practices. Even the strictest interpretation of Pauline texts can provide no theological justification for why a man could not serve as a church secretary. Simple, secular patriarchy—which values women's work less than men's—provides the answer.

Patriarchy by any other name is still patriarchy. Complementarians may argue that women are equal to men, as does the Southern Baptist Convention's 1998 amendment to the "Baptist Faith and Message": "The husband and wife are of equal worth before God, since both are created in God's image."[16] Yet their insistence that "equal worth" manifests in unequal roles refutes this.

18

Historian Barry Hankins quotes the "key passage" of the controversial statement approved at the Southern Baptist Convention (SBC) meeting in June 1998: "A wife is to submit herself graciously to the servant leadership of her husband even as the church willingly submits to the headship of Christ. She, being in the image of God as is her husband and thus equal to him, has the God-given responsibility to respect her husband and to serve as his helper in managing the household and nurturing the next generation."[17] The claim is certainly that women's work (from housework to childcare to answering phones) is valuable and worthy, but when that same work is deemed unsuitable for a man to do, it reveals the truth: women's work is less important than men's. Moreover, just as men are demeaned for doing women's jobs (which often come with less authority and, consequently, lower pay), women are restricted from doing men's jobs (which garner both more authority and higher pay). In this way, Christian patriarchy models the patriarchy of mainstream society. Our pastor valued the work of a woman less than the work of a man, just as the economy of my hometown values the work of women less (almost $20,000 per year less) than the work of men. Russell Moore is right to prefer the term *patriarchy* because, realistically, it is the right term to use. But he is wrong to think that the Christian model is different.

Indeed, regarding the treatment of women throughout history, the present looks an awful lot like the past. How little the wage gap between women and men has changed over time both frightens and fascinates me as a medieval historian. Judith Bennett describes this startling reality: "Women who work in England today share an experience with female wage earners seven centuries ago: they take home only about three-quarters the wages earned by men. In the 1360s, women earned 71 percent of male wages; today, they earn about 75 percent."[18] This historical continuity—what Bennett calls the "patriarchal equilibrium"—lends superficial support to the idea of biblical womanhood. When examined carefully, however, the historical origins of patriarchy weaken rather than bolster the evangelical notion of biblical womanhood. A gender hierarchy in which women rank under men can be found in almost every era and among every people group. When the church denies women the ability to preach, lead, teach, and sometimes even work outside the home, the church is continuing a long historical tradition of subordinating women.

So let's go back to the beginning of history—or at least about as close as we can get—and see what my world history students learn about patriarchy.

The Historical Continuity of Christian Patriarchy

In 1839, a young English scholar was distracted on his way to Sri Lanka. His name was Austen Henry Layard, and the sandy mounds that waylaid his journey were located in the heart of ancient Assyria (modern-day Iraq). What he discovered turned out to be the remains of the great Assyrian cities of Nimrud and Nineveh. Remember Jonah? Nineveh is the city that God commanded Jonah to preach repentance to, a command that Jonah resisted because the Assyrians were such terrible people. They skinned enemies alive and fought captured lions, gladiator-style, for entertainment. Yet despite their fish-slapping ways (I can't resist a VeggieTales reference), they were pretty sophisticated too.

Buried deep inside the once-fierce city walls and now-crumbling ziggurats was an extensive ancient library. It housed the clay fragments of one of the oldest stories in human existence: the story of the warrior-king Gilgamesh. The surviving text dates from the seventh-century library of the last great king of the Assyrian Empire, Ashurbanipal.[19] But the story itself was well known much earlier, with versions of it peppering the ancient Near East.[20]

Gilgamesh is a god, courtesy of his goddess mother, but he is cursed with mortality, courtesy of his earthly father. His father left him the throne of the great Sumerian city of Uruk—which means Gilgamesh is a semi-historical figure. The ancient text tells us that Gilgamesh ruled as the fifth king of the First Dynasty of Uruk around 2750 BC.

I find *The Epic of Gilgamesh* riveting. The characters are deeply flawed: a bored king who makes war to enhance his reputation; a loyal sidekick who eggs on the bad behavior of his best friend; a scorned woman who tries to release a plague of zombies on earth because she is so angry. Given its dramatic twists and turns, I am surprised the story hasn't yet been made into a Hollywood blockbuster. It is action packed and filled with high drama—including lots of sex and supernatural monsters.

It isn't the supernatural monsters that draw me to the story, though. It is the continuity of human experience that makes it so compelling. Even four thousand years ago, people acted much the same as they do today. One of my favorite parts is the aftermath of Gilgamesh losing his best friend, Enkidu, to a wasting disease. In a startlingly modern cry, Gilgamesh demands that the world echo his grief:

> Weep. Let the roads we walked together flood
>   themselves with tears. . . . .
>   . . . .
> Let the river which soothed our feet overflow its banks

21

as tears do that swell and rush across my dusty cheeks.
Let the clouds and stars race swiftly with you into
death.[21]

We can see him, crumpled over the body of his friend. We can feel his grief, as it echoes our own. We still love and grieve in the same ways that people did more than four thousand years ago. We still cry out in pain.

The rawness of human grief runs throughout *The Epic of Gilgamesh*.

So does the reality of patriarchy.

From the prostitute who civilizes the wild-man Enkidu to the wise tavern keeper to the virgins Gilgamesh takes to his bed, women play significant roles throughout the Gilgamesh stories, even moving the plot forward at key moments. For example, when Gilgamesh is most out of control, the prostitute Shamhat seduces Enkidu, enticing him to enter Uruk and challenge the tyrannical king. Shamhat does not do this of her own accord. She is ordered by the hunter, who is tired of the wild Enkidu disrupting his traps and protecting the animals, to go to Enkidu and "let him see what charm and force a woman has."[22] Shamhat does, showing Enkidu her body (I once accidentally assigned a too-accurate translation of this encounter and had an embarrassing moment in class) and staying with him for seven nights—teaching him not only about sex but also about civilization.

This episode between Shamhat and Enkidu shifts the entire story. It is through Shamhat that Gilgamesh meets Enkidu. After a violent battle, Gilgamesh realizes he cannot defeat Enkidu and accepts him as his equal. The two become inseparable. From this point forward, instead of relieving his boredom by forcing the young men of his kingdom into endless wars and the young women (even the married ones) into his bed, Gilgamesh sets off on a series of adventures that culminate in Enkidu's death and launch Gilgamesh's quest for immortality. Shamhat, in other words, is the catalyst for the entire plot.

Women like Shamhat play critical roles throughout the story. Yet women never take the lead—as religion scholar Rivkah Harris has emphasized.[23] Even Shamhat is only doing what a male authority figure (the hunter) tells her to do. Women in the Gilgamesh narrative function primarily as helpers. The collected stories of the epic, written by men for men and about men, portray women as "supporting and subsidiary."[24] Women work and speak and move throughout the narrative, but their main role is to meet the physical needs of men and to give them advice and comfort. Siduri, the tavern keeper, perhaps provides the best example of this. Not only does she offer alcohol and comfort to Gilgamesh when he is tired from his quest and overwhelmed by grief from Enkidu's death, but she also gives him some telling advice: "What is best for us to do is now to sing and dance. Relish warm food and cool drinks. Cherish children to whom your love gives life. Bathe easily in sweet, refreshing waters. Play joyfully with your chosen wife."[25] Women were keepers of the hearth. Even in the chaotic and dangerous world of ancient Sumer, women provided the comforts of food, sex, and happy family life.

In one sense, *The Epic of Gilgamesh* supports Albert Mohler's claim that history is on the side of complementarianism. Mohler, current president of Southern Baptist Theological Seminary in Louisville, Kentucky, writes that it is an "undeniable historical reality that men have predominated in positions of leadership and that the roles of women have been largely defined around home, children, and family." Biblical evidence,

Mohler continues, drives home this historical continuity: "The pattern of history affirms what the Bible unquestionably reveals—that God has made human beings in His image as male and female. . . . We understand the Bible to present a beautiful portrait of complementarity between the sexes, with both men and women charged to reflect God's glory in a distinct way."[26] Just as women were the keepers of home and family, the domestic supporters of men, more than four thousand years ago, they would probably continue to be so today if not for the disruptive (and "unbiblical") influence of feminism. Such a grand sweep of historical continuity convinces Mohler that complementarianism must be God's design.

Patriarchy exists in *The Epic of Gilgamesh*, a story about men and women at the beginning of history, because patriarchy was designed by God—or so goes the Christian patriarchal narrative. Women should proudly claim their roles as supporting actors because this is God's divine plan. Women past were just as women present are and should continue to be: subordinate. No wonder so many complementarians are upset by recent pop culture narratives like the Marvel movies and the new Star Wars trilogy that cast women in leading roles. As Denny Burk has said, "I've noticed that in Star Wars (and in action films more generally) there is a move away from male hero/protagonists. Warrior women protagonists who save the men are the order of the day (Rey, [Jyn Erso], Wonder Woman, Eleven, etc.)."[27] To him and others, warrior women reflect a feminist agenda that subverts the order of God.

But the very continuity of patriarchy should give us pause.

Patriarchy looks right because it is the historical practice of the world. In ancient Mesopotamia, women were treated as property. They had less opportunity for education; they were mostly defined by their relationships to men; they were legally disempowered as wives; they were subject to legally sponsored physical violence; and they rarely got to speak for themselves in the historical narrative. As Marten Stol concludes in his 2016 comprehensive study titled *Women in the Ancient Near East*, "In ancient society women fared much worse than men. . . . As we come to a close we expect none of our readers to shut this book without uttering a sigh of sadness."[28]

My modern students balk at how Babylonian law allowed husbands to drown their wives for alleged adultery, but my students are also living in the state of Texas in which women make up 94 percent of the victims in domestic partner murder-suicides—not to mention the United States in which almost 25 percent of women have experienced severe physical violence by an intimate partner.[29] This evidence shows not only the continuity of patriarchy from ancient Mesopotamia to modern America but also the continuity of its dark underbelly. Instead of being a point of pride for Christians, shouldn't the historical continuity of a practice that has caused women to fare much worse than men for thousands of years cause concern? Shouldn't Christians, who are called to be different from the world, treat women *differently*?

What if patriarchy isn't divinely ordained but is a result of human sin? What if instead of being divinely created, patriarchy slithered into creation only after the fall? What if the reason that the fruit of patriarchy is so corrupt, even within the Christian church, is because patriarchy has always been a corrupted system?

Instead of assuming that patriarchy is instituted by God, we must ask whether patriarchy is a product of sinful human hands.

Flipping the Narrative

I remember the first time it occurred to me to flip the Christian narrative about patriarchy.

I had just wrapped up my evening women's studies seminar at the University of North Carolina at Chapel Hill, and I was on my way to the Chili's in Durham, where my husband was working a double shift. We were both full-time graduate students, me in the history doctoral program at Chapel Hill and he an MDiv student at Southeastern Baptist Theological Seminary. I had a stipend at Chapel Hill (about $11,000 per year), while he worked as a part-time youth minister at a local Baptist church (earning about $100 per week). Waiting tables meant we could pay the bills. It also meant he could purchase half-price meals for us. On nights like tonight, when he worked a double shift, I would sit in a booth and enjoy the only restaurant food we could afford (not to mention free refills on my half-price Diet Cokes). We were so young, so poor, and so busy. Those cheap meals were a godsend.

But that night, I wasn't thinking about dinner. I was thinking about the conversation in my women's studies seminar. We had spent the semester reading and discussing the status of women. From the ancient world through the modern world, history told a continuous story of patriarchy—of women suppressed, oppressed, devalued, and silenced.

That night the story hit home for me. The conversation turned to Southern Baptists and Paige Patterson, then president of Southeastern Baptist Theological Seminary. For the same reason Patterson became a hero in the Southern Baptist world, he became repugnant in my seminar that night: his views on gender roles.

Patterson preached that men were divinely created to lead and wield authority, women to follow and submit. The influence of men like Patterson (and, ironically, his wife) led the SBC to rewrite its faith statement, first creating the 1984 resolution that emphasizes women's secondary creation, followed by the 1998 statement about wives submitting to their husbands. The submission statement swiftly became an amendment, culminating in the final (and by that time uncontroversial) addition to the "Baptist Faith and Message 2000" that only men can serve as head pastors.[30]

Bewildered outrage bubbled in my seminar—not only about Patterson's views but also about the thousands of women who supported him. We didn't miss that it was Patterson's wife, Dorothy, who fought so resolutely on the floor of the 1998 convention to hold the line on women's submission. She argued against the phrase "both husband and wife are to submit graciously to each other" because it implied similarity, equality even, between husbands and wives. She insisted that a divine hierarchy existed in the marriage relationship and that *only* women were called to submit "graciously" to the leadership of their husbands.[31] Isn't it ironic how a woman led the charge to ban women from leadership?

But why women like Dorothy Patterson so prominently supported women's submission wasn't the question that bothered me. I knew why many women supported it: because we believed male headship was divinely ordained. I was taught that God ordained women to follow the spiritual leadership of their husbands in the home and of male pastors in the church. Because Christianity was supposed to look different from the world, it made sense that a women's studies graduate seminar at a public secular research university would object to a Christian

27

understanding of gender roles. While the world promoted feminism and blurred the boundaries between male and female roles (or so I had been led to believe), Christianity promoted a divinely ordained gender hierarchy that brought clarity and order to everyday life. I understood Dorothy Patterson's argument because I was part of Dorothy Patterson's world.

But I had concerns even then. Christians were called to be radically different in how we uphold the dignity of all people, including women. That semester I had come to realize how historically unremarkable Christian gender ideals were. Instead of looking different in how we treated women, Christians looked just like everyone else.

Kate Narveson hadn't yet written her book on early modern piety, so I hadn't yet read her beautiful description of people incorporating Scripture into their everyday lives: "Scripture phrase," she called it.[32] That night I thought in Scripture phrase. A cradle Baptist, I learned to read and study the Bible at a young age, and Scripture has always flowed through my life. It flowed through my head that night, as my heart cried out to God for answers. I remembered the words of Genesis 3:16, part of the curse of the fall, almost as if they were etched in the night sky: "In pain you shall bring forth children, yet your desire shall be for your husband, and he shall rule over you." God spoke these words to Eve in the garden of Eden after she had sinned and taken the fruit from the forbidden tree. As the Latin Vulgate (which was becoming one of the primary Bibles I used as a medievalist) phrases it, "In sorrow shalt thou bring forth children, and thou shalt be under thy husband's power, and he shall have dominion over thee."[33]

And there it was—the biblical explanation for the birth of patriarchy.

The first human sin built the first human power hierarchy. Alice Mathews, theologian and former academic dean at Gordon-Conwell Theological Seminary, explains the biblical perspective of the birth of patriarchy so well in her book *Gender Roles and the People of God*. Listen to what she says:

> It is in Genesis 3:16 (God speaking to the woman) where we first see hierarchy in human relationships. . . . Hierarchy was not God's will for the first pair, but it was imposed when they chose to disregard his command and eat the forbidden fruit. . . . Adam would now be subject to his source (the ground), even as Eve was now subject to her source (Adam). This was the moment of the birth of patriarchy. As a result of their sin, the man was now the master over the woman, and the ground was now master over the man, contrary to God's original intention in creation.[34]

Patriarchy wasn't what God wanted; patriarchy was a result of human sin.

What was new to me that night was rather old, theologically speaking. Everyone already knew that patriarchy was a result of the fall. Stanley Gundry, former president of the Evangelical Theological Society, states this matter-of-factly in a 2010 essay. The patriarchy that continues to appear in biblical text is a "mere accommodation to the reality of the times and culture; it is not a reflection of the divine ideal for humanity."[35] Patriarchy is created by people, not ordained by God.

Katharine Bushnell, a female missionary to China at the turn of the twentieth century, held a similar view. She cautioned about the danger of patriarchy for women. Instead of "desire," she preferred to translate the word in Genesis 3:16 as "turning."

29

As she translated the verse, "Thou art turning away to thy husband, and he will rule over thee."[36] Before the fall, both Adam and Eve submitted to God's authority. After the fall, because of sin, women would now turn first to their husbands, and their husbands, in the place of God, would rule over them.

I love how historian Kristin Kobes Du Mez describes Bushnell's interpretation as a "theological coup" that "upended Victorian understandings of womanhood." As Du Mez explains, "For Bushnell, male authority over women contradicted God's will and perpetuated man's original rebellion against God." Women thus "continued to commit the sin of Eve when they submitted to men, rather than to God." Patriarchy, for Bushnell, was not just a result of the curse; it was embedded in the fall itself. Adam's rebellion was claiming God's authority for himself, and Eve's rebellion was submitting to Adam in place of God.[37]

I didn't know about Alice Mathews as a teenager. I certainly didn't know about Katherine Bushnell. I joined my church youth group in the late '80s—at the height of evangelical authors and influencers like James Dobson, Pat Robertson, Tim and Beverly LaHaye (founder of Concerned Women for America), Elisabeth Elliot, and the Pattersons. Collectively the devotionals, Bible studies, marriage books, and parenting advice that had been influenced by their teachings saturated the Christian publishing world.[38] The message for women was eerily uniform: Christian women submit to the authority of their husbands, taking care of home and family while men lead, protect, and provide. Take, for example, what Dobson wrote in 1994 about why men should be sole breadwinners: "I wish it were possible for me to emphasize just how critical this masculine understanding is to family stability. . . . One of the greatest threats to the institution of the family today is undermining of this role as protector and provider. This is the contribution for which men were designed. . . . If it is taken away, their commitment to their wives and children is jeopardized."[39] About ten years earlier, Dobson had counseled a woman—terrified of her husband because he routinely beat her but still wanting to stay in the marriage— that divorce was not the solution, that she should work toward reconciliation instead.[40]

Evangelical women like me were taught that God's design for marriage was submissive wives (preferably stay-at-home) and leader husbands (preferably breadwinners). I remember attending a Disciple Now event when I was in high school. The leader explained to us that God designed women specifically to be wives and to devote themselves to their husbands. This is the first time I remember hearing that at church. But it wouldn't be the last, because that year saw the publication of what Du Mez calls "a manifesto in defense of God-given gender difference": John Piper and Wayne Grudem's *Recovering Biblical Manhood and Womanhood*.[41] While Piper and Grudem admit that the prescription in Genesis 3:16, "He shall rule over you," is a result of the fall, they still argue that male headship was ordained by God *before* the fall. They write, "But the silence at this point regarding the reality of Adam's loving leadership before the fall gives the impression that fallen 'rulership' and God-ordained headship are lumped together and ruled out. Again the Biblical thrust is ignored: Paul never appeals to the curse or the fall as an explanation for man's responsibility to lead; he always appeals to the acts of God before the fall."[42]

A few years later, Grudem published the first edition of his popular *Systematic Theology: An Introduction to Biblical Doctrine*. He amplified what had been laid out in *Recovering*

Biblical Manhood and Womanhood, arguing that "the curse brought a *distortion* of Adam's humble, considerate leadership and Eve's intelligent, willing submission to that leadership which existed before the fall."[43] The rest, as they say, is history. The fait accompli presented to evangelical women was that God's design for male headship and female submission was an eternal and divine condition.

Once I finally came face to face with the ugliness and pervasiveness of historical patriarchy, I realized that rather than being different from the world, Christians were just like everyone else in their treatment of women. When Dobson upheld a battered woman's desire to remain with her husband, he was just one more voice in more than four thousand years of history that agreed: women's place is under the power of men.

The Historical Truth about Patriarchy

In many ways, the debate between egalitarians (those who argue for biblical equality between men and women) and complementarians (those who argue for a biblical gender hierarchy that subordinates women to men) is in gridlock.[44] While complementarians like John Piper and Wayne Grudem proclaim that male headship existed before the fall, egalitarians like Alice Mathews and Philip B. Payne proclaim that it only came after. But when I had my epiphany about the beginning of patriarchy, it wasn't just the biblical text that convinced me. It was because the biblical text fit so well with historical evidence. In other words, the debate over the interpretation of Genesis 3:16 is not just a case of he said / she said. Historical evidence about the origins of patriarchy can move the conversation forward.

Let me show you what I mean.

In 1986, Gerda Lerner famously argued that patriarchy is a historical construct—linked to "militarism, hierarchy, and racism."[45] *The Epic of Gilgamesh*, according to Lerner, stands at the beginning of not only history but also patriarchy itself. The story testifies to one of the earliest emergences of complex human society: civilization. As soon as humans forged an agricultural society and began to build structured communities, they also began to build hierarchies of power, designating some people as more worthy to rule than others.

Let me pause for a moment. This book is my story—a white woman whose experiences as a pastor's wife and scholar have led me to reject evangelical teachings about male headship and female submission. I am fighting against patriarchy for women, but women are not the only ones hurt by patriarchy. Biblical scholar Clarice J. Martin reminds us that while patriarchy defines the boundaries of women's lives, it also defines "subjugated peoples and races as 'the others' to be dominated."[46] Patriarchy walks with structural racism and systemic oppression, and it has done so consistently throughout history.

It frustrates me how Christians try so hard to untangle the interlocking narratives of patriarchal oppression—loosening their hold on one group while tightening it on another. In her groundbreaking article, "The *Haustafeln* (Household Codes) in Afro-American Biblical Interpretation," Martin asks a provocative question: "How can black male preachers and theologians use a liberated hermeneutic while preaching and theologizing about slaves, but a literalist hermeneutic with reference to women?"[47] I would like to ask the same question of white preachers and theologians. When we rightly understand that biblical passages discussing slavery must be framed within their historical context and that, through the lens of this historical context, we can better see slavery as an ungodly system that stands contrary to the gospel of Christ, how can we not then apply the same standards to biblical texts about women? Martin challenges African American interpreters of the Bible to stop using "a hierarchalist hermeneutic with regard to biblical narratives about women."[48] Only then can all Black people truly be free.

She is right. Isn't it time that Christians, committed to following Jesus, recognize what historians like Gerda Lerner have known for so long? Isn't it time we stop ignoring the historical reality that patriarchy is part of an interwoven system of oppression that includes racism?

While aspects of Lerner's monumental study of patriarchy have been challenged and modified by subsequent historians, her argument that patriarchy emerged with the beginning of civilization has not. Merry Wiesner-Hanks, a leading modern scholar on gender and history, writes, "Though the lines of causation are not clear, the development of agriculture was accompanied by increasing subordination of women in many parts of the world." Both male labor and male power began to be associated with property ownership and the accompanying agricultural work. This led to boys being favored over girls for inheritance and to women becoming increasingly dependent on males who were property owners or agricultural laborers. Wiesner-Hanks continues, "Over generations, women's access to resources decreased, and it became increasingly difficult for them to survive without male support."[49] Women became increasingly dependent on men as agricultural communities became the heartbeat of human civilization. It is striking to me, as a scholar and as a Christian, that when God told Eve she would be under her husband's power, God simultaneously told Adam that agricultural labor would be necessary for human survival.

Patriarchy, according to both the Bible and historical record, emerged alongside the emergence of agricultural communities.

Rather than patriarchy being God-ordained, history suggests that patriarchy has a human origin: civilization itself. From *The Epic of Gilgamesh* in ancient Sumer to other texts like the *Ramayana* in ancient India, evidence from early civilizations reveals the development of gender hierarchies that privileged men (especially men of certain classes) and subordinated women. Patriarchy is a power structure created and maintained, literally, by human labor.

Against this backdrop, the Bible is nothing short of revolutionary.

While patriarchy certainly exists in the biblical narrative, Mathews encourages us to remember that there is a difference between "what is descriptive and what is prescriptive in the Bible."[50] Echoes of human patriarchy parade throughout the New Testament—from the exclusive leadership of male Jews to the harsh adultery laws applied to women and even to the writings of Paul. The early church was trying to make sense of its place in a Greco-Roman world, and much of that world bled through into the church's stories.

At the same time, we see a surprising number of passages subverting traditional gender roles and emphasizing women as leaders—from the Samaritan woman at the well giving Jesus a drink to Mary of Bethany learning at Jesus's feet like a disciple to Martha declaring her faith in Jesus (which counters the lack of faith exhibited by most of the disciples). I laughed recently at biblical scholar Febbie C. Dickerson's musings about Tabitha, a woman identified as a disciple in Acts 9. "I wonder," asks Dickerson, "what would happen if preachers learned Greek and so recognized that Tabitha's identification as 'a certain female disciple' probably indicates that she is one of many female disciples."[51] Biblical women are more than we have imagined them to be; they will not fit in the mold complementarianism has decreed for them.

Beth Moore recognizes this in her response to Owen Strachan in an online thread about women in ministry: "What I plead for is to grapple with the entire text from Mt 1 thru Rev 22 on every matter concerning women. To grapple with Paul's words in 1 Tim/1 Cor 14 as authoritative, God-breathed!—alongside other words Paul wrote, equally inspired & make sense of the many women he served alongside. Above all else, we must search the attitudes of Christ Jesus himself toward women."[52] Moore, who has spent her life immersed in the Bible, realizes a disconnect between the construct of biblical womanhood and the real lives of women in the Bible.

Patriarchy exists in the Bible because the Bible was written in a patriarchal world. Historically speaking, there is nothing surprising about biblical stories and passages riddled with patriarchal attitudes and actions. What is surprising is how many biblical passages and stories undermine, rather than support, patriarchy. Even John Piper admitted in 1984 that he can't figure out what to do with Deborah and Huldah.[53] The most difficult passages in the Bible to explain, historically speaking, are those like Galatians 3:26–28: "For in Christ Jesus you are all children of God through faith. As many of you as were baptized into Christ have clothed yourselves with Christ. There is no longer Jew or Greek, there is no longer slave or free, there is no longer male and female; for all of you are one in Christ Jesus." This is what is radical. This is what makes Christianity so different from the rest of human history. This is what sets both men and women free.

Isn't it ironic (not to mention tiresome) that we spend so much time fighting to make Christianity look like the world around us instead of fighting to make it look like Jesus Christ? Shouldn't it be the other way around? Sarah Bessey, the progressive Christian writer, activist, and bestselling author of *Jesus Feminist*, is absolutely right that patriarchy is not "God's dream for humanity."[54] Doesn't the world of Galatians 3 seem more like the world of Jesus? Patriarchy may be a part of Christian history, but that doesn't make it Christian. It just shows us the historical (and very human) roots of biblical womanhood.

"I HATE PAUL!"

I can't tell you how many times I have heard that from my students, mostly young women scarred by how Paul has been used against them as they have been told to be silent (1 Corinthians 14), to submit to their husbands (Ephesians 5), not to teach or exercise authority over men (1 Timothy 2), and to be workers at home (Titus 2). They have been taught that God designed women to follow male headship (1 Corinthians 11), focusing on family and home (Colossians 3; 1 Peter 3), and that occupations other than family should be secondary for women, mostly undertaken out of necessity or after their children have left the house.

A few years ago, a student came to my office ostensibly to discuss her class paper, but it soon became clear that what she really wanted to discuss was her vocation. She asked me: Did God call you to be a professor as well as a mom and a pastor's wife? Was it hard? Did you feel guilty about working outside the home? Was your husband supportive? What did people in your church think? She shared her frustrations as a career-minded Christian woman from a conservative background who was trying to reconcile church and family expectations with her vocational calling. A recent conversation with her father had exasperated her. Anxious about her major, she had asked him for advice. He tried to soothe her fears, suggesting her major didn't matter that much since she would just get married and not work anyway. Shocked, she retorted, "Dad, are you really sending me to four years of college for me to never use my degree?"

The father's attitude toward women working outside the home isn't anomalous. As we have seen, a 2017 Barna study found that while Americans in general are becoming more comfortable with women in leadership roles and more understanding of the significant obstacles women face in the workplace, evangelical Christians lag behind.[1] Perhaps the most startling gap in evangelical attitudes concerns women in specific leadership roles. I commented in 2016 that Wayne Grudem's attitude toward women—that they should never be in authority over men—made it impossible for him to support a female candidate for president.[2] The Barna study suggests I was right about this. The white evangelical leaders like Grudem who rallied to support Donald Trump's bid for the presidency correspond to the lowest levels of comfort with a female president. For at least some evangelical and Republican voters (27–35 percent), the problem with Hillary Clinton wasn't just that she is a Democrat; it was also that she is a woman (27 percent of evangelical voters and 35 percent of Republican voters said they were uncomfortable with a female president).[3] Three years later I wasn't surprised to see Elizabeth Warren's bid for presidency fall beneath the same gendered hatchet.

Ideas matter. These evangelical beliefs—why they argue for the immutability of female submission—are rooted in how they interpret Paul. The Council on Biblical Manhood and Womanhood may start with Genesis 2 in their overview of complementarianism, but their reading of this creation narrative stems from 1 Corinthians 11 and 1 Timothy 2.[4] Paul frames every aspect of complementarian teachings. Evangelicals read Pauline texts as designating permanent and divinely ordained role distinctions between the sexes. Men wield authority that women cannot.

Men lead, women follow. Paul tells us so.

Is it any wonder my students hate Paul?

But what if we have been reading Paul wrong? Early during our youth ministry years, my husband and I took a group of kids to a weekend evangelism conference. One of the speakers revealed his secret evangelism weapon—the question "What if you're wrong?" I don't remember much from that conference, but this question has stuck with me. I have found it useful in my work as a historian—what if I am wrong about my conclusions? Am I willing to reconsider the evidence? I have found it useful as a teacher, especially when a student presents me with a different idea. The question "What if I'm wrong?" helps me listen to others better. It keeps me humble. It makes me a better scholar.

So here is my question for complementarian evangelicals: What if you are wrong? What if evangelicals have been understanding Paul through the lens of modern culture instead of the way Paul intended to be understood? The evangelical church fears that recognizing women's leadership will mean bowing to cultural peer pressure. But what if the church is bowing to cultural peer pressure by denying women's leadership? What if, instead of a "plain and natural" reading, our interpretation of Paul—and subsequent exclusion of women from leadership roles—results from succumbing to the attitudes and patterns of thinking around us? Christians in the past may have used Paul to exclude women from leadership, but this doesn't mean that the subjugation of women is biblical. It just means that Christians today are repeating the same mistake of Christians in the past—modeling our treatment of women after the world around us instead of the world Jesus shows us is possible.

So when my students exclaim that they "hate Paul," I counter: it isn't Paul they hate; rather, they hate how Paul's letters have become foundational to an understanding of biblical gender roles that oppress women. Beverly Roberts Gaventa, a leading Pauline scholar, laments that evangelicals have spent so much time "parsing the lines of Paul's letters for theological propositions and ethical guidelines that must be replicated narrowly" that we have missed Paul's bigger purpose. We have reduced his call for oneness into patrolling borders for uniformity; we have traded the "radical character" of Christ's body for a rigid hierarchy of gender and power. Instead of "thinking along *with* Paul*,*" as Gaventa appeals, evangelicals have turned Paul into a weapon for our own culture wars.[5] New Testament scholar Boykin Sanders proclaims that it is time to get Paul right when it comes to women. In bold type under the heading "Neither Male nor Female," he argues, "The lesson for the black church here is that gender discrimination in the work of the church is unacceptable." Paul shows us that gender discrimination is "a return to the ways of the world," and we are called into the "new world of the Christ-crucified gospel."[6]

The truth—the evangelical reality—is that we have focused so much on adapting Paul to be like us that we have forgotten to adapt ourselves to what Paul is calling us to be: one in Christ.[7] Instead of choosing the better part and embracing the "new world of the Christ-crucified gospel," we have chosen to keep doing what humans have always done: building our own tower of hierarchy and power.

Because We Can Read Paul Differently

A medieval priest penned my favorite marriage sermon. Not many people know his name, although Dorothy L. Sayers stole my heart by quoting him in her classic murder mystery *The Nine Tailors* (another favorite of mine). His name was John

Mirk, and he lived in West England during the late fourteenth and early fifteenth centuries. His sermon collection, *Festial*, became popular in England—so popular, in fact, that the first set of official Protestant homilies in 1547 was written, in part, to counter its influence. We have evidence that *Festial* sermons were printed until the eve of the Reformation and that, despite its Catholic doctrine, *Festial* continued to be preached throughout the reign of Queen Elizabeth I.[8]

Listen to how this *Festial* sermon describes the marriage relationship between husband and wife: "Thus, by God's command, a man shall take on a wife of like age, like condition, and like birth." The text continues, "For this a man shall leave father and mother and draw to her as a part of himself, and she shall love him and he her, truly together, and they shall be two in one flesh."[9] Rather than hierarchy, the sermon stresses how the man and woman shall love "truly together" and become "one flesh." When the priest blesses the woman's ring, he declares that it "represents God who has neither a beginning nor ending, and puts it on her finger that has a vein running to her heart, showing that she shall love God over all things and then her husband."[10] The ring proclaims that a wife's allegiance belongs first to God and second to her husband. Although the sermon is filled with Scripture, quoting liberally from Genesis 1–3 as well as from Matthew 22 and John 2, it does not quote Paul. It contains no reference to Ephesians, Colossians, Titus, or even 1 Peter—the New Testament books that famously contain the call for wives to submit to their husbands. These New Testament passages, known as the "household codes" (Ephesians 5:21–6:9; Colossians 3:18–4:1; 1 Peter 2:18–3:7; Titus 2:1–10), dominate modern discussions about gender roles and laid the foundation for the change in the 1998 amendment to the "Baptist Faith and Message" that wives should "graciously submit" to the authority of their husbands.[11] But Mirk's medieval sermon "places very little stress on female subjection as the basis for living well in marriage," historian Christine Peters observes.[12] Mirk does not declare that the wife should obey her husband. In fact, his sermon emphasizes that what got Eve into trouble was loving her husband too much, and so the wedding ring isn't a symbol of the wife belonging to her husband—it is a reminder for wives to *put God first*.[13]

In my research, I have found that sermons in late medieval England rarely preach the Pauline passages that my students react against. This is shockingly different from sermons in the modern evangelical world—and rather surprising, given that the medieval world was just as prone to patriarchy as was the ancient world and as is our modern world (more about this in the next chapter).[14] It is also shockingly different from what we have been taught about Paul's writings about women—that they have been used throughout Christian history in a continuous, unbroken thread to uphold God's design for men to lead and women to follow.

This simply isn't true. Take, for example, Catholicism. Evangelicals seem to think that because the Catholic tradition does not ordain women, the Catholic tradition must also use Paul to support male headship in marriage. Not so, or at least not consistently so. Religion scholar Daniel Cere explains, "There has never been a tradition of formal doctrinal teaching endorsing [marital] subordination within the Catholic tradition."[15] Medieval historian Alcuin Blamires describes "nagging paradoxes" (both practical and scriptural) that haunted medieval Catholic teachings about gender, authority, and the body of Christ.[16] For example, because husbands sinned, they often proved poor leaders for their wives—blurring for medieval preachers the "bottom line" of male authority. As one early fifteenth-century text argued, a wife should not blindly follow her husband, because—just as Mirk's marriage sermon stated—she owed allegiance first to Jesus as her "principal husband." For medieval women, Jesus as head could trump husbandly authority; sometimes women could even take the lead. Peter Abelard, a famous twelfth-century scholastic, discusses the scriptural story of a woman anointing Jesus with oil (Matthew 26:6–13; Mark 14:3–9; Luke 7:37–50). Abelard writes that when "woman and not man is linked with Christ's headship," she "indeed institutes him *as* 'Christ.'" By allowing a woman to anoint him with oil, Jesus overturns male headship—allowing a woman to do what only men had been able to do until that moment: anoint the king. Blamires describes Abelard's argument as "a stunning dislocation of the conventional gendering of body as feminine and head as masculine." The woman's anointing of Jesus is a "naming action" for Abelard, writes Blamires. "It is this woman who anoints the saint of saints to be Christ."[17]

I could say a lot more, but this is the point: despite the evangelical obsession with male headship, Christians past and present have been less sure. Pope John Paul II's stance in his 1988 apostolic letter serves as a good case in point. He suggests that using Paul's writings in Ephesians 5 to justify male headship and female subordination in marriage would be the equivalent of using those passages to justify slavery.[18]

Because Paul's Purpose Wasn't to Emphasize Wifely Submission

So let's talk about the submission of wives, an idea that evangelicals pull from the New Testament household codes. As we've seen, historical context suggests that wifely submission was *not the point* of Paul's writings, including in the household codes. Rather than including the household codes to dictate how Christians should follow the gender hierarchy of the Roman Empire, what if Paul was teaching Christians to live differently within their Roman context? Rather than New Testament "texts of terror" for women, what if the household codes can be read as resistance narratives to Roman patriarchy?[19]

Taken at face value (a "plain and literal interpretation"), the household codes seem to sanctify the Roman patriarchal structure: the authority of the paterfamilias (husband/father) over women, children, and slaves. The text in Colossians 3 shows this well: "Wives, be subject to your husbands, as is fitting in the Lord. Husbands, love your wives and never treat them harshly. Children, obey your parents in everything, for this is your acceptable duty in the Lord. Fathers, do not provoke your children, or they may lose heart. Slaves, obey your earthly masters in everything, not only while being watched and in order to please them, but wholeheartedly, fearing the Lord" (vv. 18–22). In case you don't know much about Roman patriarchy, male guardianship was Roman law. Wives legally had to submit to the authority of their husbands; unmarried women had to submit to the authority of their fathers or nearest male relatives; women could not own property or run businesses in their own right; women could not conduct legal or financial transactions without a man acting on their behalf. From this historical perspective, it is not surprising to find discussions about wives in first-century Roman texts (the New Testament) reflecting the reality of life for wives in the first-century Roman world. Paul's inclusion of a statement for women to be subject to their husbands is exactly what the Roman world would have expected.[20]

We just don't get this as modern evangelicals.

Paul wasn't telling the early Christians to look like everyone else; he was telling them that, as Christians, they had to be different. Rachel Held Evans explains the Christian household codes as a "Jesus remix" of Roman patriarchy.[21] Scholarship suggests that the term *remix* provides a good description. New Testament scholars Carolyn Osiek and Margaret MacDonald, for example, argue that the ethical teachings embedded in the Ephesian household code are so "oppositional" to the Greco-Roman world that, rather than a sign of accommodation "the household code is presented as that which ultimately sets believers apart."[22] When read rightly, the household codes not only set women free, as Shi-Min Lu writes, but they set all the members of the household free from the "oppressive elements" of the Roman world.[23] Paul wasn't imposing Roman patriarchy on Christians; Paul was using a Jesus remix to tell Christians how the gospel set them free.

So let's look at the Jesus remix of two similar household-code passages in Paul.

Colossians 3:18–19	"Wives, be subject to your husbands, as is fitting in the Lord. Husbands, love your wives and never treat them harshly."
Ephesians 5:21–22, 25, 28, 33	"Be subject to one another out of reverence for Christ. Wives, be subject to your husband as you are to the Lord. . . . Husbands, love your wives, just as Christ loved the church and gave himself up for her. . . . Husbands should love their wives as they do their own bodies. . . . Each of you . . . should love his wife as himself, and a wife should respect her husband."

As modern Christians, we immediately hear masculine authority. *Wives, be subject to your husband.* Yet as first-century

47

Christians, Paul's original audience would have immediately heard the opposite. *Husbands, love your wives and never treat them harshly. Husbands, love your wives, just as Christ loved the church and gave himself up for her.* The focus of the Christian household codes isn't the same today as it was in the Roman world.

Take the fourth-century BC philosopher Aristotle. Aristotle wrote in *Politics* what would become one of the most influential household code texts in Western culture. Listen to what he said:

> Of household management we have seen that there are three parts—one is the rule of a master over slaves . . . , another of a father, and the third of a husband. A husband and father, we saw, rules over wife and children, both free, but the rule differs, the rule over his children being a royal, over his wife a constitutional rule. For although there may be exceptions to the order of nature, the male is by nature fitter for command than the female. . . . The inequality [between male and female] is permanent. . . . The courage of a man is shown in commanding, of a woman in obeying. . . . All classes must be deemed to have their special attributes; as the poet says of women, "Silence is a woman's glory but this is not equally the glory of man."[24]

Do you hear the differences? Aristotle is writing specifically to men about how they should rule and why they have the right to rule. He does not include inferiors within the conversation. Household governance is the domain of the Roman man—as master, father, and husband. The conversation is directed to men alone.

By contrast, the Christian household codes address all the people in the house church—men, women, children, and slaves. Everyone is included in the conversation. Theologian Lucy Peppiatt writes that this is "key" to the Christian subversion of Roman patriarchy. Because the Christian household codes are directed to all members of the Roman household, instead of presuming the guardianship of the male head, they "contain within them the overturning of accepted positions accorded to men, women, slaves, and children, and the expectations placed upon them."[25] Instead of endowing authority to a man who speaks and acts for those within his household, the Christian household codes offer each member of the shared community—knit together by their faith in Christ—the right to hear and act for themselves. This is radically different from the Roman patriarchal structure. The Christian structure of the house church *resists* the patriarchal world of the Roman Empire.

Because Paul's Purpose Wasn't to Emphasize Male Authority

How the Christian household codes frame masculine authority can also be read as a resistance narrative to Roman patriarchy. Aristotle wrote to justify masculine authority. He emphasized the permanent inequality between men and women: the nature of man is to command, while the nature of woman is to obey. The Christian household codes do something different. In Colossians 3, Paul opens his discussion of the household with a call to *wives first*—not to the man presumably in charge (as Aristotle does). Both Peppiatt and Scot McKnight highlight Paul's lack of emphasis on the power and authority of the husband. Instead, Paul emphasizes that wives should be subject *as fitting in the Lord* (not because they are inferior) and that husbands should love their wives and not treat them harshly. "Instead of grounding the instruction to the wife in her husband's authority, power, leadership or status in a hierarchy," McKnight writes, "the grounding is radically otherwise: it is grounded in the Lord's way of life."[26] Jesus, not the Roman paterfamilias, is in charge of the Christian household.[27]

Likewise, Ephesians 5 can be read as a resistance narrative to Roman patriarchy. Many scholars argue that Paul subordinates his entire discussion of the household codes under verse 21: "Be subject to one another out of reverence for Christ." When this verse is read at the beginning of the Ephesians household codes, it changes everything. Yes, wives are to submit, but so are husbands. Instead of underscoring the inferiority of women, Ephesians 5 underscores the equality of women—they are called to submit in verse 22, just like their husbands are called to submit in verse 21. Instead of making Christians just another part of the Roman crowd (emphasizing female submission), the mutual submission in verse 21 "is characteristic of a way of life that sets believers apart from the nonbelieving world."[28] Because of its radical implications, verse 21 must be distanced from verse 22 in Bible translations that wish to uphold complementarian views. The English Standard Version (ESV) includes verse 21 at the end of the section the translators have titled "Walk in Love." This separates verse 21 from the beginning of the next section, titled "Wives and Husbands," which then begins with verse 22: "Wives, submit to your own husbands, as to the Lord." In this way, the ESV chooses to highlight female submission in verse 22, literally separating it from Paul's subversion of Roman patriarchy in verse 21.

What the ESV translators have done in Ephesians 5 reminds me of a critique made by archaeologist Ian Morris about Athenian men in classical Greece. It is not accidental, writes Morris, that archaeologists find little material evidence for women in ancient Athens. "Women and slaves remain invisible," but this isn't because of "methodological problems" or misattribution of evidence by scholars. The "unusually pervasive male citizen culture" of the Greek city-state not only subjugated women but so well controlled the spaces in which women lived that little evidence of them is left. Women remain invisible because "Athenian male citizens wanted it that way."[29] The subjection of women is highlighted in the ESV translation of Ephesians 5, and the call for husbands to submit is minimized—not because Paul meant it that way but because the complementarian translators of the ESV wanted it that way.

Ephesians 5:21 isn't the only radical subversion of Roman patriarchy in the chapter. Paul also demands that men love their wives as they love their own bodies. Did you know that in the Greco-Roman world, female bodies were considered imperfect and deformed men? In his *Generation of Animals*, Aristotle writes that "the female is as it were a deformed male" and that "because females are weaker and colder in their nature . . . we should look upon the female state as being as it were a deformity."[30] Women were literally monstrous. Of course, Aristotle did admit that the female deformity was a "regular" and useful occurrence. Galen, in the second century BC, likewise proclaimed women imperfect men who lacked the heat to expel their sex organs.[31] But, like Aristotle, he conceded it was a good thing that deformed men existed because otherwise procreation would be impossible.

By contrast, Paul reflects none of this disdain for the female body. He proclaims that male bodies are not any more valuable or worthy than female bodies. Women, like men, can be "holy and without blemish," and men are to love the female body just as they love their own male body (Ephesians 5:27–29). I tell my students how easily a study of Paul overturns John Piper's claim that Christianity has a "masculine feel."[32] We might think that Paul would glory in his masculine authority, but he doesn't. Seven times throughout his letters, as Beverly Roberts Gaventa has found, Paul uses maternal imagery to describe his ongoing relationship with the church congregations he helped found. "Statistically that means that Paul uses maternal imagery more often than he does paternal imagery, a feature that is impressive, especially when we consider its virtual absence from most discussions of the Pauline letters."[33] Paul describes himself—a male apostle—as a pregnant mother, a mother giving birth, and even a nursing mother.

Not only does Paul consider the female body valuable, but he is willing to "hand over the authority of a patriarch in favor of a role that will bring him shame, the shame of a female-identified male."[34] How beautiful, how radical is Paul's message! I can't even imagine how welcome his words would have been to women in first-century churches. What made female bodies weak in the Roman world made them strong in the writings of Paul. By taking on the literary guise of a woman, Paul embodied the radical claim of his own words in Galatians 3:28 that, in Christ, "there is no longer male and female."

Medieval Christians picked up on Paul's maternal imagery in a way that modern Christians do not. Gaventa notes how few modern scholars have paid attention to Paul's startling maternal imagery.[35] In contrast, historian Caroline Walker Bynum was so struck by the frequency of maternal imagery used by male clergy in the twelfth century that she wrote the groundbreaking study *Jesus as Mother: Studies in the Spirituality of the High Middle Ages.* "The question I would like to ask," she writes, "is why the use of explicit and elaborate maternal imagery to describe God and Christ, who are usually described as male, is so popular with twelfth-century Cistercian monks."[36] She identifies Anselm of Canterbury, a Benedictine monk who is rather patriarchal in his attitudes toward women, as one of the first medieval clergy to pick up on Paul's maternal imagery. Clearly echoing Paul's writings in 1 Thessalonians 2:7 and Galatians 4:19, Anselm writes, "You [Paul] are among Christians like a nurse who not only cares for her children but also gives birth to them a second time by the solicitude of her marvelous love."[37] Just because modern evangelicals overlook Paul's radical use of maternal imagery doesn't mean it isn't there. It just means that, once again, we have gotten Paul wrong.

Because Paul's Purpose Wasn't the Roman Gender Hierarchy

One more piece of evidence that convinces me that the household codes should be read as resistance narratives to Roman patriarchy is how early Christians were perceived by the Roman world: as "gender deviants." Osiek and MacDonald remind us that Pliny the Younger, after discussing the torture of two Christian women whom he called deacons, described Christianity as a "depraved and excessive superstition."[38] As they write, "In drawing attention to some kind of female leadership in the group—to the exclusion of references to male leaders—Pliny was implying that the ideals of masculinity were being compromised. Women were in control."[39] And this, in Roman terms, was shameful. Not only did early Christians place women in leadership roles; they met together on equal footing—men, women, children, and slaves—in the privacy of the home, a traditionally female space. Christianity was deviant and immoral because it was perceived as undermining ideals of Roman masculinity. Christianity was repugnant to Pliny because it didn't follow the Roman household codes—not because it followed them.

To many modern Christians, the household codes are what make us different from the world. While feminism rages chaotically around us, as many believe, the evangelical church stands like a well-groomed tree planted by streams of water—firm and serene with a hierarchy of branches. Indeed, this is how John Piper and Wayne Grudem frame it in *Recovering Biblical Manhood and Womanhood*. As they write in the introduction, "We want to help Christians recover a noble vision of manhood and womanhood as God created them to be. . . . We hope that this new vision—a vision of Biblical 'complementarity'—will both correct the previous mistakes and avoid the opposite mistakes that come from the feminist blurring of God-given sexual distinctions."[40] Except that viewing the Roman gender hierarchy as a "new vision" isn't how Paul's first-century world would have seen it. The Roman patriarchal structure echoed by Paul's household codes was *not* the "new vision." Recognizing the power of the paterfamilias was what the Roman world already did. Patriarchy wasn't something that made Christians different; it was something that made them the same.

The New Testament household codes tell a story of how the early church was trying to live within a non-Christian, and increasingly hostile, world. They needed to fit in, but they also needed to uphold the gospel of Christ. They had to uphold the frame of Roman patriarchy as much as they could, but they also had to uphold the worth and dignity of each human being made in the image of God. Paul gave them the blueprints to remix Roman patriarchy. Instead of being directed toward men as the primary authority, the Christian household codes include everyone in the conversation. Instead of justifying male authority on account of female inferiority, the Christian household codes affirm women as having equal worth to men. Instead of focusing on wifely submission (everyone was doing that), the Christian household codes demand that the husband do exactly the opposite of what Roman law allowed: sacrificing his life for his wife instead of exercising power over her life. This, writes Peppiatt, is the "Christian revolution."[41] This is what makes Christians *different* from the world around us.

Could we have gotten Paul exactly backward? What if his focus was never male headship and female submission? What if his vision was bigger than we have imagined? What if instead of replicating an ancient gender hierarchy, Paul was showing us how the Christian gospel sets even the Roman household free?

Because Paul Didn't Tell Women to Be Silent

A few years ago, my husband was out of town on a retreat with many of our high school youth. The man who normally taught youth Sunday school, which included all the kids who didn't go on the retreat that weekend, called in sick. I was the only available option. This was fine with me. I love teaching, and at this point, I was at the height of my game. Every week I taught not only six undergraduate class sessions at Baylor but also the high school girls on Wednesday night, as well as the graduate students, undergraduate students, and youth I met with to mentor. Teaching, even on the fly, was second nature.

But the leaders at our church had made it clear that women could not teach men, period. And they defined manhood as beginning at age thirteen. So I had to call the pastor. I had to explain the situation and ask for a special dispensation to be able to stand in for a male teacher in a classroom filled with teenage boys and girls. After a long pause, I was told it would be okay as long as I simply went through the sermon questions from the week before and acted as a facilitator—not as a teacher. It took everything in me to simply say thanks and hang up.

I am sure part of it was my pride. Here I was, a professor with a PhD from a major research university (my secondary field is religious studies), being told I couldn't teach high school Sunday school. Yes, it hurt my pride. But that wasn't the only reason I was upset. It was also because I believed the pastor was wrong. I could not teach because of his belief that Paul told women to be silent and not to exercise authority over men. What if Paul never said this? Just like with the household codes, what if we have simply misunderstood Paul because we have forgotten his Roman context? What if we have confused Paul's refutations of the pagan world around him with Paul's own words?

Because I am a historian, I know there is more to Paul's letters than what his words reveal. Paul was writing to churches with which he had intimate knowledge. He knew them. "These issues do not arise of out of thin air," Gaventa reminds us about 1 Corinthians.[42] Paul knew the struggles, the people, the troublemakers. We don't need a deep historical dive to understand the basics of Paul's message. We can tell that competition had emerged within the Corinthian congregation over the value of different spiritual gifts (as one example). We may not know firsthand details—like who had become prideful and who was championing prophecy over speaking in tongues—but we know how Paul rebuked them: their gifts all come from the same Spirit, their gifts all function within the same body, and none of their gifts work independently. We hear Paul's message clearly: in the body of Christ we are all equally important. The distance of more than two thousand years doesn't obscure his meaning.

And yet, when we ignore the historical context of Paul's letters, we can disrupt his meaning and turn his molehills into mountains. First Corinthians 14:33–36 provides an excellent example: "As in all the churches of the saints, women should be silent in the churches. For they are not permitted to speak, but should be subordinate, as the law also says. If there is anything they desire to know, let them ask their husbands at home. For it is shameful for a woman to speak in church. Or did the word of God originate with you? Or are you the only ones it has reached?" Paul declares that women are to be silent, subordinate, and reliant upon the spiritual authority of their husbands. Right? This passage has become a major mountain for modern evangelicals, emphasized more than I think Paul ever intended it to be. It has become a foundational verse for complementarian teachings. Let's look at how a better understanding of Roman history can change how we interpret this passage.

In 215 BC, a defeated and cash-strapped Rome passed a new law. The context was their greatest military defeat ever. The year prior, on August 2, the Carthaginian general Hannibal had destroyed their army at Cannae during the Second Punic War. Sources tell us that between fifty thousand and seventy thousand Roman soldiers died that day. That is more than some of the bloodiest battles in World War II. As the first-century Roman historian Livy cried, "Certainly there is no other nation that would not have succumbed beneath such a weight of calamity."[43] Except Rome wasn't like other nations (which was Livy's point). Rome did not succumb. They tightened their belt, raised a new army, and kept going. Rome epitomized grit.[44]

My students know I don't like straight military history. So when I start telling a story like this, they know that women will soon enter the picture. And indeed they do. Rome's belt-tightening led to a crackdown on a growing group of independently wealthy women—the wives and daughters who profited from the sudden reduction in male guardians. Rome did this for probably two reasons (historians still argue about it). One reason was certainly the war effort. Rome needed money from everyone. So they passed the Oppian Law. Women could no longer dress in luxurious clothes, ride in carriages (in Rome) except on special occasions, or possess more than half an ounce of gold. Some even had to turn over their wartime inheritances to the state. These women were encouraged to spend more money for Rome and less on themselves.

The second reason Rome likely passed the Oppian Law was to limit women's public displays of wealth. Rome was in mourning after the Battle of Cannae. It wasn't a time to have parties and wear fancy clothes. It was a time to batten down the hatches and fight to the death (which is pretty much what they did). It was especially not a time for women to have more money than men did. Rome was a patriarchal society, as we have already seen, and Roman matrons—safely married women under the guardianship of their husbands—symbolized the success of Roman society. Independently wealthy women free from male leadership did not.

Rome won, by the way.

But when the crisis was over, the law restricting women's wealth continued, while laws restricting men's wealth did not. By 195 BC, women in Rome had had enough. They protested, blockading the streets and even the pathways to the Forum, demanding that the law be repealed.

One consul, Cato the Elder, opposed repealing the law. Listen to what he said, and remember that Livy is probably recording his speech during the reign of Caesar Augustus (approximately 30 BC to AD 17):

> At home our freedom is conquered by female fury, here in the Forum it is bruised and trampled upon, and because we have not contained the individuals, we fear the lot. . . . Indeed, I blushed when, a short while ago, I walked through the midst of a band of women. . . . I should have said, "What kind of behavior is this? Running around in public, blocking streets, and speaking to other women's husbands! Could you not have asked your own husbands the same thing at home? Are you more charming in public with others' husbands than at home with your own? And yet, it is not fitting even at home . . . for you to concern yourselves with what laws are passed or repealed here." Our ancestors did not want women to conduct any—not even private—business without a guardian; they wanted them to be under the authority of parents, brothers, or husbands; we (the gods help us!) even now let them snatch at the government and meddle in the Forum and our assemblies. What are they doing now on the streets and crossroads, if they are not persuading the tribunes to vote for repeal? . . . If they are victorious now, what will they not attempt? As soon as they begin to be your equals, they will have become your superiors.[45]

Livy recorded this speech by Cato in his *History of Rome*. Pliny the Younger, writing toward the end of the first century, depicts Livy as a celebrity. Livy was a popular writer, and his *History* would have been well known.

So, as a historian, it doesn't surprise me that echoes of Livy ended up in the New Testament. Listen again to 1 Corinthians 14:34–35: "Women should be silent in the churches. For they are not permitted to speak, but should be subordinate, as the law also says. If there is anything they desire to know, let them ask their husbands at home. For it is shameful for a woman to speak in church." No, it isn't word for word. But it is close. A definite echo. In other words, Paul's words are drawing from his Roman context.

Cato's speech isn't the only Roman text to convey this sentiment about women. New Testament scholar Charles Talbert reminds us that Juvenal (early second century AD), in *Satires* 6, also condemns women who run around publicly intruding on male governance instead of staying at home.[46] The Roman world viewed women as subordinate to men. The Roman world declared that men should convey information to their wives at home instead of women going about in public. The Roman world told women to be silent in public forums.

Paul was an educated Roman citizen. He would have been familiar with contemporary rhetorical practices that corrected faulty understanding by quoting the faulty understanding and then refuting it. Paul does this in 1 Corinthians 6 and 7 with his quotations "all things are lawful for me," "food is meant for the stomach and the stomach for food," and "it is well for a man not to touch a woman."[47] In these instances, Paul is quoting the faulty views of the Gentile world, such as "all things are lawful for me." Paul then "strongly modifies" them.[48] Paul would have been familiar with the contemporary views about women, including Livy's, that women should be silent in public and gain information from their husbands at home. Isn't it possible, as Peppiatt has argued, that Paul is doing the same thing in 1 Corinthians 11 and 14 that he does in 1 Corinthians 6 and 7?[49] Refuting bad practices by quoting those bad practices and then correcting them? As Peppiatt writes, "The prohibitions placed on women in the letter to the Corinthians are examples of how the Corinthians were treating women, in line with their own cultural expectations and values, against Paul's teachings."[50]

What if Paul was so concerned that Christians in Corinth were imposing their own cultural restrictions on women that he called them on it? He quoted the bad practice, which Corinthian men were trying to drag from the Roman world into their Christian world, and then he countered it. The Revised Standard Version (RSV) lends support to the idea that this is what Paul was doing. Paul first lays out the cultural restrictions: "As in all the churches of the saints, the women should keep silence in the churches. For they are not permitted to speak, but should be subordinate, as even the law says. If there is anything they desire to know, let them ask their husbands at home. For it is shameful for a woman to speak in church" (1 Corinthians 14:33–35). And then Paul intervenes: "What! Did the word of God originate with you, or are you the only ones it has reached? If anyone thinks that he is a prophet, or spiritual, he should acknowledge that what I am writing to you is a command of the Lord. If anyone does not recognize this, he is not recognized. So, my brethren, earnestly desire to prophesy, and do not forbid speaking in tongues; but all things should be done decently and in order" (vv. 36–40).

I often do this as a classroom exercise. I have a student read from their own translation, usually the ESV or NIV. Then I will read from the RSV, inflecting the words appropriately. When I proclaim, "What! Did the word of God originate with you?"

I can usually hear their gasp, their collective intake of breath. Once a student exclaimed out loud, "Dr. Barr! That changes it completely!" Yes, I told her, it does.

When 1 Corinthians 14:34–35 is read as a quotation representing a Corinthian practice (which D. W. Odell-Scott argued for in 1983, Charles Talbert argued for in 1987, and Peppiatt has argued for again more recently[51]), Paul's purpose seems clear: to distinguish what the Corinthians were doing ("women be silent") and to clarify that Christians should not be following the Corinthian practice ("What!"). While I cannot guarantee this is what Paul was doing, it makes a lot of (historical) sense. First Corinthians includes several non-Pauline quotations already, and the wording of verses 34–35 is remarkably close to Roman sources. As Marg Mowczko observes, "The view that 14:34–35 is a non-Pauline quotation is one of the few that offers a plausible explanation for the jarring change of tone which verses 34–35 bring into the text, as well as the subsequent abrupt change of topic, tone, and gender in verse 36."[52] If Paul is indeed quoting the Roman worldview to counter it with the Christian worldview, then his meaning is the exact opposite of what evangelical women have been taught.

Could it be that, instead of telling women to be silent like the Roman world did, Paul was actually telling men that, in the world of Jesus, women were allowed to speak? Could we have missed Paul's point (again)? Instead of heeding his rebuke and freeing women to speak, are we continuing the very patriarchal practices that Paul was condemning?

As a historian, I find it hard to ignore how similar Paul's words are to the Greco-Roman world in which he lives. Yet, even if I am wrong and Paul is only drawing on Roman sources instead of intentionally quoting them for the purpose of refutation, I would still argue that the directives Paul gave to Corinthian women are limited to their historical context.[53] Why? Because consistency is an interpretative virtue. Paul is not making a blanket decree for women to be silent; he allows women to speak throughout his letters (1 Corinthians 11:1–6 is a case in point). Paul is not limiting women's leadership; he tells us with his own hand that women lead in the early church and that he supports their ministries (I will discuss Romans 16 in the next section). Maintaining a rigid gender hierarchy just isn't Paul's point. As Beverly Roberts Gaventa reminds us from earlier in 1 Corinthians (12:1–7), Paul's "calling to service is not restricted along gender lines so that arguments about complementarity find no grounding here."[54] By insisting that Paul told women to be silent, evangelicals have capitulated to patriarchal culture once again. Instead of ditching Aristotle (as Rachel Held Evans once encouraged us to do[55]), we have ditched the freedom in Christ that Paul was trying so hard to give us.

Because Paul's Biblical Women Don't Follow Biblical Womanhood

It was Paul's women in Romans 16 who finally changed my mind.

I still remember the Sunday it clicked. I was upset after the sermon. So upset that I was doing the dishes. The running water soothed my mind as I scrubbed lunch plates. My husband knew something was wrong (the dishes were a dead giveaway). He walked into the kitchen. He didn't say anything. Finally, I spoke. "I don't believe in male headship." He leaned against the counter. I couldn't look at him. More time passed, and then he asked, "You don't believe that men are called to be the spiritual leaders of the home?" I shook my head. "No." He stood there for another minute, and then he just said "okay" and walked away. I knew he didn't agree with me then—he had been raised in a complementarian church and attended a complementarian seminary. Yet he was willing to listen and consider a different theological perspective. I am forever grateful for the trust he showed me that day.

It wasn't actually the sermon that pushed me over the edge, although I do remember it had been about male leadership. What pushed me over the edge was a recent lecture I had given in my women's history class. We were talking about women in the early church, as we moved chronologically from the ancient world to the medieval world. On a whim, I asked one of the students to open their Bible and read Romans 16 out loud (at a Christian university I can always count on at least one student to have a Bible in hand). I asked the class to listen and to write down every female name they heard.

It was a powerful teaching moment—for the students and for me. I knew women filled those verses, but I had never listened to their names being read aloud, one after the other.

Phoebe, the deacon who carried the letter from Paul and read it aloud to her house church.

Prisca (Priscilla), whose name is mentioned before her husband's name (something rather notable in the Roman world) as a coworker with Paul.

Mary, a hard worker for the gospel in Asia.

Junia, prominent among the apostles.

Tryphaena and Tryphosa, Paul's fellow workers in the Lord.

The beloved Persis, who also worked hard for the Lord.

Rufus's mother, Julia, and Nereus's sister.

Ten women recognized by Paul.

Seven women are recognized by their ministry: Phoebe, Priscilla, Mary, Junia, Tryphaena, Tryphosa, and Persis. One woman, Phoebe, is identified as a deacon. Kevin Madigan and Carolyn Osiek write that Phoebe "is the only deacon of a first-century church whose name we know."[56] Another woman, Junia, is identified not simply as an apostle but as one who was prominent among the apostles.

Did you know, I asked my students, that more women than men are identified by their ministry in Romans 16? We sat there, looking at the names of those women. "Why?" a student suddenly interjected, so involved in the lecture she didn't even raise her hand. "Why have I not noticed this before?" Probably because the English Bible translation you use obscures women's activity, I told her, launching into another explanation.

I listened to myself lecturing that day. I listened to myself laying out evidence for how English Bible translations obscure women's leadership in the early church. I listened to myself as I talked the class through different translations of Romans 16.

Take, for example, *The Ryrie Study Bible*, published by Moody Press in 1986. My grandfather owned this Bible, and I have his copy on my shelf. Instead of recognizing Phoebe as a deacon, it translates her role as "servant." Listen to the study note: "The word here translated 'servant' is often translated 'deacon,' which leads some to believe that Phoebe was a deaconess. However, the word is more likely used here in an unofficial sense of helper."[57] Did you catch that? I asked my students. No evidence is given for why Phoebe's role should be translated as "servant" rather than as "deacon." No evidence is given to explain why the word is more likely used in "an unofficial sense of helper." We can guess the reason for the translation choice: it is because Phoebe was a woman, and so it is assumed that she could not have been a deacon. If the phrase "a deacon of the church in Cenchreae" had followed a masculine name, I seriously doubt that the meaning of "deacon" would ever have been questioned.

As I taught, I thought about my own church. About how women rarely appeared on stage other than to sing or play an instrument. I thought about how women ran our children's ministry and men ran our adult ministry. I thought about the time I had been asked to teach an adult Sunday school class, and the pastor had come to look through my material. Since I was just teaching on church history, he let me do it. If I had been discussing the biblical text, though, it would have been a different story.

I remember feeling like such a hypocrite, standing before my college classroom.

Here I was, walking my students through compelling historical evidence that the problem with women in leadership wasn't Paul; the problem was with how we misunderstood and obscured Paul. Here I was, showing my students how women really did lead and teach in the early church, even as deacons and apostles. Junia, I showed them, was accepted as an apostle until nearly modern times, when her name began to be translated as a man's name: Junias. New Testament scholar Eldon Jay Epp compiled two tables surveying Greek New Testaments from Erasmus through the twentieth century.[58] Together, the charts show that the Greek name *Junia* was almost universally translated in its female form until the twentieth century, when the name suddenly began to be translated as the masculine *Junias*. Why? Gaventa explains: "Epp makes it painfully, maddeningly clear that a major factor in twentieth-century treatments of Romans 16:7 was the assumption that a woman could not have been an apostle."⁵⁹ *Junia* became *Junias* because modern Christians assumed that only a man could be an apostle. As a historian, I knew why the women in Paul's letters did not match the so-called limitations that contemporary church leaders place on women. I knew it was because we have read Paul wrong. Paul isn't inconsistent in his approach to women; we have made him inconsistent through how we have interpreted him. As Romans 16 makes clear, the reality is that biblical women contradict modern ideas of biblical womanhood.

I knew all this. Yet I still allowed the leaders of my church to go uncontested in their claim that women could not teach boys older than thirteen at our church. I still remained silent.

I continued my lecture. The historical reality is the same for Phoebe, I told my students. Paul calls her a deacon. No one disputes the text—they can only dispute the meaning of the text. Phoebe was recognized as both a woman and a deacon by early church fathers. Origen, for example, wrote in the early third century that Phoebe's title demonstrates "by apostolic authority that women are also appointed in the ministry of the church, in which office Phoebe was placed at the church that is in Cenchreae. Paul with great praise and commendation even enumerates her splendid deeds."⁶⁰ While we can certainly question what Origen meant by the "ministry of the church," it is clear that Origen accepted Phoebe's appointed role. A century later, John Chrysostom, the "golden-tongued" preacher, wrote of how great an honor it was for Phoebe to be mentioned "before all the others," called "sister," and distinguished as a "deacon." "Both men and women," concludes Chrysostom, should "imitate" Phoebe as a "holy one."⁶¹ In his homily on 1 Timothy 3:11, Chrysostom makes it clear that he understands women to serve as deacons just as men do. As he writes, "Likewise women must be modest, not slanderers, sober, faithful in everything. Some say that [Paul] is talking about women in general. But that cannot be. Why would he want to insert in the middle of what he is saying something about women? But rather he is speaking of those women who hold the rank of deacon. 'Deacons should be husbands of one wife.' This is also appropriate for women deacons, for it is necessary, good, and right, most especially in the church."[62]

If this frank understanding of female leadership by a fourth-century presbyter and deacon surprises you, church historians Madigan and Osiek remind us that it shouldn't: "In John's churches in Antioch and Constantinople," they write, "female deacons or deaconesses were well known."[63] Describing Phoebe as a deacon wasn't surprising to Chrysostom because some of his good fourth-century friends were female deacons. Indeed, Madigan and Osiek have uncovered 107 references (inscriptions and literary) to women deacons in the early church.

Of course, I told my students, not everyone in the early church supported women in leadership. The office of presbyter testifies loudly to how patriarchal prejudices of the ancient world had already crept into Christianity. Remember how Aristotle considered the female body to be monstrous and deformed? Ecclesiastical leaders imported these ideas into their council decisions, declaring as early as the fifth century that female bodies were unfit for leadership. As Madigan and Osiek write, "Cultic purity becomes associated with males, impurity with females. This was the biggest argument against women presbyters."[64] By the sixth century, while the church was moving across the European landscape and replacing the old secular seats of Roman power with the sacred offices of bishop and priest, women were also on the move, back into their prior place under the authority of men.

"Dr. Barr, why don't they teach us this in church?"

I looked at the student, my heart twisting. Most people simply don't know, I said. Seminary textbooks are often written by pastors—not by historians (and especially not by women historians). Most people who attend complementarian churches don't realize that the ESV translation of Junia as "well known to the apostles" instead of "prominent among the apostles" was a deliberate move to keep women out of leadership (Romans 16:7). People believe that women were banned from leadership in the early church just as they are banned from leadership in the modern church. The church teaches what it believes to be true.

These were the things I said out loud.

What I didn't say—and what made the tears roll down my cheeks as I stood in front of my sink that day—was that I knew the truth. I knew the truth, and still I stayed silent at my church.

I stayed silent because I was afraid of my husband losing his job. I was afraid of losing our friends. I was afraid of losing our ministry.

Complementarianism rewards women who play by the rules. By staying silent, I helped ensure that my husband could remain a leader. By staying silent, I could exercise some influence. By staying silent, I kept the friendship and trust of the women around me. By staying silent, I maintained a comfortable life.

Except I knew the truth about Paul's women. I knew the reality that women who are praised in the Bible—like Phoebe, Priscilla, and Junia—challenge the confines of modern biblical womanhood. As a historian, I knew that women were kept out of leadership roles in my own congregation because Roman patriarchy had seeped back into the early church. Instead of ditching pagan Rome and embracing Jesus, we had done the opposite—ditching the freedom of Christ and embracing the oppression of the ancient world.

I turned the water off in the sink and stacked the dishes.

It was time for me to stop being silent.

I WAS MOWING THE LAWN when my husband walked out into the backyard. I couldn't hear his words over the roar of the mower, but I could see his face. I knew it was bad. I let go of the mower handle, and it began to putter out.

"The elders just met," he said, holding his phone toward me. "They called to tell me that they will not reconsider their position on women."

I had almost reached him, newly cut grass dusting my ankles and shoes. I was expecting bad news, given his face, but I wasn't expecting this. We had decided to speak out and had asked the elders to allow a woman to teach high school Sunday school. We were optimistic, knowing at least two of the four elders were supportive. I had allowed myself to hope.

It proved a vain hope.

I don't remember what I replied. I am not even sure I got words out. But my husband understood me. "If we force this," he said, "I will lose my job." The silence around us grew louder.

Did we really want to go down this path?

I could hear my children inside the house. Then just six and twelve, they were blissfully ignorant. This church was their home. It was filled with their friends. It was all they had ever known.

Did we really want to go down this path?

Almost twenty years my husband and I had been married and had served in ministry together, the bulk of which had been at this church. It was our home too. It was filled with our best friends. The women and men who had prayed with us as I finished my dissertation and interviewed for jobs; celebrated with us at the birth of our son; supported us as we waited five long years for the birth of our daughter; laughed with us over inside jokes about margarita machines and empty Starbucks gift cards.

Did we really want to do this?

I finally nodded, letting him know that I understood. Then I wiped the sweat off my face and went back to mowing. The familiar rumble of the mower focused my racing thoughts. I tried to concentrate only on the grass in front of me.

But of course I couldn't.

I was angry. I was tired. I was scared.

And for some strange reason, all I could think about was Margery Kempe.

Why Margery Kempe Matters

My husband and I were about to make a very difficult decision, and all I could think about was a fifteenth-century woman. (Any of my students reading this will surely laugh.)

I couldn't get her off my mind for two reasons. First, I was teaching a graduate seminar on medieval sermons that semester, and I had just reread her book in preparation. That certainly explains why she was on my mind.

But the second reason was that Kempe was helping answer my most burning question: *Did I really want to challenge complementarian teachings about women at our church?*

She certainly wasn't the only factor I was considering (far from it). But because I am a medieval historian and because I knew the story of Margery Kempe, I knew my answer to this question was yes, I wanted to try.

72

One day in 1417, Margery Kempe was arrested in the medieval English town of York. Her extravagant worship style, which included disrupting services with crying and sobbing, together with her tendency to debate theology with clergy and even preach to local people, meant that she was often a person of suspicion. This time she found herself facing the second most important ecclesiastical figure in medieval England, the archbishop of York. The archbishop knew Margery was traveling around the countryside without her husband; he knew she was acting like a religious teacher without any training; and he knew she had been disrupting local church services with her ecstatic worship.

His words to her were harsh and clear: "I hear it said that you are a very wicked woman."[1]

At this moment in the story, conventional wisdom about the medieval church would tell us that medieval women were subject to masculine authority. Conventional wisdom tells us that because women could not be priests, they could not preach. It tells us that women were always subordinate to the men in their lives—husbands, fathers, brothers. Conventional wisdom about medieval Christianity tells us that Margery was an aberration. She was also a very likely candidate for being burned at the stake as a heretic.

But conventional wisdom isn't always true. When the archbishop of York confronted this middle-aged woman, she stood her ground in a room full of masculine authority. When the archbishop called her a "very wicked woman," she fought back, responding directly: "Sir, I also hear it said that you are a wicked man. And if you are as wicked as people say, you will never get to heaven, unless you amend while you are here."[2]

Do you hear what she said?

Margery Kempe told the second most important ecclesiastical figure in medieval England that he wasn't going to heaven unless he repented.

She also used the Word of God to defend her right as a woman to teach about God. She preached from the Bible to a room full of male priests—including the archbishop of York—defending her right to do so as a woman. Quoting from Luke 11, she explained, "For God Almighty does not forbid, sir, that we should speak of him. And also the Gospel mentions that, when the woman had heard our Lord preach, she came before him and said in a loud voice, 'Blessed be the womb that bore you, and the teats that gave thee suck.' Then our Lord replied to her, 'In truth, so are they blessed who hear the word of God and keep it.' *And therefore, sir, I think that the Gospel gives me leave to speak of God.*"[3]

When Margery stopped speaking, a priest, horrified by her condemnation of the archbishop, ran to get his copy of the Pauline epistles. He read aloud one of the "women be silent" passages—either 1 Corinthians 14 or 1 Timothy 2—proclaiming that "no woman should preach."[4]

It didn't work.

"I do not preach, sir," she said. "I do not go into any pulpit. I use only conversation and good words, and that I will do while I live."[5] For this medieval woman, Paul didn't apply. She could teach the Word of God, even as an ordinary woman, because, she argued, Jesus endorsed it.

We have to admire her nerve. Margery Kempe not only argued with the archbishop of York; she also taught him theological truths. She defended her right to speak the Word of God, and she accused the archbishop of being a wicked man, going on to tell a story of a gross bear who eats beautiful pear blossoms and publicly defecates them in the face of a priest. When confronted with Scripture that demanded her silence as a woman, Margery explained how that Scripture did not apply to her. When the archbishop demanded that she leave immediately, she argued with him until he accepted her terms. Finally, in frustration, he paid a man five shillings to escort her from the room. Her friends met her back in the city, rejoicing, as the text reads, because God "had given her—uneducated as she was—the wit and wisdom to answer so many learned men without shame or blame, thanks be to God."[6] Indeed, the archbishop admitted that he had examined her and found no fault with her faith. He even wrote a letter endorsing that she was not a heretic, which he gave to her to carry on her travels.

Some scholars have argued that Margery Kempe's position as a well-off woman with a politically important father protected her (John Brunham was mayor of Bishop's Lynn, her hometown, and a member of Parliament). Class trumps sex, and Margery gets away with more than she should have in her time. This is absolutely correct. How Margery achieves a chaste marriage provides a good example (in book 11 of her text). According to the medieval church, husbands and wives both owe the "conjugal debt" (sex).[7] One cannot withhold sex from the other. Margery, in pursuit of a holy life (and perhaps also motivated by her previous fourteen pregnancies), wants to be free of the conjugal debt. Her husband bargains with her, asking in part that she pay off his financial debts. Margery has more money than he does, and she controls it herself (which often surprises many of my students). Her husband, John, calls her "no good wife" when she admits she would rather him be decapitated by a murderer than sleep with him again, but reluctantly he agrees to a chaste marriage.[8] In her insightful discussion of this encounter, Isabel Davis observes that Margery's willingness to pay off John's debts shows "the kind of autonomy Margery can buy with her independent finances."[9] Without a doubt, Margery's money and position smoothed her unconventional path.

But Margery Kempe went free from the archbishop of York because of more than just her financial standing. She was also helped by the fact that when she faced him, she didn't stand alone. A great cloud of female witnesses, not only remembered but revered by the medieval Christian world, stood with her.

Unlike modern evangelicals, medieval Christians remembered the female leaders of their past. Medieval churches, sermons, and devotional literature overflowed with valiant women from the early years of Christianity. Women who defied male authority, claiming their right to preach and teach, converting hundreds, even thousands, to Christianity. Women who received ordination as deaconesses and took vows as abbesses—perhaps at least one woman ordained as a bishop. Women who performed miracles and publicly taught the apostles, and even one woman who won an argument with Jesus (Matthew 15:21–28). This cloud of witnesses stood alongside Margery Kempe as she faced the archbishop, imbuing her with both the strength and the familiarity of the past.

At one point in *The Book of Margery Kempe*, God promises Kempe that the powerful female leaders from early Christianity would be with her and would escort her to heaven when she died. "I promise you," God said to her, "that I shall come to your end, at your dying, with my blessed mother, and my holy angels and twelve apostles, St Katherine, St Margaret and St Mary Magdalene, and many other saints that are in heaven. . . . You shall not fear the devil of hell, for he has no power over you."[10]

Like Margery Kempe, Christine de Pizan—a professional writer who lived in late fourteenth-century France and was employed by the French court—also remembered the strong female leaders from Christian history. Beyond using these women to defend her individual right to speak, Christine used these women to authorize female speech more broadly. As she wrote,

> If women's language had been so blameworthy and of such small authority as some men argue, our Lord Jesus Christ would never have deigned to wish that so worthy a mystery as His most gracious resurrection be first announced by a woman, just as He commanded the blessed Magdalen, to whom He first appeared on Easter, to report and announce it to His apostles and to Peter. Blessed God, may you be praised, who, among the other infinite boons and favors which You have bestowed upon the feminine sex, desired that woman carry such lofty and worthy news.[11]

In a feminine twist on apostolic authority, Jesus's authorization of Mary Magdalene "bestowed upon the feminine sex" the right not only to speak but to speak with authority.

When Margery Kempe reminded the archbishop about the conversation between Jesus and a woman in Luke 11, she was reminding him that, in the world of medieval Christianity, she didn't have to be silent.

Jesus had already given women the freedom to speak.[12]

Margery Kempe's Cloud of Female Witnesses

I am a women's retreat dropout. I really tried to go during the early years of our ministry—I knew it was important in my role as a pastor's wife to spend time with other women and build community. But I grew to dread such retreats. One retreat in particular scarred me. Around thirty women from our church went. The accommodations at a nice encampment in the East Texas woods provided a lovely, peaceful setting. The food was delicious. I relished the chance to spend time with friends.

The speaker was a different story. She had one message: women are divinely called to be stay-at-home moms dedicated to childrearing and keeping the home. She reduced the story of Luke 10, in which Jesus tells Martha that her sister has chosen the "better part," to a lesson about a woman so self-absorbed with being the perfect host that she almost ruins Jesus's dinner. Instead of emphasizing the strength of women's faith and how central women's discipleship was to the success of the early Christian movement, she focused her message almost entirely on a very narrow interpretation of Titus 2. I couldn't take it for long, and I skipped the next session to grade papers.

That semester I had assigned Larissa Tracy's *Women of the Gilte Legende: A Selection of Middle English Saints Lives*. This book is a collection of Middle English stories about female saints, drawn from one of the most popular religious texts in the medieval world, Jacobus de Voragine's *Golden Legend*. I love introducing these women to my students because the stories shatter stereotypes about medieval women. They are Margery Kempe's great cloud of witnesses; the group includes several women Kempe mentions in her own book.

As I sat on the front porch of the cabin, reading essays about women who broke free from marriage to serve God, whose preaching brought thousands to salvation, and whose words openly defied the patriarchy around them, I couldn't escape the irony. Not far from me, a roomful of women were being told that their highest calling as Christian women was to be wives and mothers—which implied that women who found meaning or calling apart from being wives and mothers were defying God's call for them. Yet I knew medieval women who were told the exact opposite—women's primary calling was to serve God first, which for some meant eschewing traditional family life and for others meant working around it.

I wondered what the speaker would think of women like Saint Paula, who abandoned her children for the higher purpose of following God's call on her life. Paula's story tells of how she set sail for Jerusalem—after the death of her husband—on a pilgrimage, leaving three of her children alone, crying on the shore. Maybe the speaker would have claimed that Paula was not following biblical womanhood, as she did not exemplify Titus 2. But Paula seemed to believe she was practicing biblical womanhood, drawing strength from Jesus's statement that "whoever loves son or daughter more than me is not worthy of me" (Matthew 10:37). Saint Jerome, her biographer, tells us that as the ship drew away from the shore, Paula "held her eyes to heaven . . . ignoring her children and putting her trust in God. . . . In that rejoicing, her courage coveted the love of her children as the greatest of its kind, yet she left them all for the love of God."[13] Paula founded a monastery in Bethlehem and worked alongside Jerome to translate the Bible from Hebrew and Greek into Latin. The Bible she helped translate became the Vulgate, the first major translation of the Bible into an everyday language outside of Greek and Hebrew. It became the most commonly used Bible throughout the medieval era.

What would the speaker think about Saint Margaret of Antioch, an alleged Christian martyr, also from the fourth century? Margaret's story was not only told in collections of saints' lives like the *Gilte Legende* but was also repeated in sermons. John

Mirk's *Festial* explains how Margaret's beauty complicated her vow to remain a virgin and serve God. According to the text, "she was fair surpassing all other women" and caught the eye of a Roman governor. When she refused his sexual advances and his demand for her to forsake Christianity, the governor tortured her and threw her into prison. *Festial* records that despite the "great plenty of blood" that poured from her body, Margaret steadfastly prayed that God would empower her to resist.[14]

At this point the story gets interesting, because God answers her prayer.

A devilish creature appears in the corner of her cell—"a great horrible dragon." Without much delay, it eats Margaret. The text reads, "His mouth was on her head, and his tongue stretched down to her heel." Margaret remains surprisingly calm, despite being "all in the mouth" of a demonic dragon. She simply makes the sign of the cross, calling on the power of God to aid her. The dragon bursts apart and Margaret steps free.[15]

In this brief but dramatic moment, the scene in the prison cell shifts from that of a dragon towering over Margaret to Margaret standing tall above the dragon. With the last of his strength, the devil confesses his failure: "Alas, I am undone forever, and all my might is gone, now such a young woman has overcome me; for many a big and a strong man I have defeated, but now such an inferior has gotten mastery and put me under her feet."[16] Although the story concludes with Margaret's martyrdom (she gets her head chopped off), it first tells how her final act involves a great earthquake followed by the Holy Spirit descending from heaven as a dove to anoint her. The thousands of people who have gathered to watch her tortured death convert on the spot to Christianity, proclaiming, "There is no God but [the God] in which Margaret believes."[17]

Again, I wondered what the conference speaker would do with Margaret, a woman who defied marriage, defied male authority, fought and killed a dragon, and was anointed by God in the same way that Jesus was anointed. Margery Kempe would have had special affinity with Margaret, not only because of Margaret's reputation as a preaching dragon-slayer but also because Margery's home church in Lynn was dedicated to Saint Margaret—and the name Margery is probably a diminutive of Margaret, showing how well medieval Christians remembered women like Margaret.

Of course, modern evangelicals don't forget all the women in Christian history. Take, for example, Mary and Martha, the sisters from Bethany. I heard the conference speaker talk that day about Martha, who was praised as a homemaker. She cooked, cleaned, took care of the domestic space, and showed hospitality to Jesus and his disciples. This understanding of Martha is popular in devotional resources for today's Christian women. Author Katie M. Reid describes Martha this way in her 2018 book, *Made Like Martha: Good News for the Woman Who Gets Things Done*:

> Martha welcomed Jesus into her home. Some versions of the Bible say she "opened her home to him" ([Luke 10:38], NIV) or "received him into her house" (KJV).
> Welcome. Opened. Received. These words paint a bright picture of hospitality.[18]

Martha was the hostess of Jesus, making her the ideal housekeeper for author Sarah Mae. In 2016, Mae published *Having a Martha Home the Mary Way: 31 Days to a Clean House and a Satisfied Soul*. Mae includes "Mary Challenges" to encourage the spiritual development of women, and she offers "Martha Challenges" to inspire women to clean different parts of their home. As Mae writes, "My goal is to inspire you and give practical help to get you moving and cleaning, so that ultimately your house will be nice and tidy by the end of the thirty-one days."[19]

I sat there in the fading sunshine, the pages of Larissa Tracy's book on medieval women ruffling in the breeze. I could hear a rumble of voices as the afternoon session ended.

I wondered what the women at the conference would do with the medieval conception of Mary and Martha. Since the seventh century, Martha of Bethany has often been identified as the sister of Mary Magdalene—the most recognizable female saint in the late medieval world (next only to Mary, mother of Jesus). Not until the sixteenth century does Mary Magdalene begin to be separated from her medieval identification as Martha's sister, the sinful woman possessed by seven devils, and the repentant woman with the alabaster jar.[20] So, for medieval Christians, Mary of Bethany was not just a woman who sat quietly at the feet of Jesus; she was a repentant prostitute and former demoniac. She was the apostle of the apostles—the first apostle who carried the good news of the resurrection. She was a missionary of Christ, affirmed by Peter. She preached openly, performed miracles that paralleled those of the apostles, and converted a new land to the Christian faith.

Even though we may doubt the historical accuracy of Mary's missionary journey to France, medieval Christians didn't. As one Cistercian monk wrote, "Just as she had been chosen to be the *apostle* of Christ's Resurrection and the prophet of his world . . . , she preached to the unbelievers and confirmed the believers in their faith."[21] Mary Magdalene was an exemplary

Christian leader—a brave woman who had repented of her sinful life and now shared the good news about Jesus where men lacked the courage to do so.

Martha accrued an elaborate medieval backstory that wasn't limited to homemaking. The *Golden Legend* describes her as a noble single woman who accompanied her famous sister to Marseilles.[22] While Mary Magdalene was preaching to the people, Martha encountered a dragon on the nearby beach. She faced a gruesome sight: a dragon that was described as a giant half-beast, half-fish with long, sharp teeth. When Martha happened upon the scene, the frightening monster was eating a man. Martha was undaunted. She sprinkled holy water on the beast, confronted the demonic creature with the cross, and calmly tied it up. When she presented the now-subdued dragon to the people of Marseilles, they stabbed it to death with their spears. Martha performed additional miracles, interspersed with a preaching agenda similar to that of Mary Magdalene's.

Mary and Martha look rather different from the medieval perspective, don't they? Today both women, especially Martha, are most associated with traditional female duties. But neither medieval woman is limited to the domestic sphere. Martha could be both a superb hostess and a preacher who slew dragons. Mary could both sit quietly at her devotions and be the apostle of the apostles whose preaching spread the gospel in France. "The legends of female saints, especially in vernacular collections like the *Gilte Legende*," writes Tracy, "provided strong, visible role models for medieval women through the diversity of their speech and the eloquence of their silence, elevating women above the traditional roles assigned to them and giving them a power of their own."[23]

I watched the women stream from the meeting space. Soon,

a friend sat down in the rocking chair next to me, dropping her Bible and session notes on the same table where I had stacked my essays. "What are you reading?" she asked, nodding at the blue cover of the *Gilte Legende*.

"Just something for class," I told her, pushing Tracy's book to the side.

I wasn't ready yet. I still wasn't sure what to do with what I knew. But I also knew that the women remembered by medieval Christianity undermined modern biblical womanhood. I knew the problem wasn't a lack of women leading in church history. The problem was simply that women's leadership has been forgotten, because women's stories throughout history have been covered up, neglected, or retold to recast women as less significant than they really were.

Because Women Couldn't Be Written Out of the Story

In fall 2016, I was teaching one of my favorite graduate courses, a course on medieval sermons. That was the semester my husband was fired from his pastoral job, three weeks after we had asked the church elders to reconsider their position on women. At first we were paralyzed. One of our best friends had helped the pastor deliver the verdict to my husband, making it exponentially more painful. Now, instead of a ministry job, we had only severance pay that was dependent on our good behavior—that is, not telling anyone the truth. We had lost our church family and some of our best friends. We were told to walk away from the youth group of about seventy kids whom we loved and had discipled for the past fourteen years.

Just three weeks to completely upend our lives. And we couldn't tell anyone why.

It took everything in me to appear normal for my children that first day. By the time we left my son's afternoon football game, finished homework with the kids, and cleaned up after dinner, I had nothing left. I had already broken down in tears at the football game after one of my Baylor colleagues simply asked how I was. I just wanted to go to sleep and forget everything for a few hours.

But I couldn't. I had a three-hour seminar the next day filled with graduate students from the history, English, and religion departments. I had to teach. Life didn't stop, especially since we were suddenly a one-income family.

So I grabbed my books, left my husband watching *Star Trek* with the kids, and climbed up to my son's treehouse in our backyard. It was cooler by then, the oak leaves shimmering in the fading light. Texas has glorious summer sunsets. Glowing pink and golden fingers of light reached out across the dusty blue horizon, quieting my fears, strengthening my heart.

Our story wasn't over. I knew God was working. I took a deep breath and started reading.

I was preparing a background article that night. I hadn't assigned it for the students, but I wanted to review the material for discussion. The article, "Prophecy and Song: Teaching and Preaching by Medieval Women," is by the insightful historian Carolyn Muessig. Listen to what Muessig writes (the long quotation is worth it):

> The notion of women teaching and preaching was deemphasized in favor of women's educating privately within the family or a cloister. However, examples of women preaching and teaching publicly were found in biblical stories and legends. Mary Magdalene offered a biblical example of a woman preaching

in her announcement of the "Good News" to the apostles. But this biblical model was often portrayed by theologians as an exception and not the rule. . . . In a sermon for the feast of Mary Magdalene it is written: "And this glorious sinner, just like the star of the sea, illumined the world with the joy of the dominical resurrection." However, the implications of this feminine exemplar of preaching are quickly restricted and defined: "And although it is prohibited for other women to preach, this woman had dispensation from the highest pope, therefore, she is called the apostle of the apostles, for she taught not only the simple but also the doctors." The implication of Mary Magdalene as a precedent for female preaching is underscored by the statement of why her pastoral activity was more an anomaly than an exemplar.[24]

I read that about three times. My fuzzy brain knew something vitally important was in those words, but it was slow to click. When it finally did, I stood up, knocking the article onto the acorn-strewn floor. What I felt was not yet hope; it was more like grim determination. But the paralyzing, barely suppressed fear that had gripped me all day faded just a little.

Did you catch what Muessig says that took so long to click in my slow brain that night? *The implication of Mary Magdalene as a precedent for female preaching is underscored by the statement of why her pastoral activity was more an anomaly than an exemplar.* If women couldn't preach, then Mary Magdalene shouldn't have preached. Except medieval Christians believed that she did preach, and they used the Bible as undisputed evidence. So either women could preach, or Mary Magdalene had to be explained away.

Guess which option most medieval theologians chose?

As Muessig writes, "Mary Magdalene offered a biblical example of a woman preaching. . . . But this biblical model was often portrayed by theologians as an exception and not the rule."[25] So the problem wasn't a lack of biblical and historical evidence for women in leadership. Mary Magdalene carried the news of the gospel to the disbelieving disciples. In a world that didn't accept the word of a woman as a valid witness, Jesus chose women as witnesses for his resurrection. In a world that gave husbands power over the very lives of their wives, Paul told husbands to do the opposite—to give up their lives for their wives. In a world that saw women as biologically deformed men, monstrous even, Paul declared that men were just like women in Christ.

No, the problem wasn't a lack of biblical and historical evidence for women to serve as leaders along with men in the church. The problem was male clergy who undermined the evidence.

The medieval clergy couldn't explain away Mary Magdalene preaching, so they made her an exception. Because she was an extraordinary rather than an ordinary woman, ordinary women's ability to follow her example was diminished. I couldn't help remembering a favorite quotation from New Testament scholar Ben Witherington: "No, the problem in the church is not strong women, but rather weak men who feel threatened by strong women, and have tried various means, even by dubious exegesis, to prohibit them from exercising their gifts and graces in the church."[26] Instead of following a clear and plain reading of the biblical text, the medieval world grafted their imported Roman patriarchy onto the gospel of Jesus.

As I sat back down in the treehouse that evening, brushing the acorns out of my seat and picking up my spilled Diet Coke can, I realized that what had just happened to me in our twenty-first-century evangelical church was a rerun for Christian women.

You see, the story starts with women as strong leaders.

Take, for example, Margery Kempe's great cloud of female witnesses. The medieval church was simply too close in time to forget the significant roles women played in establishing the Christian faith throughout the remnants of the Roman Empire. Along with early saints like Mary Magdalene and Margaret of Antioch (Margery Kempe's great cloud of female witnesses), female missionaries, preachers, and ecclesiastical leaders crowded the historical landscape.

Among the great cloud of female witnesses were missionaries like Clotilda, the Burgundian princess who defied her pagan husband Clovis, king of the Franks, in the late fifth century. Her faithfulness convinced him to convert (after he prayed and won a critical battle), and in 508 he was baptized along with three thousand of his Frankish warriors. Historian Jane Tibbetts Schulenburg remarks that Clotilda assumed the primary role in converting her husband, as Clovis invoked the "Christ of Clotilda."[27] Medieval historians and clergy also recognized Clotilda's leadership, giving her, rather than the officiating priests, the credit.

Bishops like Genovefa of Paris and Brigit of Kildare were also part of the great cloud. Historian Lisa Bitel recounts the hagiographical stories of how Genovefa became the de facto ecclesiastical leader of Paris. She protected the city from the ravages of the Huns, just as the bishop of Rome, Leo the Great, had done. She enhanced the Christian prestige of the city through her miracles and her patronage of the first bishop of Paris (Saint Denis), and she refused to submit to other episcopal authorities. As Bitel writes, "Because she was a saint, she could take the place of a man, Paris's bishop. Because she acted as a bishop, she was able to build."[28] Genovefa established Paris as a Christian stronghold just as effectively as male bishops did throughout Europe.

Genovefa acted like a bishop, but Brigit of Kildare (according to hagiography) was actually ordained as a bishop. The bishop presiding over her consecration accidentally read the episcopal orders. After realizing his mistake, he announced, "This virgin alone in Ireland will hold the episcopal ordination."[29] Brigit journeyed the island several times, performed miracles, practiced ecclesiastical authority (such as blessing houses), and established spiritual equality with Saint Patrick himself. What is really fascinating about Brigit is that even though she received ordination like a man would have, she exercises her authority in a distinctly feminine way. As Bitel explains, "She was at once a typical woman, caring for her men's needs and ministering their deaths, and a visionary who could see even what Ireland's apostle [Saint Patrick] could not."[30] Like the medieval Martha of Bethany, Brigit could be both a domestic goddess and a public religious leader.

The great cloud of female witnesses included even preachers, like Hildegard of Bingen. Kings and princes also sought the advice of the twelfth-century German mystic, author, theologian, Benedictine abbess, composer, and preacher. Hildegard preached regularly in Germany, undertaking four preaching tours between 1158 and 1170. We know beyond doubt that clergy as well as ordinary people filled her audiences. We also know that she spoke with authority to the clerical members of her audience—calling them to repentance. Barbara Newman wrote how "astonishing" it was that Hildegard preached against bishops and priests so vehemently, yet none of them invoked "St. Paul's authority against her." Instead, Newman writes, "they actually invited her to preach and then wrote to her afterward, begging for transcripts of her sermons."[31]

So when Elaine Lawless writes that "women have been preaching in the Christian tradition from the earliest historical moments, perhaps only days after Jesus Christ was crucified and his resurrection announced," she is absolutely right.[32] And the medieval church agreed—both recognizing women as preachers, teachers, and leaders in Christian history and accepting that women continued to preach, teach, and lead throughout the medieval era.

Qualified Female Leadership

The medieval church, even though it accepted women's roles as leaders, was nonetheless uncomfortable with women actively serving in these roles. The church had been uncomfortable for a long time—almost from the beginning. While medieval Christians couldn't forget the truth about female leaders in Christian history—Jesus made certain of that through his interactions with Mary, Martha, and even the Canaanite woman—medieval Christians also couldn't accept female leadership as normative.

Why? Because the medieval world inherited the patriarchy of the Roman world. Remember the Aristotelian belief that women were defective (incomplete) men, making them passive and weak compared to strong and active men? These "pre-Christian ideas," writes historian Jacqueline Murray, "meshed with Christian theology."[33] Beliefs about female inferiority haunted Christianity from the beginning, influencing early church fathers like Clement of Alexandria and Jerome to characterize spiritual maturity for women as a progression

90

to manliness. "As long as a woman is for birth and children, she is as different from man as body is from soul," explained Jerome. "But when she wishes to serve Christ more than the world, she will cease to be a woman and will be called a man."[34] If women are imperfect men, then only by becoming men can women achieve spiritual equality. These ideas affected stories about women in the early church, resulting in female martyrs described as behaving like men and virginity praised as the highest calling for women.

This brings us to the next part of the rerun—the part where women get pushed out of leadership.

As the church waxed in power, opportunities for women waned. Male leadership became the norm. But because of the long history of women in leadership roles, excuses had to be made for why women could lead in the past but could no longer do so in the present. Women's actions, in other words, had to be qualified to justify male-only authority.

One particularly effective move to qualify women's leadership happened during the eleventh and twelfth centuries. A renewed interest in ancient ideas about women (namely their inferiority and impurity) collided with a reform movement trying to strengthen ecclesiastical leadership.[35] Christianity had a long history of associating sexual activity with impurity. Augustine argued that original sin was transmitted to every human through sexual intercourse that created new life, firmly connecting sex with sin. As the priesthood and sacramental theology evolved, elevating the priest as having special spiritual powers and duties, so too evolved clerical celibacy. While it was technically heretical to claim that an impure priest couldn't properly perform the sacraments (baptism, absolution, Eucharist, etc.), people feared it was true and resented their married clergy.[36]

It is important to note that this represented a change in Christian theology. Before the eleventh and twelfth centuries, ordination was less clearly established and less critical for leadership. Evidence suggests that at least some women were ordained in the early medieval church, like Brigit of Kildare, but this practice disappeared in the Western church after the reforms of the central Middle Ages. Gary Macy writes that the twelfth-century French philosopher and theologian Peter Abelard, perhaps the most famous student of Anselm, championed the "last defense" for the ordination of women in the Western church. Abelard settled into a monastic teaching life after an HBO-worthy love affair with Heloise, his student-turned-wife, ended badly: Abelard was castrated by Heloise's angry uncle (lest you think medieval history is boring), and both Abelard and Heloise spent the remainder of their lives apart, in separate monasteries, as steadfast pen pals. Abelard championed women's ordination, building on the historical precedent of women carrying the title of deaconess in the early Middle Ages and on the New Testament story of the prophetess Anna. As he wrote, "We now call abbesses, that is mothers, those who in early times were called deaconesses, that is, ministers." And similarly, "This *ordo* of women began a long time ago because we read in the Old Testament and in the New that there were deaconesses, that is women who ministered to the saints." Abelard argued that female ordination "was established by Jesus himself and not by the apostles, specifically rejecting the teaching that only the male priesthood and diaconate were part of the original church."[37] Of course women could preach, argued Abelard, because women already did preach, including in the Bible (Anna, Elizabeth, Mary Magdalene, and even the Samaritan woman in the Gospel of John).

Abelard lost this battle.

But he didn't lose it on the same grounds he argued it. He used Christian history as a defense for why women could lead, and this the church leaders deemed acceptable. The battle was lost because the historical circumstances had changed. The lines had been redrawn. To increase the authority of clergy, medieval church leaders needed women out of the way. You see, Christianity had a long history of secular lords and powerful families controlling clerical positions. Sons and nephews inherited the ecclesiastical jobs of their fathers and uncles. Powerful families sought to control important bishoprics and the papacy itself, often by purchasing clerical positions. The church fought back, cracking down on both clerical celibacy and simony (the buying and selling of church offices). If priests couldn't marry, and if priests could be assigned to clerical positions only by other clergy, rather than by rich noblemen, it would greatly diminish secular control over the church.

The result strengthened the church but weakened the position of women.

The period of church reforms spanning the eleventh century through the early thirteenth century redefined the ecclesiastical structure of the Western church—legitimizing the power of the papacy, promoting the authority of bishops, and establishing the unique status of the local priest. "Churches were redesigned to emphasize clerical status; celibacy was demanded, legislated for, and pursued; parochial tithes allowed churches to be free from direct secular control," explains historian Ian Forrest. "A common culture of priesthood created a clear status group whose basic position in relation to secular authorities, bishops, and the ordinary laity gave more-than-superficial unity to the institutional Church."[38] Priests were defined as men who were not polluted by the sexual impurity of women. Not only could women not be priests, but women's bodies were seen as potentially threatening to male leaders.

To help my students better understand how these reforms affected women, I often use a visual example from Durham Cathedral. A line, made from marble and marked with a center cross, stretches across the westernmost part of the cathedral's nave. Local guides proclaim that the misogyny of the cathedral's seventh-century patron, Saint Cuthbert, led him to institute the line to bar women from the sacred space of clergy. Unlike men, women were forbidden to enter either the nave or the cemetery.[39] Harrowing stories from the twelfth century tell of the consequences for women who challenged Saint Cuthbert. One woman was struck with madness just for trying to take a shortcut. She was upset about the poor quality of the traveling road, as her feet kept sinking into the deep puddles. So she decided to cut through the well-kept churchyard of Durham Cathedral. "She was seized with some kind of indefinite horror, and cried out that she was gradually losing her senses." After falling down in a fit, she was carried home, where she died. Another female transgressor was "inflamed woman-like" to see the beautiful decorations within the church. "Unable to bridle her impetuous desires, for the power of her husband had elevated her above her neighbours, she walked through the cemetery of the church." Her punishment, perhaps because she was motivated by pride, was even more horrific. She went mad, bit out her own tongue, and then committed suicide by slitting her throat.[40]

Yet the historical Cuthbert didn't have a problem with women. Evidence suggests he worked well and closely with women during his lifetime. He didn't become a misogynist until four hundred years after his death. The stories blaming him for forbidding women from entering Durham Cathedral stem from the eleventh- and twelfth-century church reforms. In 1083, after the Norman conquest in England, the married clergy at Durham were forced out and replaced with celibate Benedictine monks. This was a difficult change to enforce, as you might imagine. Schulenburg writes that, in order to smooth the transition, "the famous seventh-century patron St. Cuthbert was conveniently provided with a posthumous abhorrence of females. Thus the reform writings of Symeon of Durham served to reshape the patron saint of Durham according to the blatant prejudices of the period."[41] Cuthbert became a misogynist to further the ecclesiastical campaign for clerical celibacy.

The exclusion of women from the space of Durham Cathedral stemmed from a local attempt to enforce reform. Indeed, the bereaved husband of the woman who died because of her "impetuous desires" to see the beauty of Durham Cathedral took on "the dress of a monk."[42] Her death-by-exclusion literally forced him to accept clerical celibacy.

The reforms bolstering clerical status and ecclesiastical authority—and emphasizing the impurity of female bodies— distanced women from leadership in the medieval church. It's true that historical memory about female leadership empowered later women like Margery Kempe to preach, teach, and lead. But it's also true that patriarchal beliefs about the inferiority and impurity of female bodies made it more difficult for women to exercise these spiritual gifts.

Women had led in Christian history, and women could continue to lead—but it would be harder and mostly not in official positions. And the reason for this seemed to have less to do with women themselves and more to do with protecting the power of men, especially men in the church.

Writing Medieval Women Out of Church History

Historical memory of female leaders, past and present, empowered medieval women. Christine de Pizan proclaimed these words in her early fifteenth-century defense of women against misogynistic literature: "What strong faith and deep love those women possess who did not forsake the Son of God who had been abandoned and deserted by all His Apostles. God has never reproached the love of women as weakness, as some men contend, for He placed the spark of fervent love in the hearts of the blessed Magdalen and of other ladies, indeed His approval of this love is clearly to be seen."[43] The great cloud of female witnesses that empowered Margery Kempe to speak out against the archbishop of York also empowered Christine de Pizan to argue that women were of equal worth before God. Indeed, as the words of Lady Justice (one of the three women who visit Christine and tell her to build a city of ladies filled with worthy women) explained to Christine, "I tell you that, in spite of what you may have found in the writings of pagan authors on the subject of criticizing women, you will find little said against them in the holy legends of Jesus Christ and His Apostles."[44]

As I continued to mow my lawn on that day almost four years ago, I considered the vibrant history of women as leaders, teachers, and preachers in the medieval church. I also thought about how modern evangelicals have mostly forgotten this history. Take, for example, the popular Christian history textbooks *Church History in Plain Language* and *The Story of Christianity: The Early Church to the Dawn of the Reformation*, as well as the popular Sunday school church history textbook *Christian History Made Easy*. Not only do these texts contain very few references to female leaders in the medieval church; they minimize the authority of these women.

In *Christian History Made Easy* (which also has a leader's guide, a participant's guide, and a video series), I found thirteen women listed in the index, including four medieval women: Julian of Norwich, Joan of Arc, Hilda of Whitby, and Hildegard of Bingen. The author, Timothy Paul Jones, praises Hilda of Whitby as training "hundreds of nuns and even some monks—five of whom became overseers." But his discussion of Hildegard of Bingen, while accurate, has significant omissions. She was a "Renaissance woman in the Middle Ages. . . . a musician and mystic, artist and author, proclaimer of truth and prophet of reform. Popes and emperors praised her. Only Bernard surpassed her prestige," the author writes. Hildegard of Bingen proclaims, reforms, and writes; she does not, in *Christian History Made Easy*, preach. She is also "praised" by popes and emperors instead of providing advice and instruction to them.[45]

The Story of Christianity has a much more developed index, with over one thousand entries. The author worked to include women, explaining in the introduction that he sought "to acknowledge the role of women throughout the life of the church in a way that most earlier histories did not."[46] I did count at least thirty-two individual women listed in the index, as well as an index entry for women. Once again, Hildegard of Bingen is not described as preaching. She is an abbess with popular writings.[47] Catherine of Siena receives a more in-depth discussion. Carolyn Muessig argues that Catherine of Siena was a preacher, achieving "the conversion of the listeners and the spiritual refreshment of both the audience and the preacher herself.[48] Yet *The Story of Christianity* describes her only as a famous "teacher of mysticism" who "gathered around her a circle of men and women, many of them more educated than she, whom she taught the principles and practice of contemplation."[49] Hildegard and Catherine could teach, but they didn't preach. Both texts do discuss some noteworthy women in church history, but the male-female ratio of the indexes suggest that their narratives focus more on men.

The fourth edition of *Church History in Plain Language*, which seems to be one of the best-selling church history books, includes the fewest women. It contains over 280 index entries for people, eight of whom are women. Moreover, despite the book covering the first century through the twentieth century, the index mentions only one woman from the ancient church and only one woman from the modern church. The remaining six women are all from the Reformation era. Not only are women lacking representation in *Church History in Plain Language*, but their window of appearance is surprisingly narrow.[50]

Despite the significant role women play in church history, and despite clear historical evidence of women exercising leadership, these popular, modern church history texts present a masculine narrative of church history that minimizes female leadership.

Could it be that another building block for modern biblical womanhood is simply that evangelicals have rewritten Christian history?

Once, after I finished a lecture on women in the church, a lecture whose audience included both academics and church members, a pastor stopped me.

"Why don't they teach us this in seminary?" he asked. "I have never learned any of this."

I told him I didn't know.

But that wasn't true. I do know. I think it may be for the same reason that the medieval church pushed women out of leadership: to protect and enhance the authority of men.

Indeed, rather than Margery Kempe's great cloud of female witnesses, what modern evangelicals seem to remember most about medieval Christianity are the limitations placed on women. Women couldn't be priests, and this lends credence to evangelical arguments that women can't preach.

Margery Kempe stood with a host of female witnesses who helped authorize her voice, pushing back against male authority and even the limitations placed on her.

Evangelical women, thanks to our selective medieval memory, stand comparatively alone.

MY HUSBAND DROPPED THE FLYER on the counter. "Don't you want to sign up?" he asked, grinning. It was an invitation from Dorothy Patterson to enroll in her seminary class for pastors' wives. During the years my husband was a student at Southeastern Baptist Theological Seminary, I was eligible to take the class. I rolled my eyes. "One day you will wish you had!" he said, laughing.

He was right. I do wish I had taken the class, because it would have been fascinating to see the syllabus firsthand and participate in the conversations. As it stands, I can speak only as an outsider and rely on secondhand information.

But I did hear things about the class (it was pretty famous).

First, it emphasized equipping women to serve alongside their husbands in ministry—a task that Dorothy Patterson embodied. Historian Elizabeth Flowers writes, "The spirited and highly visible Patterson reigned throughout the 1990s as the 'matriarch of complementarianism,' becoming as well known and as controversial as her husband, Paige."[1] Second, the class emphasized women's roles as focused on the household and caring for the family. Even though Dorothy Patterson had earned a master of theology (New Orleans Baptist Theological Seminary), a doctorate in ministry (Luther Rice Seminary), and a doctorate in theology (University of South Africa), she always introduced herself publicly as a wife and mother. "She was, in her words, 'primarily a wife, mother, and homemaker,' with grandmother added in years to come," writes Flowers.[2] In line with how Patterson presented herself, the class for pastors' wives focused on homemaking.

I also heard the rumor that the final exam tested the domestic hospitality skills of each woman in the class: Dorothy Patterson would randomly show up at your house during the week, inspect your housekeeping skills, and stay while you served her tea. I shudder to think what would have happened if she had shown up at my house during some weeks of graduate school (my disinclination to do dishes has been a consistent pattern in my adult life; it was worse when I was a stressed-out, newly married graduate student).

Finally, I knew that Patterson's training class for pastors' wives was rooted in Paul's writings about women. For "nearly two millennia," Patterson argued, Christians have agreed that Paul's writings barred women from leadership. She accused academics who argued otherwise of "jesuitical casuistry" and "historical hanky-panky."[3] Only complementarians like herself preserved "the pure Word of God as enduring across cultures and throughout history and as appropriating itself from age to age with vigor and relevance." Biblical womanhood, as she argued in her dissertation, was a timeless continuity throughout church history, divinely ordained by God and clearly articulated by Paul.[4] From everything I knew about her and her husband, I am quite sure that she stressed the importance of biblical womanhood to her students.

I will never know firsthand what Dorothy Patterson's class was like. But I do know that the roots of what Patterson taught and embodied about women's roles lay not in the past "nearly two millennia" but rather in the past five hundred years.[5]

Women have always been wives and mothers, but it wasn't until the Protestant Reformation that being a wife and a mother became the "ideological touchstone of holiness" for women.[6] Before the Reformation, women could gain spiritual authority by rejecting their sexuality. Virginity empowered them. Women became nuns and took religious vows, and some, like Catherine of Siena and Hildegard of Bingen, found their voices rang with the authority of men.[7] Indeed, the further removed medieval women were from the married state, the closer they were to God. After the Reformation, the opposite became true for Protestant women. The more closely they identified with being wives and mothers, the godlier they became.

The Holy Household

The late afternoon light slanted gray through the window of the small room. It was empty, apart from a few chairs and a seminar-style table—everything I needed so that I could work while my husband was in class. I piled several books next to me, an optimistic habit. It wouldn't be possible to get through more than one or two books that afternoon. I had at most three hours while my husband was in class. But hope springs eternal, especially for history doctoral students in the midst of comprehensive exam prep. We had driven together that afternoon to Wake Forest, North Carolina, where my husband was working on his MDiv. I could hear the hum of conversation from his nearby classroom as I sat alone with my pile of books. I picked up the top one from the stack and began reading. The book was *The Holy Household: Women and Morals in Reformation Augsburg* by Lyndal Roper.

Two hours later, my world had shifted.

From childhood, conservative Protestant Christians like me are taught that the Reformation is a story of success, of freedom, of faith revived and reinvigorated. This is why we use Halloween as an occasion for a Reformation Day costume party, in honor of Martin Luther nailing his Ninety-Five Theses to those doors in Wittenberg on October 31, 1517. It is why a tiny plastic Martin Luther—complete with quill and Bible—became the fastest-selling Playmobil figure ever. (The first thirty-four thousand figures sold out within seventy-two hours.) It is why *Foxe's Book of Martyrs* and John Calvin's *Institutes* are still household titles, despite publication dates close to five hundred years ago.

For evangelical Christians, the story of the Reformation is a story of triumph. Roper's scholarship tells a different story. Instead of focusing on the dramatic moments, such as Martin Luther declaring "Here I stand," she focuses on the aftermath of the Reformation in the German town of Augsburg. Instead of focusing on the Reformation heroes, Luther and Calvin and Zwingli, she focuses on how the Reformation affected the lives of ordinary women.

Her very different perspective produces a very different story—a story of loss rather than a story of gain, of increased subordination rather than of liberation.

According to Roper, the male political and economic leaders of Augsburg found Reformation theology supportive as they worked to strengthen control over the city and make it more financially stable. These economic and religious changes hardened a "theology of gender" for women that, far from improving their lives, placed women more securely under the household authority of their husbands. Marriage guaranteed women stability and significance, but their increasingly subordinate role confined them to low-status domestic work, increased their dependence on their husbands for economic survival, and curtailed their economic and social opportunities outside the household structure. Women were encouraged to be chaste, modest, obedient, and passive, while men were encouraged to be aggressive, domineering, controlling, and active. "The heritage of Protestantism for women was deeply ambiguous," writes Roper. While it could have affirmed women's spiritual equality with men, the Reformation instead ushered in a "renewed patriarchalism" that placed married women firmly under the headship of their husbands.[8]

I put the book down. I could hear the buzz of conversation from my husband's classroom. I don't remember what course he was taking that day, but I remember the opposition many of his professors and fellow students held toward women in ministry. One professor was known to divide his students into permanent small groups in his class, and each student was tasked with leading a group discussion. The professor would then pronounce in front of the entire class that if a male student was uncomfortable with a woman leading, the student should let him know. The professor would switch that student into a group without women. The message was clear: any man could lead in this class, regardless of his qualifications or how uncomfortable he made women, but the position of every woman in his class was precarious. A woman's ability to complete the course requirements depended on whether the male students would grant her the permission to do so.

Unfortunately, this professor's stance was not anomalous, even if his tactics were more blatant than those of other professors. It had been a few years since the conservative SBC takeover, and Paige Patterson reigned supreme at Southeastern Seminary. Women were not allowed in preaching courses, and the emphasis was on men as leaders and teachers and women as stay-at-home wives and mothers. From the classes offered to the professors who taught them to the preachers in chapel to the president overseeing it all, Southeastern rooted itself firmly in a gender hierarchy that elevated men over women.

Yet I had just read a compelling historical argument that the roots of this gender hierarchy had more to do with politics and economics than with divine order. As Europe shifted from the medieval era to the early modern era, political ideas about state governance and economic ideas about business management also shifted. These shifts started well before Luther nailed up his Ninety-Five Theses, so they were not launched by the Protestant Reformation per se. But the changing political and socioeconomic landscape of Europe found a supportive partner in Reformation theology. The language of God, argues Roper, married the gender hierarchy of early modern Europe, and subordinate wifedom became synonymous with being a godly woman. Biblical womanhood is rooted in human patriarchal structures that keep seeping back into the church, but the emphasis in biblical womanhood on *being a wife* was strengthened and reinforced during the social changes wrought by the sixteenth century.

Was Roper Right?

I knew I wasn't going to get the job.

I was in the middle of my teaching presentation for a tenure-track position in a religion department. For the topic of my lecture, I had chosen (rather poorly, in hindsight) the less-often-told story of the Reformation: how it affected women. The students, lining the first two rows of the theater-style room, were engaged. The Baptist professors filling the back row were a different story.

106

I focused on how the Reformation elevated the status of wives, but I also talked about what women lost—like the ability to choose a religious life in the convent among a community of women. Instead of focusing exclusively on the success of Luther, I also talked about the narrowing of economic options for women—as trades like medicine became more professionalized, female practitioners found themselves pushed out. In addition to discussing the priesthood of all believers, I talked about the increasing authority of men as heads of spiritual households—women no longer sat with their friends in church, as they had done for so long, but now sat next to their husband under his visible care. I didn't teach the narrative most often found in seminary textbooks and Protestant histories. Instead, I taught the narrative I had learned from my training as a historian at the University of North Carolina at Chapel Hill.

I didn't get the job.

Now, let me be clear. I know a lot about Catholic theology, especially medieval Christianity, and I am both understanding and sympathetic. Theologically, though, I agree with the Reformation. I am a Protestant—not just because I grew up as a Protestant but also because, as an adult, I have chosen to remain Protestant. I think Luther was right—about faith, Jesus, the priesthood of all believers, and the Bible. At the same time, the Reformation wasn't perfect. Glorifying the past because we like that story better isn't history; it is propaganda. Just because I agree with the outcome of the Reformation theologically doesn't mean I think everything that happened during the Reformation era was good.

So let's talk about how the Reformation affected women.

Merry Wiesner-Hanks—a highly respected historian of the early modern world—has summed up the different scholarly positions on how the Reformation affected women: "Some see it as elevating the status of most women in praise of marriage, others see it as limiting women by denying them the opportunity for education and independence in monasteries and stressing wifely obedience, and still others see it as having little impact, with its stress on marriage a response to economic and social changes that had already occurred, and not a cause of those changes."[9] Historians disagree in their interpretation of the evidence, but they agree about the evidence itself.

For example, women's alternatives to marriage decreased, and their dependence on their husbands (economic, political, legal, etc.) increased. Katharina von Bora (Katie Luther) exemplifies this. She was a runaway nun who married the ex-monk Martin Luther. Luther taught that marriage was God's best for both men and women, and his writings helped popularize the godly role of wife and mother. As Katherine French and Allyson Poska explain in *Women and Gender in the Western Past*, "Unlike Catholicism, Luther did not promote female models of spiritual power. Luther's God was not influenced by the Virgin Mary or supported by the work of female saints. Instead of the Virgin Mary, Luther extolled the virtues of Martha, the sister of Lazarus, who stayed in the kitchen, prepared the food, and oversaw the household." Katharina von Bora embodied Martha, turning the Luther household into a domestic sanctuary for their family (she birthed six children) and hosting dinner parties that furthered the fame and influence of her husband. Her husband's theology about marriage was so influential that, as French and Poska write, "every Protestant territory passed a marriage ordinance that stressed wifely obedience."[10] Women's identity, both inside and outside the church, became more firmly intertwined with the household. As Luther said in his lectures on Genesis, "For just as the snail carries its house with it, so the wife should stay at home and look after the affairs of the household, as one who has been deprived of the ability of administering those affairs that are outside and that concern the state."[11]

Katie's reputation as a domestic goddess helped her family while her husband was alive. Their dinner table (enhanced by her conversational wit as well as the fame of her husband) became the place to be for everyone in Europe—from politicians and leaders to university professors, exiled clergy, and ex-nuns. But this fame didn't help her earn a living after his death.[12] Luther's death deprived his family of income, and Katie and her children faced financial challenges. Few economic options existed for a sixteenth-century widow and ex-nun who lacked family support. While Katie's difficulties would have been common even for medieval women (women's work remained low status and low pay), they were intensified by changing perceptions about work. As the household became more firmly established as a woman's space, professional work became more firmly identified as a man's space. The European economy had been swiftly commercializing since the late Middle Ages—success now required deeper pockets and broader networks. Professional status was more clearly identified, often requiring more intentional training, and trade regulations were more clearly established by civic authorities. None of these trends favored women working for pay.

Judith Bennett tells the story of how English brewing went from being the work of medieval women to being the professional job of early modern men. In the fourteenth-century brewing town of Oxford, for example, women dominated the trade. When women brewed for their families, they brewed extra to sell to their neighbors and made a little extra cash. Brewing for sale was mostly small scale, but it helped women contribute to their household needs. Over time, brewing in Oxford became more regulated—by the university, by a brewers' guild, and then by the professionalization of the trade. By 1600, instead of dozens of housewives brewing for their neighborhoods, a few brewers began to supply the city. These few brewers were men. They had deeper pockets and more resources; they invested more money and developed new techniques. They also made close friends with the local government. Women couldn't compete with these bigger, more professional brewers because they had less investment capital and less social clout.[13] A woman who sometimes sold ale to her neighbors might have made a tasty beer, but she couldn't compete with the big boys—just like the woman next door who sells donuts out of her garage on Saturdays can't compete with Krispy Kreme (or Shipley's, which is my family's favorite). Even if women were better brewers than men, they simply couldn't keep up in this changing world.

Of course, increasing professionalization and commercialization didn't really change the kind of work women did. Women in the medieval era mostly worked in low-pay and low-status jobs, and this continued throughout the Reformation era. What seems to have shifted (or at least started shifting for Protestant women)—and this is what is important for modern evangelicals—is how working wives were perceived. In the medieval era, women who brewed ale were ale-wives. They were often identified as such in the records. They were identified by their work as well as by their marital status. They could have more than one identity. But later, in the early modern era, a Protestant wife who brewed was a good wife working alongside her husband (or taking over her deceased husband's trade).[14] Her primary identity was her marital status, and her job was secondary. Indeed, her husband even stood in for her as the public face of the business.

The implications of these shifting ideas about women's work would not be fully realized until the eighteenth and nineteenth centuries, as we will see in chapter 6. But the increasing emphasis on a woman's primary role as *wife*, trumping all other callings, would have a profound impact for modern evangelical women.

Take, for example, the emphasis placed on marriage for conservative evangelical women today—it's often considered more important than a career. Marriage, from the evangelical perspective, ranks right after salvation in regard to the most important life decisions for women. Contemporary Christian musician Wayne Watson's hit song "Somewhere in the World" illustrates this well. Released on his 1985 *Giants in the Land* album, the song is still listed as one of his top songs on Apple Music. Watson sings, "A little girl will go out to play, / All dressed up in mama's clothes." This little girl is brought up in the godly ways of her mama to love Jesus and—the song later implies—to learn how to become a wife. Watson prays for the little girl to come to Jesus because someday "a little boy will need a Godly wife."[15] This heartfelt song enshrines the goals for Christian women: salvation and marriage.

Marriage (followed by motherhood) completes us. I will never forget a story told by one of my early mentors. She was a single woman who became a missionary. Once, when she was younger and still training for the mission field, she was given a pair of men's pants. She was advised to hang them on her bed and pray for God to fill them. I can still see her laughing while she told us the story.

111

While women can aspire to other goals, marriage and family should be the priority. As the ESV proclaims in its resources for marriage and sexual morality, "The union of one man and one woman in marriage is one of the *most basic* and also *most profound* aspects of being created in the image of God."[16] The emphasis on "most basic" and "most profound" are mine, but these words are also the crux of the sentence: because we are created in the image of God, implies the ESV resource, we desire the union of marriage. Marriage—from the evangelical perspective—completes us. This becomes clear in current debates about the Trinity, which I will discuss in chapter 7. Some of the evangelical scholars and pastors who are most vocal about male headship and female submission argue that the relationship between husband and wife models the relationship between God the Father and God the Son. Wives follow the leadership of their husbands, just as Jesus follows the leadership of the Father. The marriage hierarchy, like marriage itself, they argue, is embedded in the *imago Dei*.

Indeed, evangelical Christians focus so much on marriage that we neglect the vocational callings of career women and the choices of single women. This is very shortsighted given how many evangelical women continue to work outside the home. "Christians who are worried about feminism's influence, or about the breakdown of the family, will not have much luck telling married women to stop working," writes Katelyn Beaty in *A Woman's Place*. "Women are already working—in the home, outside of it, for their families, for their neighbors, for the glory of God."[17] It is also shortsighted given how many evangelical women remain unmarried. My friend and fellow Baylor historian Andrea Turpin writes about "singleness microaggressions" in evangelical churches—"Like when someone at church asks,

'Why aren't you married?' before adding, 'You're great!'"[18] The Reformation world elevated marriage as the ideal state for women, and evangelicals, who identify strongly with the Reformation legacy (remember how well the Martin Luther figurine sold?), have done the same—to the detriment of not only single women and working women but also married women.

The Irony of Reformation Theology for Women

Reformation theology should have set women free, but it didn't.

When I teach the second half of my European women's history course, covering roughly 1215 to 1918, I use my own interpretation of Virginia Woolf's phrase "a room of one's own" to explain historical differences within the continuity of women's lives.[19] Women, throughout history, live within the confines of patriarchy. Bennett describes this as the patriarchal equilibrium. Regardless of how much freedom women have, they always have less than men. Yet the patriarchal equilibrium is a continuum, not a fixed standard. The boundaries of patriarchy wax and wane; the size of a woman's room—the space where she is able to make her own choices—changes. Some women have bigger rooms, such as wealthy women with husbands and fathers among the highest social classes. Some women have smaller rooms, such as poorer women from families with little political and social influence. Historical circumstances, such as the aftermath of the Black Death in Europe, temporarily expanded women's rooms by increasing their independence as wage earners, while other historical circumstances, such as Athenian democracy, made women's rooms smaller.

If we look at the broad sweep of history, we find some interesting patterns regarding the size of women's rooms. When

113

political and social structures are less centralized and less clearly defined, women often experience greater agency; their rooms are bigger. It is no accident that the stories of the most authoritative women in Christian history stem from the fourth century through the tenth century, when the authority structures of Christianity—not to mention the political structures to which Christianity became attached—were more fluid. It is also no accident that, after the ecclesiastical hierarchy became more centralized and more powerful during the central Middle Ages, women's ability to exercise formal authority diminished; women's rooms became smaller. There are always exceptions, of course, but these general patterns are clear.

Consider, for example, the modern missions field. Power structures and centralized authority are often less accessible and less clearly defined, leaving room for conservative evangelical women to lead as preachers and teachers on the mission field in ways that they cannot when they return to their home churches. Margaret Bendroth, in her classic *Fundamentalism and Gender, 1875 to the Present*, notes that "when the China Inland Mission called for two hundred volunteers in 1929, 70 percent of those who left for China the following year were women, and all but four were single."[20] But the home offices that sent them were run predominantly by men, and when the women came home, they were reminded quickly of their place—beneath male authority.

The Reformation ushered in a theology about ecclesiastical leadership that, ironically, made evangelical women's rooms smaller. Taken at face value, Reformation theology should have expanded women's rooms. Priests were no longer necessary, as all believers had direct access to God. While the female body was still the "weaker sex," it was no longer considered impure.

114

Men and women were both understood to be created in the image of God, and the union of man and woman in marriage was considered the ideal state intended by God—even for clergy.

Medieval women had to transcend their sex to gain authority in the medieval church. But Protestant women didn't have to do this—their bodies were not a spiritual problem. Indeed, Protestant women were celebrated for their roles as wives and mothers. So couldn't women now preach and teach just like men? Didn't the priesthood of all believers apply to women just as it applied to men?

Some women thought so.

They insisted that Reformation teaching made their rooms bigger.

For example, Katherine Zell, wife of the Strasbourg reformer Matthew Zell, demanded that she be judged "not according to the standards of a woman, but according to the standards of one whom God has filled with the Holy Spirit."[21] Argula von Grumbach, a German woman who converted to Protestantism despite her husband remaining Catholic and who became one of the most outspoken supporters of the Reformation (even publishing eight works between 1523 and 1524 in defense of Lutheranism), certainly thought that she had the God-given right to teach and preach. In a letter to the University of Ingolstadt defending the Lutheranism of a young teacher, she proclaimed, "What I have written to you is no woman's chit-chat, but the word of God; and [I write] as a member of the Christian Church against which the gates of Hell cannot prevail."[22] She knew the writings of Paul, but she did not believe they applied to her. "I am not unfamiliar with Paul's words that women should be silent in church," she announced, "but when I see that no man will or can speak, I am driven by the word of

God when he said, 'He who confesses me on earth, him will I confess, and he who denies me, him will I deny.'"[23]

Anne Askew, an English reformer, likewise believed women had the authority to speak. Accused of heresy, she argued back when Paul's directive for women to "be silent" was quoted at her. Preaching only took place behind a pulpit, and since she wasn't behind a pulpit, she wasn't preaching. As she explained, after the bishop of London Edmund Bonner's chancellor (1539–49 and 1553–59) quoted Paul at her, "I answered him, that I knew Paul's meaning so well as he, which is, 1 Cor. xiv. that a woman ought not to speak in the congregation by the way of teaching. And then I asked him, how many women he had seen go into the pulpit and preach? He said he had never seen any. Then I said, he ought to find no fault in poor women, unless they had offended against the law."[24] In other words, she argued that she had the right to speak God's Word and teach men, as long as she stayed out of the official preaching space. Moreover, because she had stayed out of the official preaching space, the chancellor had no right to accuse her because she hadn't broken any law.

The early modern world didn't agree with these women. "Zell's wish was never granted," writes Wiesner-Hanks, "and women's writings were always judged first on the basis of gender. Argula von Grumbach's husband was ordered to force her to stop writing."[25] As for Anne Askew, she was burned at the stake for heresy.

So what was the problem? Why didn't Protestant theology sanction women to teach and preach, even though it had declared the priesthood of all believers and sanctioned the marriage bed? The response to von Grumbach gives us a clue. Instead of being ordered herself to stop preaching and writing, her husband was ordered to stop her. She was under his authority. The problem was what Roper calls the "holy household."

Reformation theology might have removed the priest, but it replaced him with the husband. The 1563 Tudor homilies, a series of sermons authorized by the Anglican Church, clearly show this: "Let women be subject to their husbands as to the Lord, for the husband is the head of the woman, as Christ is the head of the Church. Here you understand, that GOD has commanded, that you should acknowledge the authority of the husband, and refer to him the honor of obedience."[26] The sermon continues, emphasizing that wives should cover their heads as a sign of submission. In an eerie echo of the ancient Roman paterfamilias, the orderly household once again became the barometer for both the state and the church, and the waning power of the Catholic priest was balanced by the waxing power of the Protestant husband.

A Refashioned Paul

The medieval world argued for women's exclusion from ecclesiastical leadership based on the inferiority of the female body and the subordinate role of wives. But since not all women were wives, and since some women could transcend their bodies, special allowances existed for women to preach and teach and lead. Historian Nicole Beriou describes how the thirteenth-century Franciscan priest Eustache of Arras explained women preaching. According to Eustache, the Holy Spirit did indeed inspire women like Mary Magdalene and Thecla to preach and gave them spiritual authority, just like men. But these women were exceptions. They were not married, and so, Eustache explains, "Saint Paul's interdiction did not concern them, but it was directed against married women only." Women in general did not have the right to preach, but "a certain right to speak authoritatively might be recognized for women who had the special gift of prophecy" and were not married.[27]

This changed after the Reformation.

The early modern world argued for women's exclusion on the basis of an emerging gender theology that emphasized differences between women and men rather than their spiritual sameness and on the basis of an expanded understanding of Pauline prescriptions and household codes. Paul's words now applied to all women, not just wives, and the importance of women being wives was underscored.

I confess, as an evangelical woman, it surprised me that the Reformation introduced so much emphasis on the Pauline texts about women. I remember reading an offhand comment from medieval church historian R. N. Swanson that the Pauline household codes were not nearly as important to medieval Christians as modern historians thought they were.[28] I marked exclamation points and underlined the comment. "Seriously?" I wrote in the margin. I couldn't imagine a world without gracious submission filling the pages of women's Bible studies and the authority of husbands preached regularly from the pulpit. I couldn't imagine a world of marriage sermons not focused on Ephesians 5.

But my own research into late medieval English sermons showed me that such a world existed.

Medieval preachers did preach Paul. In fact, the most frequently cited Scripture passages in late medieval English sermons, after Matthew 25:31–41 (which is cited in more than fifty sermon manuscripts), are Pauline texts. Yet these sermons are almost completely silent about the Pauline prescriptions and household codes for women. As I revealed in my presidential address to the Conference on Faith and History in 2018, I have found that the usual-suspect Pauline texts (1 Corinthians 11:3; 14; Ephesians 5; Colossians 3; 1 Timothy 2; Titus 2) appear in only a handful of the 120 late medieval English sermon manuscripts I have studied.[29] On the few occasions when these Pauline texts are used in medieval sermons, their focus is mostly not on female roles.

Take, for example, 1 Timothy 2:15: "Yet she will be saved through childbearing." In one of the only two medieval sermons to discuss this verse, the sermon casts the woman (the "she" in the verse) as an example for *all* Christians, who must go through the pain (like childbirth) of cleansing themselves of sin before experiencing the joy of salvation (the child itself). In other words, the sermon interprets Paul's claim that women "will be saved through childbearing" not as a way to enforce strict gender roles or to emphasize women's domestic responsibilities or even to highlight women as mothers. This medieval sermon author is clearly aware of Paul's words in 1 Timothy 2:15, but he uses them to encourage all Christians to face the pain of repentance and penance so that they might be reborn into the joy of salvation.

Medieval preachers preached Paul, but their primary focus was to teach parishioners how to find redemption through involvement in the sacraments and practices of the medieval Catholic Church. Paul was used to reinforce these medieval lessons, and women as exemplars of faith became much more important to the medieval religious agenda than women as exemplars of submission and domesticity. The woman saved through childbearing as an exemplar of the sanctification process for all Christians was more important to medieval theology than tethering the salvation of literal women to their reproductive capabilities.

For the most part Paul was not preached in medieval sermons to reinforce women's subordinate role.

Early modern preachers also knew their Paul. But unlike their medieval counterparts, they preached Paul to enforce women's subordinate role within the household. Early modern sermons emphasize godly behavior as reflective of spiritual status. Adherence to the Pauline prescriptions became a barometer for the spiritual health of families, and women as models of submission and domesticity became critical exemplars for Protestant theology. This was a departure from sermons of the medieval world.

Lancelot Andrewes, in a sermon published posthumously in 1657, interprets 1 Timothy 2:15 thus: "The domesticall duty of preserving the household pertaineth to her, as it is in Proverbs 31:21. She should be of the property of the Snail, still at home. . . . The house in holy Scripture is taken for the children, whom she must bear and bring up in the fear of God; *The Wife through bearing of Children shall be saved, saith Paul in 1 Tim. 2. 15.*"[30] The medieval sermon author uses Paul's words in 1 Timothy 2:15 to encourage all Christians to face the pain of repentance and penance so that they might be reborn into the joy of salvation. Andrewes, in stark contrast, uses Paul's words as evidence for the divinely ordained subjection of women and their divinely ordained calling as—if I may use a modern term—homemakers.

Let me provide one more example.

In 1690, Isaac Marlow, a member of minister Benjamin Keach's Baptist church, published a tract that countered Keach's teaching that congregational hymn singing was important.

Marlow argued that singing was unbiblical because if the entire congregation sang, women would sing too:

> That Women ought neither to teach nor pray vocally in the Church of Christ, is generally believed by all Orthodox Christians, and is asserted from *1 Cor.* 14.34, 35. *Let your Women keep silence in the Churches: for it is not permited unto them to speak* and *1 Timothy* 2, 11, 12. *Let the Women learn in Silence with all Subjection: but I suffer not a Woman to teach, nor to usurp Authority over the Man, but to learn in silence.* I therefore greatly marvel that any Man should assert and admit of such a Practice as Women's Singing; and that any Woman should presume to sing vocally in the Church of Christ, when he positively and plainly forbids them in his Word: for Singing is Teaching, *Coloss.* 3.16. and Speaking, *Ephes.* 5.19. both of which are plainly forbidden to Women in the Church.[31]

Although agreeing that Paul's injunction banned women from church leadership, Keach argued that singing "doth not lie in a Ministerial way, and therefore not intended by the Spirit of God here; Preaching or Teaching is not Singing, nor Singing Preaching or Teaching. You [Isaac Marlow] must learn better to distinguish between different Duties and Ordinances, before you take upon you to teach others."[32]

From my medieval perspective, I find this sermon-inspired dialogue striking. While Keach defended women's right to sing, he did so by accepting the Pauline ban against women teaching and preaching. Women could sing only because singing did not fall within the purview of 1 Corinthians and 1 Timothy. In other words, a shift occurred across the Reformation era in how preachers used Paul. Rather than always having serious consequences for women, Paul had less impact on attitudes toward women within late medieval English sermons. In the aftermath of the Reformation, however, Paul came to define Christian womanhood. Remember, it was the 1563 Tudor homilies that declared women's position in the church and household to be subordinate: "Let women be subject to their husbands as to the Lord, for the husband is the head of the woman, as Christ is the head of the Church. Here you understand, that GOD has commanded, that you should acknowledge the authority of the husband, and refer to him the honor of obedience."[33] The godly woman was submissive and silent, just as Paul declared she should be.

The question, of course, is why?

Why the shift in how Pauline texts were used in regard to women?

First, the preaching program put forward in the thirteenth century and reinforced in the fifteenth century dictated teaching focused on the basics of the faith. It actively discouraged preaching to ordinary people on more complex and potentially controversial topics. Second, the theological emphasis on redemption through penitence as rooted in the sacramental community of the medieval church profoundly shaped how preachers preached Paul in medieval sermons, emphasizing women's faith as more important than their sex.[34]

Finally, the medieval reality was that most men would never be priests, placing them—strangely enough—on more spiritually equal footing with women. The spiritual headship of a husband didn't matter so much in a patriarchal world where both husbands and wives had to go as individuals through a priest for the necessary sacraments. But it did matter in a world in which patriarchy was already the norm and women potentially had as much spiritual power as men did. Patriarchy had to shapeshift to adapt to the new Reformation world. As Roper explains, "The values of evangelical moralism were harnessed to an older conservative tradition which defined women as wives in submission to their husbands. . . . Far from endorsing independent spiritual lives for women, the institutionalized Reformation was most successful when it most insisted on a vision of women's incorporation within the household under the leadership of their husbands."[35] The emphasis on Pauline texts by early modern reformers was born into a secular world already supported by a gender hierarchy. Rather than Protestant reformers reviving a biblical model, they were simply mapping Scripture onto a preceding secular structure. Instead of Scripture transforming society, Paul's writings were used to prop up the patriarchal practices already developing in the early modern world.

A Refashioned Family

We stumbled on the church by accident.

It was March 2003. I was writing the final chapter of my dissertation and made a last-minute trip to England with my parents. I was hunting seven sacrament fonts on England's east coast. Ann Eljenholm Nichols has written about these "seeable signs," arguing that parishioners carved the stone baptismal fonts in an attempt to combat fifteenth-century heresy. The parishioners literally reinscribed orthodoxy by inscribing scenes of their faith in stone.[36] Several of the images depict women interacting with priests, which is why I wanted to see them. So off we went—my parents and I driving around the British countryside for seven full days tracking down fifteenth-century baptismal fonts.

We only made a couple of mistakes as we hunted down the churches, and this was one of them. There were two different churches in two different towns but with the same town name: Wilby. We drove to the wrong Wilby.

But it was a worthwhile mistake, stumbling into the church of All Saints, Wilby.

It was the first time I had seen a church with seventeenth-century box pews. Not much remains of what medieval churches looked like in England before the Reformation. The aftermath of Henry VIII's reformation (1533–36), which included the dissolution of the monasteries (a nice way of describing the looting and destruction of medieval churches), combined with the chaos of the English Civil War (1642–49) and the so-called Victorian "restorations" (1840–75), left little that medieval parishioners would recognize. The vibrant colors of medieval stained glass windows and the interior paintings on the church walls are mostly lost, smashed and whitewashed over. The medieval naves that used to be crammed with chantries and separated from the altar with elaborate rails and rood screens are now filled with chairs and pulpits. The church we had just walked into was about as far removed from the colorful, noisy, incense-filled churches of medieval England as our full English breakfast was from medieval porridge. But All Saints, Wilby, mostly escaped Victorian restorations, so it still stands as a testament to the Anglican Church on the eve of the Civil War.

Two features dominated the small, bright space: the large double-decker pulpit fixed on the wall, accessed by a circular staircase, and the remaining box pews partially lining the aisle. I stared at those boxed spaces, envisioning the families that filed into each one, closing the door to "box" them in for the duration of the service.

My medieval history–trained eyes stared hard at those box pews. I caught a glimpse, maybe for the first time, of how vastly the Reformation had changed Christian worship. In medieval churches, women and men gathered on opposite sides of the church regardless of their family affiliations. This is probably why the salutation "Good men and women" was a favorite way medieval preachers opened their sermons—I can almost see them looking first to their left, welcoming the "good men" before turning to their right and welcoming the "good women." Weddings today still echo this old medieval arrangement, as the bride stands to the right of the pastor and the groom to the left. Grouping women and men by their sex instead of by their families encouraged the single-sex parish communities that flourished in late medieval England. One of the first articles I ever read by historian Katherine French told me about medieval church communities for women. These groups, argues French, not only built community but also expanded women's agency in late medieval churches while reinforcing accepted gender norms. As she writes, "We can imagine that in wives' groups, women found both comfort and advice to help them through difficult marriages, the birth and death of children, and the running of a household. Through these groups women could create their own hierarchies, based somewhat on family status and wealth, but also on less visible criteria, such as piety, fertility, or personality."[37] French shows how through these female communities women expanded their domestic authority into the space of the church. "Together they created opportunities for collective action and created visibility in the name of salvation."[38]

But these groups were lost with the Reformation as the family unit became paramount.

Instead of sitting with their female communities, women now sat with their families. Instead of the preacher directing his sermon to "Good men and women," he now mostly directed it to the spiritual leaders of the household—the "men, fathers, and brethren" as one preacher addressed his audience.[39] Standing in that refashioned church, I could almost hear the changes wrought in the Reformation aftermath. I could almost see the women lined up with their children in the boxed pews, sitting literally under the increased authority of their husbands. French is not talking about box pews in churches when she describes the impact of the Reformation on women in the English parish, but her words still ring true. As women's activities were redirected into the household, women became less "collective, visible, and active" in the late medieval parish. "The lay agency that was at the heart of women's ability to turn the parish into a forum for their own spiritual practices ended, as the family became increasingly a religious unit that was on display in the parish."[40]

Women's identities were now subsumed within the family. Yes, the role of wife had been elevated but at a price.

I love how French concludes her book *The Good Women of the Parish*:

To be sure, some women rejoiced at the abolition of guild dues, the veneration of saint images, and the pomp and ritual of the Sarum Manual. However, those who were going to find meaning in this new Church needed to develop a new set of skills and actions from which to create religious meaning. For some, literacy, a personal relationship with God, and the increased role of faith rather than works were the new skills and actions. For others, unable to read, and unable to hear the Word of God

126

with their friends who supported them through difficult times, it was not enough.[41]

I am a Protestant woman, and I am thankful for the theological changes wrought by the Reformation world. But as a historian, I know these changes came with a cost. As the role of wife expanded, the opportunities for women outside of marriage shrank. The family became not only the center of a woman's world but her primary identity as a good Christian.

The subjugation of women is indeed a historical constant—but that doesn't make it divinely ordained. While Paul's writings about women were known consistently throughout church history, it wasn't until the Reformation era that they begin to be used systematically to keep women out of leadership roles. Instead of Scripture transforming society, society transformed how early modern Christians interpreted the Bible—and this was compounded (as we will see in the next chapter) by the proliferation of the English Bible.

I STILL REMEMBER how frustrated I was. At our church, I led Wednesday night youth group, but because of the pastoral stance on male headship, I could only teach teenage girls. Usually, my husband and I avoided teaching directly on women's roles in the church. We worked hard to not publicly contradict the pastoral position.

Tonight one of the teenage girls was leading. Part of our philosophy was to teach the youth the skills they would need to become leaders in the church, which included teaching the Bible. So we worked with them on how to prepare lessons, find resources, and actually lead a lesson. This student taught on what it meant to be a Christian wife. Because of the complementarian stance of the church, I couldn't refuse her choice. I also couldn't contradict her. I could only listen.

I sat staring at the Bible in front of me. It was my Today's New International Version (TNIV), which my husband had given me early in our marriage. I listened as she read from the ESV. I listened as she argued from Scripture that women's primary calling was to be a wife and a mother. I listened as she said that men were called to lead, because only men were mentioned in the Bible in leadership positions, while women were called to follow.

When it was over, I got in my car and sat there. Many of the verses the girl had read were shaped by the translation she was using. The picture of submissive wives and mothers, who sat under the leadership of their husbands and male leaders in the church, may have seemed crystal clear. But her translation, her very modern English Bible translation, made her believe that what she was teaching was a plain reading of Scripture, whereas as a historian, I know that all biblical translations are shaped by human hands.

Translations matter. And for women, translations of the English Bible have mattered more than most modern evangelicals realize.[1]

The Gender-Inclusive Bible Debate

It was the 1996–97 academic year when I graduated from Baylor University with a bachelor's in history. This was also the year I got married to an ordained Baptist pastor and started a graduate program in medieval history at the University of North Carolina at Chapel Hill. It was a big year for me.

The year 1997 was also a big year in the world of Bible translation. It was the year *World* magazine published the article "Femme Fatale: The Feminist Seduction of the Evangelical Church." Writer Susan Olasky told readers that the New International Version (NIV) was "quietly going 'gender neutral.'"[2] The result, she wrote, could be catastrophic—a gender-neutral Bible could "cloud the uniqueness of men and women" and hamper the "uphill" struggle of complementarians for a return to biblical gender roles. The catalyst for the change, argued Olasky, was not "new discoveries about the Bible" but rather "social changes occurring in culture." One month later, Olasky published a second article, "The Battle for the Bible." In it, she accused Zondervan of being more committed to "unisex language" than to faithfulness to the biblical text. Because Zondervan authors were supposed to avoid using masculine pronouns as "generic placemarkers" and instead use gender-inclusive terms like *humanity* and *people*, because Zondervan already published other gender-inclusive Bible translations (such as the NRSV), and because Zondervan was contractually bound to support the International Bible Society's Committee on Biblical Translations (which had been promoting gender-inclusive language since 1992), Olasky painted Zondervan as letting culture change the Word of God.[3]

The uproar among evangelicals was instantaneous. Gender-inclusive language was no longer just an argument over proper translation; it was the slippery slope of feminism destroying biblical truth. "I do not think this is an issue that should be swept under the rug," wrote Wayne Grudem, then professor at Trinity Evangelical Divinity School. "The accuracy and integrity of many words of Scripture are at stake, and these are the very words of God."[4]

One month after Olasky's second article was published, twelve men met in Colorado Springs. Led by James Dobson (founder of Focus on the Family) and including Grudem and Piper, the group produced guidelines for "Gender-Related Language in Scripture."[5] Sometimes, they conceded, gender-inclusive language could improve the accuracy of translations, but most gender-inclusive language, they concluded, was not biblically accurate. Shortly after the Colorado Springs meeting, the SBC met in Dallas. In June 1997, the nearly sixteen-million-member denomination unequivocally condemned gender-inclusive language in biblical translations. Their resolution proclaimed that such translations resulted from "those who do not hold a high view of Scripture" and those who gave in "to accommodate contemporary cultural pressures."[6] By fall 1997, the battle lines were drawn. Secular culture, especially the feminist movement, was changing Scripture in a dangerous way, and it was time for Christians to fight back.

131

When Zondervan released their gender-inclusive translation (TNIV) in 2002, Grudem wrote a scathing review. According to him, "The heart of the controversy is this: The TNIV people have decided to translate the general idea of a passage and to erase the male-oriented details."[7] The website for the Council on Biblical Manhood and Womanhood, of which Grudem was president, listed more than one hundred challenges to the textual renderings of the TNIV. The same article reports Dobson's prepared statement about the TNIV: "Like most evangelical Christians, I want my Bible to contain an accurate translation of the canonical Hebrew and Greek texts. Accordingly, I will continue to speak out against any effort that alters God's Word or toys with translation methodology for the sake of 'political correctness.'"[8]

Before the TNIV was even released, the Colorado Springs group had begun working on their own translation. Directly after Dobson's meeting in May 1997, Grudem entered translation negotiations with Crossway and the National Council of Churches; in 1998, permission was secured to revise the 1971 RSV and release a new translation that would get rid of "de-Christianing translation choices."[9] In 2001, a year before Zondervan published the TNIV, Crossway released the ESV, along with a slew of endorsements from evangelical megachurch pastors, musicians, and authors.[10]

The ESV was a direct response to the gender-inclusive language debate. It was born to secure readings of Scripture that preserved male headship. It was born to fight against liberal feminism and secular culture challenging the Word of God.

As a medieval historian who specializes in English sermons, the debate over gender-inclusive translations amuses me. It amuses me because the accusers depict gender-inclusive Bible translations as a modern, secular trend fueled by the feminist movement. Yet, as a medieval historian, I know that Christians translated Scripture in gender-inclusive ways long before the feminist movement.

I'll admit that the debate also scares me. It scares me for the same reason that it amuses me: because gender-inclusive language has a long history in the church, the debate shows how much modern evangelical Christians have forgotten church history. Indeed, the debate underscores how dangerous many evangelicals' lack of understanding about the past affects women in the present. While it is certainly true that second-wave feminism in the 1960s contributed to greater concern for gender-inclusive language in American culture, it is also true that concern for gender-inclusive language in the biblical text existed long before modern feminism.

So let me tell you what I know as a historian about the translation of the English Bible—what I wish I had told those girls long ago at Wednesday night youth group.

The English Bible before the Reformation

I was recently given the Baylor Annotated Study Bible. The gold-trimmed pages shine between the dark green leather cover. It is beautiful. It is easy to carry around. It has an attached green ribbon so I won't lose my place. It has study notes by some of my favorite biblical scholars, including Scot McKnight, Todd Still, and Mikeal Parsons. When we think of a Bible, we visualize a bound book like this.

Historically speaking, the Bible as a bound book is new. A single bound volume that can be purchased and carried around by ordinary people was birthed more than fifteen hundred years after the death and resurrection of Jesus. The ingenuity of a fifteenth-century German blacksmith launched the printing revolution in early modern Europe, including mass-market distribution of the Bible. The production of what we now know as the Gutenberg Bible marks a significant turning point in history. The Word of God, from Genesis to Revelation, became readily available to the people of God for the first time.

One of my favorite churches in London enshrines the English Bible as born in 1535. The church, St. Magnus the Martyr, stands steps from Thomas Farriner's bakehouse on Pudding Lane, where the Great Fire of London began in 1666. Dedicated to Saint Magnus the Martyr, this church was the second church destroyed by the fire and the most expensive church restored under the direction of Christopher Wren. The pricey steeple is now nearly obscured by surrounding buildings, including the monument to the Great Fire itself.

But if you duck inside St. Magnus the Martyr, on the east wall near the altar you will find a nineteenth-century plaque marking the remains of Miles Coverdale. Coverdale is best known for his English Bible translation, printed in 1535. The plaque inscription reads, "To the memory of Miles Coverdale: . . . With the view of affording the means of reading and hearing, in their own tongue the wonderful works of God, not only to his own countreymen, but to the nations that sit in darkness. . . . The first complete English printed version of the Bible was published under his direction."[11]

In one sense, the plaque is correct. The Coverdale Bible was the first complete printed Bible in English (from Old Testament to New Testament) in the sense of our modern understanding—a complete text bound in a single volume. (Of course, William Tyndale had printed an English translation of the New

Testament in 1525. Because Tyndale was executed before he could finish translating the Old Testament, the designation "first complete English Bible" went to the Coverdale Bible, printed ten years after Tyndale's New Testament.)

In another sense though, the plaque is wrong. The Coverdale inscription proclaims that the English Bible is a result of the Reformation. It suggests that medieval people before Coverdale did not have access to the biblical text in English. They sat in (biblical) darkness—as the nineteenth-century inscription reads. This isn't true.

Medieval historian Beryl Smalley opens her classic *The Study of the Bible in the Middle Ages* with this sentence: "The Bible was the most studied book of the middle ages."[12] The Protestant Reformation changed how the Bible was used by Christians, but it didn't introduce the Bible to Christians. English translations of biblical text existed long before the Reformation. By the eleventh century, English translations had been made of the Psalms, the first six books of the Old Testament (the Old English Hexateuch), and the Gospels (the West Saxon Gospels). Although this biblical text circulated in clerical circles, scholars argue that they were also intended for use by "literate laymen." Frans van Liere, a medieval historian who authored my favorite book on the medieval Bible, notes that Matthew Parker (archbishop of Canterbury from 1559–75) used the existence of Middle English biblical manuscripts to argue for his right to publish an English Bible (a 1568 translation known as the Bishops' Bible). Because the Bible had a long history of being translated into English, Parker argued, it was appropriate for the Church of England to continue translating the Bible into English.[13]

While complete translations of the English Bible were uncommon, they did exist in the medieval era. A fifteenth-century sermon collection that I work with frequently, known as the *Longleat Sunday Gospels*, contains a provocative claim that "since it is lawful to preach the Gospel in English, it is lawful to write it in English, both to the teacher and to the hearer, if he knows how to write."[14] The preacher (probably a Franciscan friar) admits that he personally has been told not to write the Gospel in English, but that shouldn't keep anyone else from creating vernacular translations. We know that by the late fourteenth century, followers of John Wycliffe had translated the entire Bible into English. Modern Protestants often think of this as a "heretical" Bible that was used only by those dissatisfied with English Catholicism. But more than 250 extant copies of the Wycliffe Bible exist today (the copies range from just New Testaments to complete Bibles), showing that the Wycliffe Bible was in common use.[15] Catholic sermons from the fifteenth century confirm this as they preach.[16] That Catholic clergy used this "heretical" Bible shows a broad approval for English Bibles. Indeed, Henry Ansgar Kelly writes that the regular use of the Wycliffe Bible in late medieval English church services "is one of the strongest indications for the widespread acceptance of the translations by the general populace."[17]

Before the printing press made books more widely available, it was difficult to own complete versions of the Bible. Copies of the Bible took a long time to create and were thus costly and rare. Yet for most medieval people, the proliferation of Scripture in literature, sermons, and excerpts of the Bible like the Psalms (Psalters) gave them plentiful access to the Word of God. James H. Morey, in his *Book and Verse: A Guide to Middle English Biblical Literature*, shows how rapidly English translations of Scripture proliferated in late medieval culture.[18] *Book and Verse* includes six appendixes, composed of 264 printed pages, which list every instance of biblical text that he could find in Middle English literature—including Gospel accounts, Psalters, biblical overviews, commentaries, poems, religious treatises, and even two complete Middle English translations of Revelation. Ordinary Christians in late medieval England were not strangers to the Bible in their own tongue.

I had a student one semester who had a hard time staying awake during lectures. I imagine he would be asleep by now. So let me get to the point: the Bible existed in English before the Reformation, despite what the plaque at St. Magnus the Martyr claims. Certainly, the Reformation ushered in broader use of the vernacular Bible through its emphasis on *sola scriptura* and encouragement of printed Bibles. But the Reformation's emphasis on biblical access was preceded by the access medieval Christians already had to biblical text.

The English Bible in Medieval Sermons

Sermons provided the most consistent access to the Bible for medieval people. Now, I know what you are thinking—medieval people heard sermons? Anti-Catholic rhetoric combined with Protestant glorification of the Reformation combined with poor methods of measuring medieval church attendance by modern scholars have warped our understanding of medieval Christianity. To this day I grind my teeth over the church history series used by Capitol Hill Baptist Church. It paints a grim picture of a sordid, corrupt medieval church in which few people, except for a remnant of "scattered monks and nuns," found salvation. For the sake of my sleepy student, I will save Protestant myths about medieval Christianity as material for a future book and will point out only this sentence from the online curriculum: medieval Christianity "reminds us what happens when people are illiterate of our Bibles—we drift from knowing what constitutes acceptance with God."[19] Medieval people did not know their Bible, this Protestant church history curriculum states, and consequently most of them were eternally damned. (I had to take a deep breath after writing that sentence.)

Evangelicals should know that medieval people knew Scripture at least as well, if not better, than we do today. Frans van Liere reminds us that biblical knowledge was not confined to the clergy. The Bible revolution wrought by the Reformation among ordinary Christians began with ordinary Christians in the medieval world (and not just with the three men listed by the Capitol Hill Baptist Church curriculum).[20] As van Liere writes, the medieval church had a "long tradition of lay access to biblical texts."[21]

Take, for example, Margery Kempe. Along with the help of Lynneth Miller Renberg, I have counted about fifty Scripture references, direct and indirect, in *The Book of Margery Kempe*. Her fifteenth-century life story overflows with English Scripture. From her retelling of Mary's visit to her cousin Elizabeth in the Gospel of Luke (chap. 6, book 1 of Margery's book) to her cry that she loves God with all her heart and with all her strength (chap. 13, book 1; echoing Deuteronomy 6:5; Matthew 22:37; Mark 12:30–33; Luke 10:27) to her reflection on the encounter between Jesus and the woman accused of adultery in John 8 (chap. 27, book 1), Margery Kempe knew her Bible. Her life testifies that she, a fifteenth-century woman, had access to "Holy Writ" (as medieval folk described it). Instead of carrying a Bible in her hands, she carried biblical text inscribed on her heart and spoken through her words. Instead of learning Scripture by reading it during her daily quiet time and memorizing verses at Awana, she learned it from going to church: talking with clergy, listening to them read religious texts, memorizing her prayers, and—most importantly—listening to sermons.

Late medieval people listened to sermons. A boom in the production of sermon manuscripts and changes to the physical space of churches testify to the popularity of late medieval preaching. Historian Larissa Taylor describes sermons as the "mass medium" of the Middle Ages, and Beverly Kienzle calls them the "central literary genre" for medieval Christians.[22] Margery Kempe describes how people ran to hear popular preachers, and records from some medieval cities reveal that thousands went to hear them. Crowds like these were often too large to fit inside local churches, and so—long before the Great Awakening and Baptist tent revivals—medieval preachers had already mastered the outdoor arena.[23]

Scripture flows through medieval sermons, with the Latin text translated so that ordinary Christians would understand the Word of God. Notable for our purposes is the fact that this biblical text often includes gender-inclusive language. Long before either the TNIV or the ESV—or even the King James Version (KJV), for that matter—priests in late medieval England were already erasing "the male-oriented details" from Scripture as they preached to the men and women crowding the naves of their churches.[24]

Gender-Inclusive Language before the TNIV

In the Latin Vulgate (Jerome's fourth-century translation and the primary Bible used throughout the medieval world), Genesis 1:27 reads, "Et creavit Deus hominem ad imaginem suam ad imaginem Dei creavit illum masculum et feminam creavit

139

eos." Or, as the Wycliffe Bible (an English translation directly from the Vulgate) reads, "And God made out of nothing a man in his image and likeness; God made out of nothing a man in the image of God; yea, God made them out of nothing, male and female." Or as the KJV renders it, "So God created man in his own image, in the image of God created he him; male and female created he them." Or, as the modern NIV renders it, "God created mankind in his own image, in the image of God he created them; male and female he created them."

In 2012, Vern S. Poythress of Westminster Theological Seminary expressed great concern that the TNIV had altered Genesis 1:27.[25] Instead of following the NIV translation, "God created mankind in his own image," the TNIV rendered "mankind" as "human beings." As Poythress wrote, "The change to a plural obscures the unity of the human race." For Poythress, "human beings" was not an acceptable substitution for "mankind."[26]

Except that it is. The Hebrew word *'adam* is a gender-inclusive word for "human." Indeed, the text of Genesis 1:27 explains this for us: God created *humans* in his image, both men and women. The Vulgate picks up on the gender inclusivity of the Hebrew word, rendering it with a gender-inclusive Latin word: *homo* or *hominem*. While the word *homo* can apply to a single male, it is not a gender-specific term. Instead, *vir* is the word used exclusively for "man." The word *homo*, by contrast, applies to humanity. So the Vulgate translates the Hebrew word *'adam* (human) as *hominem* (human).[27]

Many late medieval English sermons do the same. The fifteenth-century author of a collection of sermons found in the archives of Salisbury Cathedral includes a more succinct English translation of Genesis 1:27. In a passage comparing how a person's face reflects the bright morning sun with how a clean

140

soul reflects the likeness of God, the author underscores that humanity was created for this purpose: to reflect the image of God. The sermon quotes Genesis 1:27 to emphasize this point: "For God made *man and woman* in his likeness."[28]

To make sure the medieval audience understood that all people were included, the sermon author omitted translating the first part of the verse and translated only the words *masculum et feminam*: man and woman. Those who heard this sermon would have found no difference between the text read in the sermon, "for God made *man and woman* in his likeness," and the words of the Wycliffe Bible itself, "God made them out of nothing, male and female." For medieval people, Genesis 1:27 proclaimed how each man and each woman was made in the image of God.

Middle English sermons so frequently translate biblical text in gender-specific ways that I suspect many medieval people perceived gender-inclusive language as commonplace in the Bible. John 6:44 provides another example. The Wycliffe New Testament renders it like this: "No man may come to me, but if the father that sent me, draw him." But a fifteenth-century sermon from the Bodleian Library archives in Oxford adds the phrase "nor woman" into the verse—that is to say, "no man *nor woman* comes to me, but my Father that sent me, draw him."[29] This is significantly more gender inclusive than the KJV's "no man can come" and is even one step further than the modern gender-attentive translations, like the NIV (and, interestingly, the ESV also), which has "no one can come."

Another fifteenth-century sermon, from a Dominican compilation, also writes women into biblical text. The sermon recites Luke 14:11: "For every man that exalts himself, he shall be lowered, and he that humbles himself, he shall be raised."

The sermon then addresses the "male-oriented details" of the text and rewrites the verse: "For *every man and woman* that exalts himself in this sin of pride, he shall be made low."[30] Piper and Grudem accused the translators of the TNIV of intentionally "obscuring" biblical text to make it more gender inclusive; authors of Middle English sermons apparently thought that writing women into the biblical text made the translation more accurate.

These changes were made in late medieval manuscripts, for *accuracy*. The inclusion of "woman" and "every man and woman" had nothing to do with political correctness or a feminist agenda. Preachers were concerned that Scripture teachings be taken to heart by all church members, so they changed and sometimes even "obscured" the "male-oriented details" for the benefit of women. That way, both men and women could better hear the Word of God. And for medieval women, they heard Scripture speak directly to them.

Certainly not all preachers did this, but enough did that it is easy to find examples. I discovered the rendition of Genesis 1:27 during an impromptu lesson with one of my graduate students. I had purchased a digital copy of the Salisbury Cathedral manuscript and was looking at it for the first time. I pulled up the sermon in question as an example to show her what a medieval sermon looked like, as well as to show her how to understand medieval pagination. I almost immediately zeroed in on the gender-inclusive rendition of Genesis 1:27.

On the one hand, this is just another example of how Middle English sermons translated biblical text in gender-inclusive ways. On the other hand, it is a striking example of how modern the concept of biblical womanhood really is. The medieval world was far from promoting equality for women in everyday life. Yet medieval English clergy, charged with communicating the Bible to ordinary Christians, seemed more concerned about including women in biblical text than about emphasizing masculine authority.

Modern evangelicals denounce gender-inclusive language as a dangerous product of feminism.

Medieval clergy used gender-inclusive language to better care for their parishioners.

Leaving Women Out

So what happened? Why didn't the gender inclusive renditions used by some medieval clergy continue into full-text translations of the Bible itself?

The answer is easy: because the world that produced the English Bible was not the same as the world that produced middle English sermons. The English Bible is a historical artifact as much as it is the Word of God. It tells the timeless and divinely inspired story of God's plan to rescue humanity; it tells that story *through* the timebound hands of human translators. Grudem may complain that the TNIV capitulates to non-Christian culture (feminism), but the ESV also capitulates to non-Christian culture (patriarchy). People are products of the world in which they live, and translators are no exception. What any translator or interpreter brings to the Bible influences how we understand the Bible.

As a historian who studies manuscript transmission, the miracle of the Bible is the consistency of its message (and its text) throughout history. Even Bart Ehrman, an agnostic and a serious critic of the New Testament, acknowledges that most of the textual variations in early Christian New Testament manuscripts "have nothing to do with theology or ideology." As he explains, "Far and away the most changes are the result of mistakes, pure and simple slips of the pen, accidental omissions, inadvertent additions, misspelled words, blunders of one sort or another."[31] It always amazes me how *little* human translators have affected God's story of salvation, despite centuries of us messing about with it. As much as I disagree with Ehrman on other points, I do agree with his assessment of textual changes. When words are changed in biblical text, whether by accident or by translation decisions, it changes how we understand that text. Even if these changes do not affect the big story of Christianity (as Ehrman affirms), they do affect little stories—like if Junia is a prominent apostle in the early church or simply a noteworthy woman.

The early modern English Bible was translated in a context that politically, legally, economically, and socially obscured women behind the identities of their husbands and fathers. The world of early modern England treated women as dependent on men, and this cultural attitude was translated into the English Bible.

Let me show you what I mean.

English Bible translations multiplied during the sixteenth and seventeenth centuries—from Tyndale's and Coverdale's versions to the Great Bible of 1539, the Geneva Bible (complete by 1560), the Bishops' Bible of 1568, and the KJV of 1611. The most influential of these versions were the Geneva Bible (which has three main editions) and the KJV.

The KJV, in fact, was a direct response to the Geneva Bible— sort of like the ESV was a direct response to the TNIV. King James, the successor to the throne of Elizabeth I, declared in 1604 that it was time for a new authorized version of the English

Bible. He was irritated with the Geneva Bible, which was then the most popular translation in Elizabethan England. Translators influenced by reformers like John Calvin and John Knox had shaped the study notes of the Geneva Bible with their more extreme views, especially concerning the nature of the church and the role of government. For example, the third and most extreme edition of the Geneva Bible (1608) contains an explanatory note for Romans 13:5. This verse urges Christians to be subject to authority for conscience's sake. The study notes, however, counter that this is true as long as the authorities are lawful; otherwise, "we must answer as Peter teacheth us, It is better to obey God, than men."[32] Just as the twentieth-century Scofield Study Bible normalized an obscure theory about the end times (dispensationalism), the Geneva Bible normalized dissenters who were critical of royal authority and Anglican theology.

And King James was tired of it, even before the extreme 1608 edition.[33]

He said that the Geneva Bible was "partial, untrue, seditious, and favouring too much of dangerous and trayterous conceits."[34] So he charged fifty-four learned men throughout England to create a new translation. The rules were straightforward: create an accurate English translation using language accessible to ordinary people and with no marginal notes. The KJV was born. It not only surpassed the Geneva Bible in popularity but also became the most popular Bible translation of all time.

As the popularity of both the Geneva Bible and the KJV soared, early modern English people absorbed the language therein into everyday life, speaking and writing in Scripture phrase.[35] From a "fly in the ointment" to "the salt of the earth"

145

to the "Land of Nod" to even "giving up the ghost," the KJV helped create the language used by early modern (and even modern) people. As linguist David Crystal notes, the KJV popularized at least 257 phrases still in use today.[36] How the English Bible was translated in early modern England changed the English language for us today.

And this had repercussions for women. One goal of the KJV translators was to use everyday language to make the Bible more readable. Anyone who has read Shakespeare knows that everyday English in early modern England overflowed with male generic language. Hilda Smith calls it "false universal language." Early modern English *pretended to include women* through male generic words (like the universal "man") but *excluded women* by gendering examples, metaphors, and experiences in masculine ways. Dorothy L. Sayers explains it this way: "*Vir* is male and *Femina* is female; but *Homo* is male and female." The problem is that "Man is always dealt with as both *Homo* and *Vir*, but Woman only as *Femina*."[37]

This is false universal language. It pretends to include women, but really doesn't.[38] Words for men were used interchangeably in reference to kings, politicians, preachers, household heads, philosophers, and even to represent all "mankind," while specific words for women were used exclusively for women and mostly regarding the domestic sphere. "Man" in early modern English could represent humanity, but the humans it described were political citizens, decision-makers, leaders, household heads, theologians, preachers, factory owners, members of Parliament, and so on. In other words, "man" could include both men and women, but it mostly didn't. It mostly just included men.

Let me give you an example of the false universal in action. The seventeenth-century preacher William Gouge upset his female church members with his new sermon series, "Domesticall Duties." They were especially upset over him accusing women of stealing money from their husbands when they gave to charity without asking permission first, so Gouge clarified for them what he meant. Gouge also found it important to clarify why he excluded women in some of his language. In a section directed to the masters and mistresses of a house, he referred only to the masters. "I have according to the Scripture phrase comprised Mistresses under Masters," he wrote.[39] Gouge sanctified his false universal language by quoting Ephesians 6. He claimed that the masculine language "masters" referred to women. But for Gouge, it was okay to use language that excluded women, because the Bible translators did it too.[40]

This is a relatively innocuous example. It may have upset the women in Gouge's congregation, but the ramifications were small. Let me give you a more significant example of how the false universal language of early modern England continues to influence English Bible translations today.

A few months ago, I rewatched Steve Lipscomb's documentary *Battle for the Minds*, which is about the conservative takeover of the SBC. I was struck by how SBC leaders harped on 1 Timothy 3:2 and 3:12 that overseers should be husband of one wife. They used this as ironclad proof that senior pastors had to be men. Yet Lucy Peppiatt shows us how 1 Timothy 3, the chapter so often cited by the male leaders of the conservative resurgence as articulating why only men can preach, was shaped by English-language translations to look more masculine than it actually is.[41] We assume 1 Timothy 3:1–13 is referencing men in leadership roles (overseer/bishop and deacon). But is this because of how our English Bibles translate the text? Whereas the Greek text uses the words *whoever* and *anyone*, with the only specific reference to *man* appearing in two verses (a literal Greek translation of the phrase is "one woman man," referencing the married state of deacons), modern English Bibles have introduced eight to ten male pronouns within the verses. None of those male pronouns in our English Bibles are in the Greek text. Peppiatt concludes that the problem with female leadership is not actually the biblical text; it is the "relentless and dominant narrative of male bias" in translations.[42]

The KJV may have been free of the study notes that King James despised, but that didn't make it any freer from cultural influences than the Geneva Bible was. As Rodney Stark reminds us, the main reason we have forgotten that women served as deacons in the early church is that "the translators of the King James Version chose to refer to Phoebe as merely a 'servant' of the church, not as a deacon, and to transfer Paul's words in 1 Timothy into a comment directed towards the *wives* of deacons."[43] The context in which all the early modern English Bibles arose championed a language that excluded women. The emphasis on masculine language continued throughout English Bibles until Zondervan's attempt to restore gender-inclusive language to the text. From this perspective, gender-inclusive language isn't distorting Scripture. Gender-inclusive language is *restoring* Scripture from the influence of certain English Bible translations.

Translating Marriage in the Bible

Leaving women out of the biblical text wasn't the only way that English Bible translations affected women. They also affected women by changing how we understand marriage in the Bible.

The culture that created the KJV championed marriage as the ideal state decreed by God. The holy (male-headed) house-

148

hold formed the center of English society, from the household of the urban merchant to the lordly estates of the members of Parliament. Law codes favored husbands and male heirs by excluding women from inheritance, reducing married women to the legal status of children, and elevating marriage as key for securing masculine social rank and authority.

Yet early modern biblical scholars found that marriage was puzzlingly absent from the Old Testament (the Hebrew Bible), especially for an institution thought to be championed by God. Historian Naomi Tadmor explains that the primary word for *woman* in the Old Testament was complex, applying to both an adult woman and a woman "belonging" to a man—as a wife, a concubine, a wife within a polygamous relationship, and even a slave. Although certainly aware of these complexities, translators of the English Bible simplified matters by reducing the Hebrew word to two English words: *woman* (used 259 times in the KJV) and *wife* (used 312 times in the KJV). Hence Rebekah became Isaac's "wife," and Laban's daughters, Rachel and Leah, became Jacob's "wives." Even the raped woman in Deuteronomy 21 became a "wife."[44] Tadmor writes, "The polygamous social universe of the Hebrew Bible was rendered in terms of a monogamous English marital discourse."[45] Women became wives in the early modern English Bible, mirroring the marital arrangements in early modern English society.

What does this mean?

It means that early English Bible translations did not accurately reflect Hebrew words or relationship but instead reflected early modern English sensibilities. Women became "wives" in English Bible translations, even when they would not have been considered wives in the biblical world. The word *marriage* never appears in the Hebrew text. But it appears fifty times in the

Geneva Bible and nineteen times in the KJV.[46] According to Tadmor, Genesis 2:22–24 provides perhaps the most striking example of how the English Bible translated Hebrew culture through a contemporary lens. As the KJV translates the verses, "And the rib, which the LORD God had taken from man, made he a *woman*, and brought her unto the man. And Adam said, This is now bone of my bones, and flesh of my flesh: she shall be called *Woman*, because she was taken out of Man. Therefore shall a man leave his father and his mother, and shall cleave unto his *wife*: and they shall be one flesh."

The word translated as "wife" in verse 24 is the same word translated as "woman" in verses 22 and 23. The reason the word is translated as "wife" in verse 24, argues Tadmor, is to emphasize a woman's "status within a social framework of marriage."[47] The 1611 KJV even places these verses under the subheading "Institution of Marriage." The English Bible makes it clear that Genesis 2:22–24 sanctifies marriage. Yet neither the word *marriage* nor the word *wife* appear in the Hebrew text. The KJV was not the first translation to infer marriage from verses 22–24, but the normalcy of these words for early modern readers made marriage in the Old Testament world seem very similar to marriage in seventeenth-century England.

The English Bible translated more than Hebrew text; it also translated early modern English ideas about marriage into biblical text, as well as a "falsely universal language" that excluded women. The translators of early modern English Bibles thus added one more layer to the growing idea of biblical womanhood. Because women were written out of the early English Bible, modern evangelicals have more easily written women out of church leadership.

"WAIT, DR. BARR, WHAT?"

I was sitting in a seminar room full of doctoral students. Most of them were training to be American historians, but they were taking my class Women and Religion in the North Atlantic World, 1300–1700. It was early in the semester, only the first or second week. We were discussing medieval perceptions of women. I had just made a passing reference to a medieval sermon about a woman who murdered her brother-in-law because she was unable to control her sexual desires. (I keep telling you, medieval history is far from boring.)

The story goes like this: Sex was considered impure, so medieval Christians were encouraged to abstain from sex during holy times (which was a lot of time on the medieval calendar). A woman wanted to have sex with her husband on Easter morning. He said no. She was so overcome by desire that she tried to seduce her brother-in-law, who also denied her. Mad with lust, she grabbed a sword and cut off his head. When her husband found her, standing with the sword dripping with blood, she declared, "Lo, all this I have done, you have made me do!"[1]

And, according to the medieval sermon, she was right.

The moral of the story was, yes, you should abstain from sex during holy times. But married people were also required to pay the marriage debt (sex), and the husband should not have denied his wife. The marital debt trumped purity regulations. Because of the natural weakness of the female body, medieval women were considered more prone to sin, especially sexual sin. The temptress in medieval lore was more likely to be a woman or a demon than a man. It was thus more important for the husband to meet the needs of his wife than to obey the prohibitions barring sex during holy times.[2] In this case, had the husband done so, it would have prevented his brother's murder.

The students were confused, because this woman was the opposite of what they knew about women from American history. You see, by the early modern era (at least in European and American history), the perception of women as more sexually lascivious than men had flipped. It was now men who were seen as less able to control their desires. Women had to be protected from predators and had to learn how to stop tempting the insatiable sexual appetites of men (such as through dressing more modestly). Historian Marilyn Westerkamp explains that, by the nineteenth century, "the average woman was no longer feared as a potential seductress; she was more likely to be seduced, since men were now seen as those more likely to indulge in sexual sin."[3] Innocence, instead, now characterized women.

As a medieval historian, women being depicted as sexual temptresses was such a norm for me that I had forgotten how foreign it would be to American history students. I had forgotten how much our understanding of women today is shaped by what happened after the Reformation.

Indeed, when we get down to it, the construction of modern biblical womanhood for Protestant women owes much more to developments after the sixteenth century than it does to all the centuries before. As we've discussed, during the Reformation era, "the ideological touchstone of holiness" changed. Instead of women finding holiness through virginity, they now found it in the marriage bed. The most sacred vessels were no longer the valiant men and women who rose above their sex to serve

God; the most sacred institution was now the holy household. As Westerkamp powerfully writes, "In place of the special spiritual status granted to a few men and women by virtue of their celibacy and consecration, the mandate for marriage gratified all men. Each became a patriarch, to follow in Abraham's footprints." As for women? "Destined to be married, to labor in the household, and to subject themselves to the rule of their husbands."[4]

I had my students' attention. I realized, as I looked around the classroom, that I had just taught them something new. Patriarchy defined the lives of both medieval women and early modern women. But at some point, across that great divide, patriarchy shapeshifted.

Medieval women moved closest to equality with men when they were furthest from the married state. Virgins received the most points in the medieval spiritual economy, followed by widows, and finally by wives, who came in last place. After the Reformation, the spiritual economy flipped, so wives received the highest honors, followed by widows. This time, virgins—now demeaned as spinsters instead of celebrated as saints—brought up the rear. As historian Merry Wiesner-Hanks writes, "Protestant denominations—Lutheran, Anglican, Calvinist, and later Methodist, Baptist, and many others—differed on many points of doctrine, but they agreed that the clergy should be married heads of household and that monastic life had no value. . . . Thus there was no separate religious vocation open to women, who were urged to express their devotion within the family as 'helpmeet' to their husband and guide to their children."[5] Women, instead of encouraged to forsake their female bodies as the highest spiritual calling, were now urged to embrace their feminine distinctiveness as their best service to God.

As womanhood became redefined and the role of wife and mother sanctified in the post-Reformation world, so too did women's subordination. Historically, women have always been subordinated to men, but now their subordination became embedded in the heart of evangelical faith. To be a Christian woman was to be under the authority of men.

Sanctifying Modesty

It was summer in the late nineties. We took our small North Carolina youth group, five girls and four boys, to a youth camp in a neighboring state. It was sticky hot. Our clothes clung to our bodies as we carried suitcases and sleeping bags to our bunks. The girls ran for the showers, trying to cool off before dinner and evening worship. Thirty minutes later we were clean and fresh and cheerful, walking across the campground. A young woman walked up beside me.

"Are you the leader for these girls?" she asked. "They need to change clothes."

I stopped and turned to look at her.

"The straps on their tank tops are too thin. Their bra straps will show. We need them to cover up."

I was in my early twenties. I hadn't learned to sweeten my words yet. "We read the dress code. Sleeveless was fine," I responded.

She wasn't happy with me, but she let us continue.

That conversation was the beginning of a weeklong modesty battle with the camp leaders. After the worship service, one of the camp directors paid me a special visit to tell me that the girls needed to comply with the recently changed dress code. Tank tops were not allowed. I challenged him. Sleeveless was allowed. Our youth had only brought so many things to wear. I was unmoved.

Apparently the camp leaders were unmoved too. They showed up at my door that night with a box of extra-large T-shirts for the girls to wear. I think my mouth fell open. I was really upset. I returned the box.

The next morning, the girls and I were called into a special meeting. One of the young men working at the camp came to talk with us. It is really important, he told us, that beautiful young women be careful in their dress. Boys have difficulty controlling their imaginations, and when they see a bra strap, well, it can cause them to sin. Modesty honors God, and didn't the girls want to honor God?

Once again, we were given a box of shirts. This time the message was clear—cover up, or we will ask you to leave.

We never went back to that camp.

The next year, when I was reading for my comprehensive exam in women's history, I discovered that my youth-camp modesty battle had roots deeper than I realized. To be sure, purity culture took on a life of its own in the 1990s, leading to purity rings, disturbing rituals like teenage girls dancing in wedding dresses with their fathers, and a strange fear of visible bra straps. But it wasn't the first time that Christians had obsessed about the sexual purity of women. During the nineteenth century, a similar fixation with female purity emerged—stemming from a new ideology about women, work, and family life—which historians call the cult of domesticity.

The cult of domesticity emerged as a phenomenon central to middle-class culture in Western Europe. It emphasized piety, domesticity, submission, and purity as characteristics of the ideal Christian woman. It cut across class and national borders,

155

affecting peasant women and queens. It developed alongside narratives of imperialism and racial oppression. Historian Lynn Abrams tells us that "everywhere a girl learned to be a good wife and mother, a thrifty household manager, a willing worker, a chaste companion to her husband, and a dutiful mother to her children. A European woman of the nineteenth century was judged primarily by her role and deportment in her home."[6] The reason the teenage girls in our youth group were forced to put on baggy T-shirts wasn't because Jesus cares that much about bra straps. It was because the leaders at that camp had confused nineteenth-century ideas about women's purity (not to mention male culpability) with what it meant to be a Christian woman. Conservative evangelicals believed that the key to reducing sexual temptation for men was emphasizing purity for women. In Margaret Bendroth's book *Fundamentalism and Gender*, she quotes a similar sentiment from a 1920s fundamentalist publication: "Every man has a quantity of dynamite, or its equivalent, in him. The matches have, as a rule, been in the hands of the world's womanhood."[7] Seeing the bra straps of teenage girls, apparently, would have ignited the dynamite of the teenage boys at camp.

The youth-camp leaders banned tank tops and short shorts to help safeguard sexual purity. The nineteenth century, in turn, demonized prostitutes, working girls, and dance halls, elevating the home as the safest space for respectable women. The teenage girls in my youth group were given T-shirts to teach them about modesty and remind them of their Christian duty to protect men from lusting after their bodies; the purity lessons for nineteenth-century working-class women were harder. Those suspected of sexual immorality, or even considered high risk for committing a sexually immoral act, could be rounded up for rehabilitation in Magdalene homes. There, writes Abrams, "they were taught to be modest, silent, hard-working and subservient through religious indoctrination and training in domestic duties." Washing clothes became a favorite occupation taught to these women—"as well as providing training for domestic service, it symbolised the cleansing of the girls' shame as well as the dirt of the urban environment and was a potent reminder of the girls' fall from grace."[8] Purity culture thus shamed women in the nineteenth century as it continues to shame women today.

Understanding that purity obsessions were nothing new in Christian history didn't decrease my frustration with the youth camp. But it did help me see how Paul's call for Christians to strive for sexual morality became tangled up with historical changes wrought by the Industrial Revolution as well as age-old patriarchal concerns about controlling the female body. Just like with Dan Brown's *The DaVinci Code* (when many Christians fell for a bit of historical truth mixed with an action-packed fictional story), Christians had once again fallen for a little bit of biblical truth mixed with a lot of human effort poured into maintaining the patriarchal equilibrium of history.

As I think about my modesty battle with those overzealous camp leaders, I can't help wondering what Jesus thought about the situation. Instead of condemning his disciples when they broke a rather strict law in Matthew 12, plucking heads of grain on the Sabbath because they were hungry, Jesus defended them from the Pharisees. Instead of condemning the bleeding woman in Luke 8, who reached out and touched him for healing without his permission, Jesus told her to go in peace—her faith had healed her. This Jesus—who let Mary learn at his feet like a male disciple, who chastised the disciples for missing the point of his message over and over while recognizing over and over the strong faith of women—would he have joined the camp leaders in shaming teenage girls for a slipping bra strap?

Once again, the world in which we live oppresses women, fighting to control their bodies from their "natural" fallenness.

Once again, the God we serve has always done the opposite. Jesus has always set women free.

Sanctifying Domesticity

"Of course!" I typed in response. The email was a request to provide a workshop on mentoring at the upcoming women's retreat. It had been a while since I had gone to a women's retreat, but the retreat committee had changed the format. Instead of relying on outside speakers, they were now running workshops facilitated by people in our community. I was excited to talk about the importance of mentoring and perhaps encourage a few more volunteers to help mentor teenage girls.

Then I saw the schedule.

The mentoring workshop was scheduled at the same time as a holiday cookie baking workshop. Mentoring was definitely going to lose out to cookies.

I wasn't upset, just resigned. A handful of women did come to the mentoring session, but baking cookies proved much more popular. One woman apologized for not coming to the mentoring session. Her explanation reinforced what I feared about the priorities of many women in my evangelical world. She told me that mentoring other women was important (Titus 2, right?), but she didn't see it as a priority. Her first job was to mentor her children, not people outside her family. Her family came first, and baking cookies was a great way for her to engage with her children. Plus, this was a retreat, and baking cookies with other women was fun.

No problem, I told her. I like cookies too.

I really do like cookies. I also like to bake. The teenagers I have been feeding for years, my own children, my students every semester, and the college students I now live with as a faculty-in-residence can all attest to this. Baking is high on my list of enjoyable things. I do not see a conflict between my feminist identity and my cooking skills. I don't have a problem with women, or men, taking pride in domestic prowess.

What I do have a problem with is how we continue to teach the cult of domesticity to modern Christian women. Paul does remind us about the significance of sexual sin for Christians, as our bodies are the temple of God, but Paul says nothing about cooking or cleaning as having unique import for women. We love to hold up Martha and the Proverbs 31 woman as exemplars of the spiritual worth of domestic work. But, historically, these are bad comparisons. While domesticity has always been important for women throughout church history—like medieval women who baked the Eucharist bread and washed the altar linens—it wasn't until the early modern world that domesticity became linked with women's spiritual calling. Instead of just being something that women usually did, domestic prowess in the home (centered on the family) now became something that good Christian women *should* do because it is what we are designed to do. It is our primary calling in this world.

Domesticity, for evangelical women, is sanctified.

To explain how this happened—how domesticity became embedded in the identity of Christian women—we have to go back a few centuries to the aftermath of the Reformation. The Reformation, if you remember, elevated the status of wives and mothers, imbuing them with spiritual dignity and even some authority. The advance of medical science, combined with the belief that women's physical bodies are made in the image of God, finally pushed women beyond Aristotle. No longer were women regarded as deformed men; now they were uniquely created by God to complement men. As historian Catherine Brekus writes, "Instead of viewing women as lesser versions of men—incomplete men whose sexual organs were turned inside out—clergymen and scientists portrayed the sexes as essentially different in both biology and temperament."[9] It is pretty much the start of *Men Are from Mars, Women Are from Venus.* Not only are women and men different; they are very different.

But, hey, I remind my students, at least women are no longer monstrous and deformed, right?

By "different" from men, however, early modern thinkers meant much more than sex organs. In the chapter "Learning to Be a Woman," Lynn Abrams provides several examples from contemporary sources of what "different" now meant for women. For example, Vicomte de Bonald, a political writer in France, wrote in his 1802 treatise on education that "women belong to the family and not to political society, and nature created them for domestic cares and not for public functions." As such, he continued, "everything in [girls'] instruction should be directed toward domestic utility, just as everything in the education of boys should be directed toward public utility." I always pause on his next statement when teaching class as it provokes great conversation among students: "It is a false education," Bonald wrote, "that gives one's inclinations a direction that goes contrary to nature, *that makes the sexes want to exchange occupations just as they would clothing.*"[10] Science declared women so different from men that the differences affected every aspect of their lives, including education and occupation.

Doesn't that sound just like what many evangelical women hear today? That women are designed to stay in the home, with paid work outside the home being temporary—that is, only when needed.

Abrams provides an example from an Irish preacher in 1856. The Reverend John Gregg preached that women are designed to be different from men, which included occupations. Men work outside the home in the "great and weighty business of life"; women work inside the home because they are not "fitted" for the work of men. As he said,

> We have features peculiar to us as men, and we also have our peculiar capabilities and responsibilities. The *great* and *weighty* business of life devolves on men . . . , but a most important portion of the duties of life, especially of private life, falls to the share of women. God has adapted our sex to the peculiar duties to which we are especially called, and for which you are not so well fitted. . . . Society does best when each sex performs the duties for which it is especially ordained.[11]

Being different for women meant being ordained for the private sphere—family life. It meant staying out of leadership and economic and political roles. It meant literally to do what John MacArthur told Beth Moore to do: "Go home."[12]

The Historical Roots of Sanctified Subordination

Where did these ideas come from?

First, they came from the Enlightenment. Historians Katherine French and Allyson Poska provide an excellent overview in

Women and Gender in the Western Past. They draw attention to how the Enlightenment, like the Reformation, could have created greater equality for women as women were no longer considered deformed men but, rather, humans and, just like men, capable of rational thought. Unfortunately, these "radical views of human equality" were tempered by the emerging theory of complementarity.[13] Patriarchy, in other words, shape-shifted again. A new theory emerged to keep women under the power of men. Isn't it interesting that it is called complementarity? French and Poska explain, "Complementarity provided the basis for the idea that women were built for domesticity and child-rearing, and men were built for rule, rationality, and public duties. This understanding of sex differences justified the different educations and political rights that men and women received."[14] Perhaps the most famous early proponent of complementarity was the philosopher Jean-Jacques Rousseau. In his famous text *Emile*, he expounded his philosophy of education for women, arguing that "the search for abstract and speculative truths, for principles and axioms in science, for all that tends to wide generalization, is beyond a woman's grasp; their studies should be thoroughly practical."[15] Women, according to Rousseau, are simply not as smart as men and therefore should not bother with more advanced learning. They are better suited to domestic work.

Second, early modern science reinforced the idea that women are so different from men that they are preordained for domesticity. Women's physical exams suggested that women were smaller and weaker than men, including having smaller heads, which in that time meant smaller and weaker brains. Women were considered to be biologically more similar to children than to men, possibly because women were less evolved than their masculine counterparts. In his 1871 *Descent of Man*, Charles Darwin explained that desirable evolutionary traits were "transmitted more fully to the male than to the female offspring. . . . Thus man has ultimately become superior to woman."[16] Not to mention that in this brave new scientific world, because women's bodies are designed for childbirth and mothering, childbirth and mothering should be women's primary occupation.

Finally, we must understand the effects of the Industrial Revolution. Enlightenment beliefs about women's physical differences went hand in hand with a world changed by machines. The eighteenth and nineteenth centuries saw the transformation of work in the West. Machines and factories sped up everything from the creation of goods to food production. Technological innovation changed not only the time it took to complete work (things got done a lot faster) but also the space in which work was done—moving it from the household to the public sphere, separating domestic space from work space.

The impact on women was significant.

On the one hand, the Industrial Revolution provided women with more job options and allowed them to earn an independent living. In factories, women often worked together in similar positions, enabling them to forge new female communities like labor unions. French and Poska note that in 1830 "three thousand female workers in a tobacco factory in Madrid rioted for five days against a wage cut and poor working conditions."[17] On the other hand, the Industrial Revolution hardened gender restrictions. While the Industrial Revolution certainly created a boom in jobs, and even precipitated the hiring of high proportions of women during the early stages, it didn't improve women's wages. Indeed, it seemed to provoke arguments that women deserved to be paid lower wages than men simply *because* they were women. As James Mitchell, a British factory commissioner, declared in 1833,

> Some persons feel much regret at seeing the wages of females so low . . . , but perhaps such persons are wrong; and nature affects her own purposes more wisely and more effectually than could be done by the wisest of men. The low price of female labor makes it the most profitable as well as most agreeable occupation for a female to superintend her own domestic establishment, and her low wages do not tempt her to abandon the care of her own children. Nature therefore provides that her designs shall not be disappointed.[18]

Women should be paid less, Mitchell argued, because that would discourage them from working too much outside the home, which is where they belonged.

Beliefs that women were ill-suited to factory work because of their weakness and that their primary job should be in the home resulted in laws passed throughout Europe that shortened women's work hours, forced them to take unpaid maternity leave, and even—in some places—prohibited them from working at all. French activist Paule Mink defended women, claiming that "by denying women the right to work, you degrade her, you put her under man's yoke and deliver her over to man's good pleasure. By ceasing to make her a worker, you deprive her of her liberty, and thereby, of her responsibility, . . . so that she no longer will be a free and intelligent creature, but will merely be a reflection, a small part of her husband."[19]

I always pause at this point in my lecture. Mink argued that by forcing women to remain in the home, by denying women the right to work if they so desired, women would lose not only their freedom but their identities.

Sanctifying the Cult of Domesticity

This brings us full circle to the cult of domesticity.

By the early nineteenth century, the separation of work from home, scientific claims about female distinctiveness and weakness, and Christian teachings emphasizing the role of wife and the natural piety of women melded together. The cult of domesticity was born. It's hard to pin down its birth date, but it had definitely emerged by the early nineteenth century. Again, the four main components of the cult of domesticity, first articulated by historian Barbara Welter and summarized here, are as follows:

1. *Piety.* Women are naturally more religious than men and more attuned to spiritual matters. This means they are better equipped than men to guide the spiritual education of children. It also means that women's education should focus on cultivating this trait.
2. *Purity.* Women are not naturally sexual creatures. Their minds and hearts are purer than men's are, and sexuality is important only because it allows women to be mothers. Women have to be covered and protected from the danger of sexual predators.
3. *Submission.* Women are not designed to lead. They do not have the mental capacity or the emotional temperament to lead in the political or economic realms. They yearn to follow the lead of strong men.
4. *Domesticity.* Women are not designed to work outside the home. The Industrial Revolution moved work-for-pay

165

outside the domestic space. Women were to stay home and manage the household while men went outside the home and earned the daily bread. This also means that women's education should focus on improving domestic skills (the origin of home economics courses).[20]

Don't these characteristics sound familiar? Doesn't it seem that the cult of domesticity is written into the core of modern evangelicalism? Indeed, doesn't biblical womanhood just seem like an updated version of the cult of domesticity? Instead of biblical womanhood stemming from the Bible, it stems from a gender hierarchy developed in the wake of the Industrial Revolution to deal with the social and economic changes wrought by work moving outside the home. As French and Poska unequivocally state, "Industrialization created the cult of domesticity."[21]

When I first learned about the cult of domesticity, all I could think about was James Dobson. His book *Love for a Lifetime* made a lasting impression on me. I clearly remember reading how women were designed to be more passive than men, how women were physically weaker and more prone to emotional instability, how women preferred the safety of the home and a breadwinning husband over the harsh working world of corporate America. Suddenly, his attitude made sense. What Dobson was teaching about women's natures wasn't biblical. It was rooted in the cult of domesticity and ancient ideas about the biological inferiority of women. Dobson was simply preaching the nineteenth-century cult of domesticity, the only difference being that he had now sanctified it.

When it comes to the evangelical endurance of the cult of domesticity—the idea that women are created for the home while men are created for public work and leadership—it seems that I should modify Judith Bennett's observation. She writes, "Patriarchy might be everywhere, but it is not everywhere the same."[22] This is usually true, but the cult of domesticity seems to be an exception. Patriarchy is everywhere, and sometimes—as in the case of the nineteenth-century cult of domesticity resurrected as modern biblical womanhood—patriarchy is the same.

How Women Adapted

I had the privilege of hearing historian Kate Bowler speak twice before she became a household name. The first time was in 2015 at a meeting of the American Historical Association. I was the upcoming program chair for the 2016 Conference on Faith and History, and I listened to Bowler present on her then-new book *Blessed: A History of the American Prosperity Gospel*. I immediately asked her if she would be a plenary speaker for our 2016 program.

Because of a bizarre turn of events during the conference—a Donald Trump rally suddenly gathered at the Christian college campus that was hosting our event—the second time I heard Bowler speak was even more memorable than the first. We had been kicked out of the buildings originally assigned for the conference, as they were too close to the Trump rally, and reassigned to the campus chapel. This meant that Bowler gave her presentation standing behind Pat Robertson's pulpit at Regent University in Virginia Beach. I am happy to report that I too got to speak from that same pulpit as I introduced her. I wasn't brave enough to raise my arms in the air, just like the stained glass Jesus behind the pulpit, but Kate Bowler was.

The second reason Bowler's presentation was memorable was because of her topic: how conservative evangelical women have carved out religious authority in traditions that prohibit women's leadership. Her research was later published as *The Preacher's Wife: The Precarious Power of Evangelical Women Celebrities*. In a rather entertaining section of her talk, she described her spreadsheet of Twitter profiles for evangelical women. Words like *coffee*, *yoga pants*, and *hot mess*, I wrote down in my notes, were favorites, but *wife* and *mother* were common identities expressed. In her book, Bowler provides the examples of Ann Voskamp, "Wife to the Farmer: Mama to 7," and Lauren Chandler, "wife to matt. mother to audrey, reid + norah." They both emphasize their role as wife first and mother second.[23] Being a wife and mother gives evangelical women credibility. As Bowler writes in the introduction to *The Preacher's Wife*, "A famous megaministry woman . . . drew fame from the familial role she held as a mother, sister, daughter, or, most often, wife of an important godly man. . . . Most women built on the poured foundation of marriage and family."[24]

Because of Bowler's work, I often think about what the Twitter profiles would be for the medieval women I study who preach and teach. They would be rather different from Bowler's evangelical women, I think. Margery Kempe's would definitely include the word *creature*. Maybe "Creature of God, professional crier, pilgrim, secondary virgin, vowess." I doubt Kempe would include any reference to her family or her husband. Julian of Norwich's would be easier to guess: "Enclosed nun, servant of God, visionary, spiritual adviser, lives alone." Probably, though, Margaret of Antioch's would be my favorite: "Defiant virgin, impervious to torture, dragon slayer, evangelist, miracle worker, friend of God." Neither marriage nor motherhood would figure significantly in the Twitter profiles of these medieval women; they wouldn't bother highlighting domestic skills either.

By the eighteenth and nineteenth centuries, the Twitter profiles of preaching women would look a lot more like the examples Bowler brings up. Their status as wife and mother would probably be expanded to "virtuous wife" and "loving mother." They would likely highlight their domestic prowess as "household manager" or "family Bible reader," and they would definitely reference their feminine distinctiveness, describing themselves as a "gentle sister," "long-suffering mother," "prophetic daughter," "quiet spirit," and perhaps even as the "weaker sex."

Women adapt to the ever-changing rules of patriarchy. The patriarchal equilibrium endures, but it is defined by the culture around us. The rules of patriarchy change as history changes (although the endurance of the cult of domesticity might be an exception!). Rejecting feminine distinctiveness authorized women's voices in medieval Europe, but that no longer worked in the post-Reformation world. Embracing feminine distinctiveness now became the best way forward for women called to preach. "Instead of justifying women's right to preach on the grounds that they had transcended their gender—that they were neither male nor female," writes historian Catherine Brekus, "a new ideology of female virtue" emerged, grounding women's authority in their feminine distinctiveness.[25]

We can take heart.

Women, despite patriarchy's ever-moving goalposts, have always found a way to preach and teach the Word of God. In one of the most encouraging appendixes to an academic text that I have ever read, Brekus charts each woman she could find in the records who preached and exhorted in American churches between 1740 and 1845. One hundred twenty-three names. One hundred twenty-three women who felt God's calling on their lives and responded. One hundred twenty-three women from approximately twenty Protestant denominations: Almira Prescott Bullock, who founded a new Baptist sect with her husband, Jeremiah, in 1821; Zilpah Elaw, who preached in an African Methodist church in 1827; Ellen Harmon White, who founded the Seventh-Day Adventists in 1844. White women and Black women preached across the landscape of American Christianity. Brekus powerfully concludes, "By preserving their faith in a world that seemed to scorn them, by trusting in the goodness of God, they hoped to inspire future generations of evangelical women to claim the pulpit as their own."[26] And as a Baptist woman, I love that about thirty of the preaching women in Brekus's appendix are Baptist.

But we can also be disheartened by this information.

In order for these women to preach, they had to conform to expectations. Turning the cult of domesticity to their advantage, women claimed that their superior piety and God-given nurturing roles empowered them to preach: "Pastoral work is adapted to women, for it is motherly work," explained Methodist preacher Anna Oliver. "As a mother spreads her table with food suited to the individual needs of her family, so the pastor feeds the flock."[27] This certainly speaks to these women's persistence in fulfilling God's calling. But it also shows how the rules changed again for women. God's calling on women's lives never seems justification enough for women to preach; they have to justify their right based on their historical context of patriarchy. For nineteenth-century women, this meant using their feminine distinctiveness to authorize their voice.

The cult of domesticity infiltrated America from its British roots and seeped into what became modern evangelical culture. From the popularity of magazines like *Godey's Lady's Book* in the 1850s (which instructed women on how to turn a house into a home) to Marabel Morgan's 1973 book *The Total Woman* (which argued that the key to a perfect marriage was for a woman to abjectly submit to her husband) to the modern True Woman conference led by Nancy DeMoss Wolgemuth, the ideal evangelical woman was one who protected her sexual purity, stayed home, nurtured the spirituality of her family, and submitted to her husband. What evangelicals have failed to realize, explains historian Randall Balmer, is that the "traditional concept of femininity" that we believe to be from the Bible is nothing more than "a nineteenth-century construct."[28]

All we have to do is read a selection from *Happily Ever After*, a book of marriage devotionals by John Piper, Francis Chan, and Nancy DeMoss Wolgemuth, among others. "He sacrifices, she submits. He leads, she follows. He initiates, she affirms. He reflects Jesus, she reflects Jesus."[29] To my women's history trained ears, these words might have come straight from the Enlightenment writings of Rousseau: "The man should be strong and active; the woman should be weak and passive; the one must have both the power and the will; it is enough that the other should offer little resistance."[30] Women are the passive partners, submitting, following, affirming, and yielding to the strength of their husbands. The only difference between Rousseau and the *Happily Ever After* marriage devotional is that now Jesus sanctifies these differences.

All we have to do is read any post on *The Transformed Wife* blog to see that, in some places, the cult of domesticity is in hyperdrive. Take, for example, the flowchart made by Lori Alexander—the woman behind *The Transformed Wife*—which compares stay-at-home moms to working moms. The chart, titled "Should Mothers Have Careers?," went viral in 2018. Her answer, clearly, was no. In Alexander's opinion, a stay-at-home mom has a "fulfilling life" and "her husband and children rise up & call her blessed," whereas a working mom has a life that is "falling apart." When Alexander worked as a teacher, she says she didn't "feel like . . . a good wife or mother,"[31] and she extrapolates from her experience to assert that all women feel this way—or should feel this way.

All we have to do is look back at the Barna poll discussed in chapters 1 and 2. The poll numbers show how resistant evangelicals still are to women's leadership. As Barna Group says about its 2017 poll results, "Within the Church—among evangelicals, especially—support for women in leadership and acknowledgment of the challenges women may face lags significantly."[32]

History matters, and for modern evangelical women, nineteenth-century history has mattered far more than it ever should have.

THE 1995 FILM *The Usual Suspects*, written by Christopher McQuarrie, directed by Bryan Singer, and starring Kevin Spacey (long before the #MeToo movement unveiled allegations of sexual assault against him), is a rather brilliant story about five criminals who meet in a police lineup and plan a heist together. Suspense builds as the evidence points toward a legendary criminal mastermind, Keyser Söze. The final, surprising plot twist is worthy of a screenplay by M. Night Shyamalan. Spacey's character delivers a line I have never forgotten: "The greatest trick the devil ever pulled was convincing the world he didn't exist."

I haven't forgotten the line, because I disagree with it. The greatest trick the devil ever pulled was convincing Christians that oppression is godly. That God ordained some people, simply because of their sex or skin color (or both), as belonging under the power of other people. That women's subordination is central to the gospel of Christ.

I am still surprised by an article Russell Moore wrote in 2006 titled "After Patriarchy, What?" I hope he no longer believes what he wrote, because in the article he argues that women's subordination belongs with the gospel: "We must . . . relate male headship to the whole of the gospel," he writes.[1] Summarizing the scholarship of several sociologists, Moore laments that evangelical households are functionally feminist, with decisions made "through a process of negotiation, mutual submission, and consensus."[2] Moore argues that while evangelicals pay lip service to male headship, most don't practice it. Because feminism pervades modern culture, bubbling up through the everyday experiences of life, it has infiltrated the evangelical family. Seeing Beth Moore preach so often has made evangelicals more receptive to women preaching and hence (he seems to imply) more receptive to egalitarianism. He concludes that it is time to cast a new vision of Christianity that "provides a biblically and theologically compelling alternative" to egalitarianism—one "that sums up the burden of male headship under the cosmic rubric of the gospel of Christ and the restoration of all things in him."[3] It is time, in other words, to write female submission into the heart of Christianity.

By the time Russell Moore wrote this article in 2006, the groundwork for his vision had already been laid. The devil had already pulled his trick on evangelical Christians. Let me tell you how it happened, just as Special Agent David Kujan finally did at the end of *The Usual Suspects*. Let me tell you why evangelicals believe that biblical womanhood is gospel truth. Maybe you, like Kujan, will drop your coffee too.

Forgetting Our Past

In June 1934, the deacons met at First Baptist Church Elm Mott, an old Southern Baptist congregation near Waco, Texas. They voted unanimously to invite Mrs. Lewis Ball of Houston to come as their revival preacher. The deacons recommended "Mrs. Lewis Ball of Houston to come and assist us one week during our coming Revival, she being a great inspiration to the young people. Mrs. Ball has been exceptionally successful as a soul-winner."[4]

On July 3, 1934, Mrs. Ball preached the morning service. Handwritten church records state that Jack Wiley and B. H. Varner both "professed Christ as their personal Saviour." When

Mrs. Ball preached the evening service for the young peoples' prayer meeting, Miss Mary Brustrum made a profession of faith. Mrs. Lewis Ball preached throughout the week, including a message titled "Is It Well with Your Soul?" on July 5, during which six people made professions of faith. The 1934 revival witnessed the largest crowd in the sanctuary yet recorded at First Baptist Church Elm Mott (139 people), and the Sunday school attendance that week broke all their records (176 present). Overall sixteen baptisms resulted. Ball proved so popular that she was asked to return in 1935 and 1938.

In 1934, no one at this Southern Baptist church had a problem with Mrs. Lewis Ball preaching. The deacons' recommendation had nothing to do with gender and everything to do with preaching ability. Ball was a "great inspiration" and "exceptionally successful as a soul-winner," so they invited her.[5] The attitude toward Ball represents broader attitudes of the SBC at this time. In 1963 the Southern Baptist denomination ordained Addie Davis, and in 1974 it sponsored a conference affirming women's role in ministry. This resulted in an edited collection published by Broadman Press: *Christian Freedom for Women and Other Human Beings*.[6] Baptist historian Charles Deweese notes how the SBC once used New Testament passages to support women in public ministry (instead of using these passages to push women out of ministry, as they do today).[7] For example, *The Broadman Bible Commentary*, a commentary that began in 1969, read Phoebe as a deaconess in Romans 16.[8] Religion scholar Timothy Larsen wrote a 2017 essay showcasing the long history of female leadership in the evangelical tradition, including the Baptist tradition. He went so far as to call women's involvement in public ministry a "historic distinctive of evangelicalism."[9]

I have to pause here to tell you about the first time I read Larsen's article.

I struggled the first year after my husband's firing. Sometimes I would find it hard to breathe inside the basement walls of my faculty office. So I would leave, walk across the street, and sit on the carved stone benches in front of Carroll Library on Baylor's campus. Every day the light surfaces of those benches soak up the hot Texas sun. I found I could breathe there, sitting in the open space with the warm stone at my back. I would often carry papers or a book to make me look busy, like I was preparing for class or grading. That way I could just sit, alone, and breathe.

One day I forgot my reading camouflage. It had been a hard morning, early in fall 2017. Much of our future was still uncertain. The wounds left by our abrupt departure from our church family of fifteen years felt all the fresher with the start of a new school year. Gone was the usual pattern of back-to-school youth ministry activities; gone was the hope of starting the children's programs our kids had been looking forward to with their friends at church; gone were the couple we had spent so much of our time with and their not-yet-replaced friendships; gone was our son's answer when friends at school asked what his father did. I was so wrapped up in the emptiness of our lives that it wasn't until a well-intentioned friend sat down next to me on that warm stone bench and struck up a conversation that I realized my mistake.

As soon as she left, I picked up my phone and clicked on an article link that a colleague sent. It was just camouflage reading, making me look busy. And then my eyes focused on the title: "Evangelicalism's Strong History of Women in Ministry." What a gift on that hard day! The question that had sparked our family trauma was whether our evangelical church would allow a woman to teach youth Sunday school, and here was a respected evangelical scholar outlining how women throughout evangelical history have been teachers, leaders, and even preachers.

Listen to what Larsen argues: "Women in public Christian ministry is a historic distinctive of evangelicalism. It is historic because evangelical women have been fulfilling their callings in public ministry from the founding generation of evangelicalism to the present day and in every period in between." He defines public ministry as "service to adult believers" and includes preaching, teaching, pastoring, and other forms of spiritual care. John Wesley, the founder of Methodism, moved from prohibiting women as preachers to embracing them. Larsen notes how Wesley affirmed the preacher Sarah Crosby (among others), writing that she had an "extraordinary call." This persuaded Wesley to accept her as a preacher, just as he accepted male lay preachers. "It is fascinating," writes Larsen, "that [Wesley] affirmed the ministries of these women in explicitly egalitarian language as of the exact same order as that of the men who had not received Anglican ordination whose public ministries he was also affirming."[10]

Despite John Piper's hardline complementarian stance, even Calvinist evangelicals of the past have affirmed women's calling by God as public ministers. Larsen explains how the first American Calvinist denomination to emerge from the eighteenth-century evangelical revival was founded by a woman, Selina, Countess of Huntingdon. The denomination still exists as a member of the Evangelical Alliance, and the denomination still bears her name: "The Countess of Huntingdon's Connexion."[11]

Many evangelicals believe that supporting women in ministry is a slippery slope leading to liberalism and agnosticism.

Wayne Grudem argues that female leaders in the church (especially pastors) disobey God's Word, opening themselves to "the withdrawal of God's hand of protection and blessing."[12] According to Grudem, female leadership erodes orthodoxy in churches, leading to misinterpretation of Scripture and lack of trust in the Bible. Female leadership also erodes proper family roles, undermining masculine authority and creating gender-identity confusion among children. Grudem even provides a specific example of a female preacher who suffered the loss of God's protection in her life—a pastor named Judy Brown. Grudem is quick to point out that Brown contributed a chapter to a book edited by Gordon Fee: *Discovering Biblical Equality: Complementarity without Hierarchy*. (The book was published in 2004; another edition came out in 2012 with Brown's article removed.) Yet Brown ended up in prison for attempting to murder the husband of her lover. When the interviewer asked if Grudem thought Judy Brown's tragic fate was "related to her views about women preaching," his answer was clear: "In this case it seems to me there's an area of disobedience to the command of scripture regarding male leadership and teaching in the church."[13] Allowing female leadership is symptomatic of cultural compromise, Grudem implies, as the push for women as preachers and elders comes from outside Christianity. Female leadership is not a part of Bible-believing evangelicalism. It is sin, and—like the trajectory of Judy Brown's life—it leads to destruction.

Timothy Larsen's essay proves Wayne Grudem wrong.

Historically, women have flourished as leaders, teachers, and preachers—even in the evangelical world. Instead of opposing women as preachers and teachers, many eighteenth- and nineteenth-century evangelicals did the opposite—they supported women in public ministry. My favorite part of Larsen's essay is how he flips our understanding of why evangelicals support women in ministry. For Grudem and Piper, women in public ministry is evidence of how evangelicals have caved to contemporary culture, succumbing to the peer pressure of modern feminism instead of remaining faithful to the timeless standard of God's Word. Indeed, their book *Rediscovering Biblical Manhood and Womanhood* is subtitled "A Response to Evangelical Feminism." Larsen inverts their argument: "When evangelicals have cared more about the Bible and the gospel than they did about being perceived as respectable by the wider society, these commitments have often led them to affirm women in public ministry."[14] When evangelicals have supported women in public ministry, they are most closely aligned with the gospel of Jesus. It is when evangelicals succumb to the peer pressure of contemporary culture that they turn against women in public ministry.

What a reframing of our perspective!

Larsen is not alone in arguing that evangelicals have a strong history of women in public ministry. Historian Bettye Collier-Thomas has found women actively preaching and leading in denominations like the African Methodist Episcopal (AME) Church, AME Zion Church, Baptist Church, Colored Methodist Episcopal Church, and in Holiness movements. She published a collection of thirty-eight sermons by fourteen Black, female preachers who worked in the US between 1850 and 1979—showing, again, a continuous thread of women as leaders, teachers, and preachers long before the rise of evangelical feminism.[15]

The title of Collier-Thomas's book is brilliant: *Daughters of Thunder: Black Women Preachers and Their Sermons,*

1850–1979. She discusses women who paved the way, like Mary J. Small (ordained an elder in 1898 in the AME Zion Church), as well as twentieth-century preachers like Texas Baptist Ella Eugene Whitfield, who became a missionary for the Woman's Convention Auxiliary National Baptist Convention and, in 1911, preached almost five hundred sermons and visited over one thousand homes and churches. (To me, the public nature and widespread visibility of Whitfield's ministry in the early twentieth century sounds like a precursor to the public ministry of her later Texas Baptist sister Beth Moore.) The voices of Black women thundered from pulpits, just like the voices of their brothers in Christ did.[16] Baptist minister Samuel W. Bacote praised Whitfield's public presence as "a woman of untiring zeal and commanding appearance." "She can hold an audience indefinitely," he wrote, "by the intensity of her earnestness and the clearness and appropriateness of her well-chosen words. The utility of her subjects and the excellence of her delivery have rendered her extremely popular as a public speaker."[17]

When Mrs. Lewis Ball preached at First Baptist Church Elm Mott in the 1930s, she did not preach because the church was succumbing to feminist pressures. She preached because the church regarded her as a great soul-winning preacher and because—like Ella Eugene Whitfield and so many other women of their time—her calling was affirmed by the Christian community around her.

The problem is that evangelicals simply do not know this history.

Instead of reading the powerful 1941 sermon "If I Were White" by ordained minister Florence Spearing Randolph or learning about the sixteen people baptized after the revival service led by Mrs. Lewis Ball in 1934, evangelicals flock to John Piper's Desiring God website (it has had six million visitors during the last six months alone), where they listen to *Ask Pastor John* podcast interviews like "Can a Woman Preach if Elders Affirm It?" or read articles like Mary A. Kassian's "Women Teaching Men—How Far Is Too Far?" Instead of reading Larsen's article "Evangelicalism's Strong History of Women in Public Ministry" and Collier-Thomas's *Daughters of Thunder*, we are listening to John Piper state unequivocally that it is not okay and never has been okay for women to teach men.[18] Because we lack a historical context in which to evaluate Piper's claims, evangelicals accept his teachings.

By forgetting our past, especially women who don't fit into the narrative that some evangelicals tell, we have made it easier to accept the "truth" of biblical womanhood. We don't remember anything different.

Redefining Holiness

Evangelical women preached to public crowds just like women preached in medieval Europe. Yet evangelical women preachers look rather different from Margery Kempe's great cloud of female witnesses. Let's look more closely at Mrs. Lewis Ball. We don't actually know her name—records simply identify her by her husband's name. She was not paid for her services. The records note that she would not be paid—although the women of Elm Mott got together and hosted a "pounding" for her to show their appreciation.

It is remarkable that First Baptist Church Elm Mott invited a woman to preach from the pulpit on several occasions during the 1930s. It is also remarkable that this preaching woman managed to do so without challenging male authority. She identified herself by the name of her husband, Lewis Ball, emphasizing that she preached with his permission. Instead of accepting money to preach (as if it was her job), she gave money back to the church, donating $25 to their Lottie Moon Missionary Fund. Mrs. Lewis Ball earned a reputation as a great soul-winning evangelist while maintaining her reputation as a conventional wife. She even managed to convey the message that preaching was just her side gig. As a married woman, of course, her primary job would be caring for her family.

If we rewind almost three centuries, to the early years of Baptist history, we can see a similar emphasis placed on another female Baptist preacher. In 1655, Katherine Sutton asked God to "pour out of his blessed Spirit" upon her, and she began to preach and prophesy through singing.[19] Sutton's Baptist pastor, Hanserd Knollys, wrote the preface to her spiritual autobiography. His purpose was to defend her public ministry, but he did so by grounding her spiritual calling in her feminine distinctiveness. Just as Mrs. Lewis Ball did not directly challenge male authority, Knollys made sure Sutton didn't either. Using John 6:12 as a framework, Knollys describes how God poured out his Spirit first on his faithful servants (men), and then the women (handmaids) came behind and gathered up the "crumbs of that spiritual bread."[20] While the men received the Spirit of Christ directly, the women followed and picked up the leftovers. Knollys justifies Sutton's right to prophesy while simultaneously emphasizing her secondary status. She was not a threat to male authority. Sutton was a preaching (well, actually, singing) prophet, but she also was a godly woman dedicated to family. Knollys justifies the extraordinariness of her spiritual gift by emphasizing her ordinariness as a woman—she was loving, gentle, wise, virtuous, maternal, and dedicated to family.

What I noticed about Mrs. Lewis Ball's leadership in the 1930s is similar to Knollys's characterization of Sutton's leadership some three hundred years prior. Both women had the right to preach and prophesy as long as they maintained their traditional female roles and did not usurp male authority.

As a medieval historian, I was really struck by this similarity. Remember Margery Kempe's great cloud of female witnesses? The leadership of medieval women was also qualified, but, instead of having to maintain their female distinctiveness, they had to rise above their sex. "Holy women and men who moved closer together, were also moving away from the extremes of sexed temperament and were becoming more similar in body and in soul," explains Jacqueline Murray.[21] Medieval women gained spiritual authority by casting off their female roles and acting more like men.

So the medieval world told stories about women like Saint Cecilia. Compare Cecilia's leadership style with those of Mrs. Lewis Ball and Katherine Sutton. One rendering of Saint Cecilia's story is found in a fourteenth-century sermon collection titled "The Mirror." The sermon concludes with a story about a man named Stephen. Stephen is a rich Roman who lived a rather ordinary life—neither completely saint nor completely sinner. For example, when he decides to add on to his luxurious villa, he steals land from his next-door neighbor—a church dedicated to the virgin martyr Saint Cecilia. He refuses to return the land or to apologize for his actions. Stephen dies before his priest can convince him to repent, and he goes to eternal judgment carrying this sin.

183

But something interesting happens on Stephen's way to judgment: "Then came St. Cecilia by Stephen, and as she passed him, she took him by the arm and pinched him. And it so greatly pained him that had he been alive, it would have killed him. Then he was called before the judge and damned for his sin against Cecilia."[22] Stephen eventually does get a second chance. The judge relents—Stephen is resurrected and immediately restores Cecilia's church. The pain caused by Cecilia's pinch, however, is never healed. For the rest of his life it serves as a constant reminder of his previous sin. Kathleen Blumreich, editor of the 2004 edition of "The Mirror," notes that Cecilia is depicted as a tormentor who prefers "vengeance over mercy" and behaves "more like a stereotypically scorned woman than one of the blessed."[23]

Yet Cecilia's behavior is not condemned. In fact, the moral of the story is to think twice before you trespass against saints. Cecilia's aggressive personality matches her medieval persona as rebellious and insubordinate (just read Chaucer's fourteenth-century rendering of her story[24]). Her harsh punishment of Stephen might not match modern notions of biblical womanhood, but—as Karen Winstead reminds us—it wouldn't have bothered medieval hearers.[25] "The Mirror" sermon concludes by praising Cecilia for her behavior: "God grant us such saints to serve and maintain Holy Church that we may come to the bliss of heaven and dwell with the saints without end."[26]

Cecilia's story vividly shows that the touchstone for female holiness shifted after the Reformation. For women in the ancient and medieval world, rising above their sex and behaving in ways we would consider unbecoming for women today buttressed women's religious authority. Chaucer, for example, praised Cecilia for her "good and prudent behavior" even while describing her as shouting rude insults at her Roman judges and preaching for three days with blood gurgling out of her throat, lying in her gore after a botched beheading.[27] I can't help but wonder what Marabel Morgan, who in her book *The Total Woman* advised women to be "feminine, soft, and touchable," would think about Cecilia.[28] By the time of the Reformation, Cecilia's brand of biblical womanhood was already disappearing and being replaced by an emphasis on female distinctiveness that included a more passive submission.

In a fascinating conclusion to her book *Women and Religion in Early America, 1600–1850,* Marilyn Westerkamp argues that from 1600 to 1850 even the words women used to describe their spiritual callings became more passive while the words men used became more active. She writes that "while men and women used many of the same descriptions, labels and formulas in their testimonies, their spiritual autobiographies were not telling the same story."[29] Women were controlled by God and spoke only when God spoke through them; men made bold choices as leaders for God and spoke with their own voices, empowered by God. Women were passive; men were active. While men were the fleet feet of Jesus carrying the good news, women were stationary vessels overflowing with what God poured into them. The touchstone of holiness had shifted so much for women that—in quite a contrast to Cecilia shouting vulgar threats at Roman officials—women's self-described spiritual callings now included being quiet and still.

Women from Katherine Sutton to Mrs. Lewis Ball could still preach, teach, and prophesy. But they had to ground their ministry in feminine distinctiveness. In fact, as women's holiness became more and more rooted in submission, passivity, and their roles as wives and mothers, women increasingly needed to demonstrate that their callings did not challenge men's authority.

Biblical womanhood teaches that women are designed by God to be different from men and submissive to (at least their husband's) masculine authority. By forgetting our long history of women in public ministry and by redefining holiness for women as rooted in both female distinctiveness and female submission (the core of biblical womanhood), evangelicals moved closer to making biblical womanhood gospel truth.

Redefining Orthodoxy

As I have argued throughout this book, it is impossible to write women's leadership out of Christian history. We can forget it and we can ignore it, but we can't get rid of the historical reality. It is also impossible to maintain consistent arguments for women's subordination because, rather than stemming from God's commands, these arguments stem from the changing circumstances of history. New reasons have to be found to justify keeping women out of leadership. Jemar Tisby accurately writes, "Racism never goes away. It just adapts."[30] The same is true of patriarchy. Like racism, patriarchy is a shapeshifter— conforming to each new era, looking as if it has always belonged. The eighteenth and nineteenth centuries emphasized women's distinctiveness from men and used this distinctiveness to justify women's subordination. Pious rhetoric described a woman as the "angel of the house" and sentimentalized her role as a domestic goddess.[31] By assigning women primarily to the household, their work outside the household held less value. In this way, employers could justify paying women lower wages than men, and thus women would be less likely to compete with men on the job market. Women could also be kept out of the political realm, allowing men to govern without women's interference. Once again, Christian patriarchy spilled out into the wider world, further limiting women's opportunities.

By the early twentieth century, advocates for women argued that women should not be categorized by their biological differences from men but should be understood by their sameness as human beings. Dorothy L. Sayers writes this in her 1938 essay "Are Women Human?": "A woman is just as much an ordinary human being as a man, with the same individual preferences, and with just as much right to the tastes and preferences of an individual. What is repugnant to every human being is to be reckoned always as a member of a class and not as an individual person." When we differentiate women because of their sex, we objectify them and deny them their humanity.[32]

Despite the traction gained by ideas like Sayers's, patriarchy within Christianity reasserted itself with a vengeance during the twentieth century. Two significant (but related) shifts happened within evangelical theology that helped seal biblical womanhood as gospel truth: the championing of inerrancy and the revival of Arianism.

Championing Biblical Inerrancy

I can still see her standing at the chalkboard, gesturing with her Bible. She was teaching my youth Sunday school class that morning. She was one of the women's Bible study leaders in our church, and she mentored many younger women. I don't remember exactly how old I was—a freshman or sophomore in high school. I still remember her claim though; it stuck with

187

me. "If you don't accept Genesis literally, creation and the flood, you might as well throw out the rest of the Bible."

I didn't know until years later that her words, rather than stemming from the Bible, stemmed from one of the sides of a theological battle that engulfed the Protestant world in early twentieth-century America: the fundamentalist-modernist controversy. I once grabbed my Baylor colleague Andrea Turpin after a conference session and made her explain the controversy to me. My evangelical life made more sense after that.[33]

The fundamentalist-modernist controversy of the early twentieth century split Protestants into liberal and conservative camps, laying the groundwork for the modern culture wars. Liberals wanted a more ecumenical approach to missions and the freedom to modernize traditional beliefs; conservatives wanted to protect traditional beliefs against encroaching cultural pressures. Margaret Bendroth gets to the point: "The central drama of the fundamentalist-modernist controversy was a conflict over the nature of biblical truth. For fundamentalists, all other debates over evolution, the conduct of foreign missions, or the coming millennium boiled down to a single principle: their insistence on the utter reliability of God's word."[34] The fundamentalist-modernist controversy helped evangelicals stake out the importance of biblical inerrancy—the belief that the Bible is completely without error, including in areas of science and history.

For many, inerrancy meant not only that the Bible was without error but that it *had to be* without error to be true at all.[35] Just like my youth Sunday school teacher, conservative evangelical leaders employed a slippery-slope mentality to weaponize inerrancy. If we can't trust the biblical account of creation, they argued, then how can we trust the biblical story of Jesus? Either we believe the Bible, literally and in its entirety, or we don't. When presented with these options and "forced to choose," as Hankins writes, it is not surprising that so many twentieth-century evangelicals chose inerrancy.[36]

Growing up Southern Baptist during the 1980s and '90s, I honestly thought inerrancy was a Baptist idea. How surprised I was to learn that Calvinist theologians at Princeton Theological Seminary actually led the inerrancy charge! This connection between Calvinism and inerrancy helped me better understand the connection between Calvinism and complementarianism. Because of their belief "that the subordination of women was inherent in the created order," explains Bendroth, "Calvinists were only guardedly optimistic about the possibilities of social amelioration in women's status." God elected women to be subordinate and domestic and elected men to be intellectual and public. Preaching women were simply "embarrassments."[37]

Indeed, the early twentieth-century emphasis on inerrancy went hand in hand with a wide-ranging attempt to build up the authority of male preachers at the expense of women. As we have seen, preaching women peppered the landscape of late nineteenth- and early twentieth-century America: they flooded the mission field as evangelists and leaders, and they achieved popular acclaim as preachers among Pentecostal and even fundamentalist denominations. As these women rose in prominence, so too rose inerrancy teachings. And these teachings buttressed male authority by diminishing female authority— transforming a literal reading of Paul's verses about women into immutable truth.[38]

"We may like what Paul says, or we may not like it," proclaimed Princeton Seminary professor B. B. Warfield in 1920, "but there is no room for doubt in what he says."[39] The divinely sanctioned patriarchy entrenched in his words would sound the death knell for preaching Baptist women like Mrs. Lewis Ball. The concept of inerrancy made it increasingly difficult to argue against a "plain and literal" interpretation of "women be silent" and "women shall not teach." The line between believing the Bible and believing a "plain and literal" interpretation of the Bible blurred. If Ephesians 5 told wives to submit to their husbands, the plain and literal interpretation demands that wives submit to their husbands. Those who disagree were not faithful to Scripture.

And just like that, evangelicals baptized patriarchy. Women could not preach and had to submit—not because their bodies were too flawed or their minds too weak, but because God had decreed it through Paul's inerrant writings. Those who doubt these biblical truths doubt the truth of the Bible itself. Inerrancy introduced the ultimate justification for patriarchy— abandoning a plain and literal interpretation of Pauline texts about women would hurl Christians off the cliff of biblical orthodoxy.

From my experience as someone who grew up Southern Baptist and remained in conservative evangelical churches throughout most of my adult life, inerrancy creates an atmosphere of fear. Any question raised about biblical accuracy must be completely answered or completely rejected to prevent the fragile fabric of faith from unraveling. After my husband was fired, for example, we pled with the elders for an audience to share our views in person. We had never been allowed to do this. We had to raise our concerns through an email to one elder (which was then forwarded without our permission to the others) and were then told to respond in writing within a certain time frame. The only part done in person was the actual firing. Eventually, my husband received an answer from one of the elders. We couldn't present our views in person because they simply would not be considered. If the elders considered allowing women to teach or exercise authority over men (i.e., teenage boys in Sunday school), it would lead to the "slippery slope" (this was the actual phrase used) of cultural compromise.

The evangelical fight for inerrancy was inextricably linked with gender from the beginning. Kristin Kobes Du Mez explains how, in the SBC specifically, the direct challenge to male headship caused by the rising number of female Baptist preachers put conservative Baptist leaders on the defensive.[40] Inerrancy wasn't important by itself in the late twentieth century; it became important because it provided a way to push women out of the pulpit. It worked extremely well.

Are you ready for the final piece in making biblical womanhood gospel truth?

Hang on to your coffee.

Reviving Arianism

If I had been holding coffee, I would have dropped it that Sunday morning. As it was, I almost fell out of my seat—which wouldn't have been a good thing since I was sitting in clear sight of the pastor. But, seriously, I had just heard him preach heresy. I am not using the word *heresy* lightly. Throughout church history, what I had just heard come from the mouth of our pastor had been declared heretical over and over and over again. Yet here was a twenty-first-century evangelical pastor boldly stating that Jesus is eternally subordinate to God the Father. This was a heresy so serious that the fourth-century church father Athanasius refused to recognize those who supported it as Christian.[41]

Heresy.

I looked around, expecting to see others reacting. No one seemed concerned. My husband hadn't come in yet (he often helped with behind-the-scenes work during services). I didn't have anything else to do but keep listening. Maybe I heard wrong? I really hoped I had.

I hadn't. That sermon was a wake-up call to how far the argument for women's subordination had gone—to the point of rewriting Trinitarian doctrine.

But before we talk about the heresy, let's talk about the historical context. Droves of women went to work outside the home during World War I and World War II while men (and a few women) fought. However, when the wars ended, the rules changed. Women were pushed out of jobs to accommodate the returning soldiers, and rhetoric once more began to emphasize women's roles as keepers of the home. Katherine French and Allyson Poska relate well how old laws subordinating women were revived after these wars. These laws put women under the household authority of their husbands, rewarded women for getting married and having children (just like in ancient Rome!), and even restricted women from working outside the home and filing for divorce. As French and Poska write, "Despite women's importance to the wartime workplace, government policies quickly reverted to prewar promarriage and pronatalist policies."[42]

But women weren't interested in going back to the way things were. Just like the suffrage movement was born during the most suffocating years of the cult of domesticity, modern feminism was born in the aftermath of World War II. Women fought to work outside the home, to receive educations equivalent to men's, to have the same legal rights as men did, and even to preach the gospel when called by God.

This is when the heresy I had just heard preached began to resurface in Christian history. Even C. S. Lewis toyed with a version of it.[43] This heresy is the eternal subordination of the Son to the Father. By the end of the twentieth century, it had a new twist: because Jesus is eternally subordinate to God the Father, wives are eternally subordinate to their husbands.[44]

Listen to how Bruce Ware describes the relationship between the Father and the Son in his children's theology book *Big Truths for Young Hearts*: "As the Son of the Father, Jesus lives always under the authority of his Father—in all times past and now in all times future . . . , the Son always stands under his Father and does the will of the Father. Jesus takes great joy in doing exactly what the Father wants him to do. The Son is not upset about this; he doesn't wish to be the one in charge."[45] The Trinity, according to Ware, is hierarchical. While the Son is equal to the Father in glory and power, the Son is unequal in his role.

This teaching, called "the eternal subordination of the Son," has infiltrated the evangelical world. Aimee Byrd describes a 2001 Council on Biblical Manhood and Womanhood document that teaches "the Son, the second person of the Trinity, is subordinate to the Father, not only in economy of salvation but in his essence."[46] She also tells of how Owen Strachan sent her a copy of his recently published book, which grounds the council's "understanding of the complementarity of men and women on a relationship of authority and submission in the nature of the Trinity."[47]

My fear is that many evangelicals have already converted without realizing that the eternal subordination of the Son is a teaching outside the bounds of Christian orthodoxy. Complementarians may claim that women preaching violates Christian orthodoxy, but the eternal subordination of the Son really does violate Christian orthodoxy. As philosophy professor Phillip Cary writes, gender egalitarians' "disagreement with the Eastern Orthodox and Roman Catholic Tradition about such matters as the ordination of women are minor . . . compared to conservative evangelicals' abandonment of the Great Tradition of the Trinity."[48] Trinitarian teachings are central to orthodox Christianity; and complementarians—in their blind pursuit to maintain control over women—have exchanged the truth of God for a gender hierarchy of human origin.

As a church historian, I immediately recognized the eternal subordination of the Son as Arianism. In the fourth century, a priest in Alexandria, Egypt, began to preach that the Son was of a different substance from God the Father, which meant the Son had a subordinate role to God the Father. God the Father gave the instructions; God the Son obeyed the instructions. When everyone else in the Christian world got wind of what Arius was teaching, they reacted with horror. If Jesus isn't of the same substance as God the Father, then his death on the cross couldn't cover sin. Only God could save, and if Jesus wasn't fully God, what did that mean for his death and resurrection? As Kevin Giles writes, "By arguing that the Son is *different in being* from the Father, [Arians] impugned the full divinity of the Son of God, the veracity of the revelation of God in Christ and the possibility of salvation for men and women."[49] Salvation itself was at stake.

So early Christians convened the Council of Nicaea in 325 to confront the teachings of Arius. They unilaterally rejected Arianism as heresy. They declared, as the Nicene Creed would proclaim, that Jesus is of the same substance as God the Father— "light from light." The Trinity is Three in One, not One followed by Two and Three. Indeed, so horrific were the implications of Arianism that the Nicene Council "intentionally excluded all expressions of subordinationism." This affirmation of the absence of hierarchy within the Triune God was reaffirmed by the Council of Constantinople in 381 and reiterated by the Athanasian Creed in 500: "We worship One God in Trinity, and Trinity in Unity; neither confounding the Persons, nor dividing the Substance," which means that "none is greater, or less than another. But the whole three Persons are co-eternal together and co-equal."[50]

What early Christians were so adamant about teaching, that no hierarchy existed within the Triune God, modern evangelicals seem adamant about forgetting. Giles writes that Christians were much more attuned to the Trinity and the significance of the doctrine of the Trinity before the modern world. Even Calvin opposed the subordination of the Son. The Reformation accepted and promoted the trinitarian teachings of Athanasius. Unfortunately, after the Reformation, both Protestants and Catholics became laxer about teaching the importance of the Trinity and often taught it in ways that were incorrect. Giles writes, "In the nineteenth and twentieth centuries, conservative evangelicals were among those with a very weak and sometimes erroneous grasp of the historically developed doctrine of the Trinity."[51] It shouldn't surprise us that these conservative evangelicals (with a "weak" and "erroneous" understanding of the Trinity) resurrected Arianism once again. Instead of striving to become more like God, these evangelicals fought to make God look more like us.[52]

It should also not surprise us that evangelicals resurrected Arianism for the same reason that evangelicals turned to inerrancy: if Jesus is eternally subordinate to God the Father, women's subordination becomes much easier to justify. Arianism, like inerrancy, proved the perfect weapon against women's equality, the perfect prop for Christian patriarchy.

Except it is *still* heresy. Arianism repackaged.

It is true that teachings about the subordinate status of Christ persisted—sometimes even flourished—from the fourth through the ninth centuries. Arianism had spread too quickly to be quickly contained. In 325, the Council of Nicaea "anathematized" those who rejected the co-eternity of Jesus and the teaching that Jesus was of the same substance as the Father. But since the Visigoth king Reccared (who ruled an early medieval kingdom in Iberia) did not convert from Arianism until 587, the road to broad acceptance of Nicene Christianity was clearly slow.[53]

Yet is also true that Arianism has always been deemed heretical. As R. P. C. Hanson writes in *The Search for the Christian Doctrine of God: The Arian Controversy, 318–381*, Arianism taught "two unequal gods, a High God incapable of human experiences, and a lesser God who, so to speak, did his dirty work for him."[54] It was condemned by early Christians just as it has continued to be condemned by many modern evangelicals today. Byrd tells the story of how she helped draw attention to the heretical revival of Arianism among complementarian leaders. The result was a conference in 2016 that upheld Nicene Christianity and condemned eternal subordination of the Son.[55]

I fear, though, that the damage has already been done. Conservative evangelical leaders, yearning to maintain traditional family values and fend off feminism, turned to an old heresy. They poured their ideas about submission and authority, embedded in the very nature of God, into the teachings imbibed by their congregations—the same evangelicals who already believe

196

that inerrancy is bound up in female submission. Evangelicals believe that biblical womanhood is the only option because we have been taught that it is tied to our trust in the reliability of God's Word as well as embedded in the Godhead itself: women are subordinate because Jesus is subordinate. Gospel truth indeed.

The Problem of Biblical Womanhood

The soft blue and green lighting shifted on the mostly naked walls. I still remember it reflecting on the speaker's face, framing her body in the colors of stained glass. She was so small in the center of that large stage. Her voice was small too, tentative as she read from her book, *Nice Girls Don't Change the World.* She was Lynne Hybels, and in 2007 everyone loved her husband, the founding pastor of Willow Creek Community Church.

Yet on that November day, most people weren't listening to her. It was almost lunchtime at the National Youth Worker's Convention, meeting that year in St. Louis. Everyone was hungry. The whole row in front of me got up, not very quietly, and left. So did almost everyone in the section next to me. Soon most people were leaving, embracing rudeness at the siren call of lunch specials.

I didn't move.

Lynne Hybels had me absolutely transfixed. She was speaking words shockingly reminiscent, at least to my historian's mind, of Betty Friedan. But instead of describing a problem for American housewives that had no name, as Friedan famously did in her 1963 *The Feminine Mystique*, Hybels was describing a problem for Christian women that had a name: the problem of biblical womanhood.

Reading excerpts from her book, Lynne Hybels—wife of one of the most powerful and admired pastors in American Christianity—confessed to being a fraud. As a woman who had grown up in American evangelicalism, she had done everything right. She professed the right beliefs; she made the right choices; she even married a pastor and became a good Christian wife and mother. Yet at the age of thirty-nine, she found herself seriously depressed. As she told her counselor, "I've been working so hard to keep everybody else happy, but I'm so miserable I want to die."[56]

Almost forty years into her life, Hybels realized she had been living a script of what she had been taught Christian girls were supposed to be, instead of becoming the woman that God had called her to be. The script taught that a woman's highest calling was to enhance the life of her husband and children. The script taught that women should practice selflessness and obedience. The script taught that women should stifle personal desires and dreams for the sake of their families. By following this script, Hybels had become a living Facebook feed—her outward perfection hiding a mess inside.

As I listened, riveted to my seat, pieces of my life clicked together. As a historian, I knew that biblical womanhood looked a whole lot like the rest of human history: women defined as less than men, oppressed, abused. But I also still believed that women and men were called to divinely ordained gender roles. So I figured the problem had to be with me—my own prideful unwillingness to submit. At least that was what I thought before I heard Lynne Hybels.

You see, Lynne Hybels had the same problem I did. As women who grew up in the late twentieth century—women who knew little about the long history of Christian women as leaders and teachers and preachers, who believed that be-coming a wife and mother was part of our Christian calling, who lived in the aftermath of the emergence of both inerrancy and renewed teaching about the eternal subordination of the Son—we believed that biblical womanhood was biblical. Even a woman like Lynne Hybels, who attended a church that sup-ported women in ministry, still seemed trapped by evangelical teachings about biblical womanhood. As I listened to her, I realized that biblical womanhood had become more than a clause in the "Baptist Faith and Message 2000."[57] It had become more than a return to traditional family values. It had become a gospel issue—intertwined with the very nature of God. It had become God's timeless truth, defended by those who remain the most faithful.

Take, for example, the Gospel Coalition. Did you know that it includes biblical womanhood in its statement of faith? "God ordains that [women and men] assume distinctive roles which reflect the loving relationship between Christ and the church, the husband exercising headship in a way that displays the car-ing, sacrificial love of Christ, and the wife submitting to her husband in a way that models the love of the church for her Lord."[58] While John Piper and Tim Keller agree that comple-mentarianism is not necessary for salvation, they argue that it is a very important aspect of the gospel and is necessary to protect a proper understanding of the gospel. As Keller says, "It indirectly affects the way we understand the Scripture which affects the way we understand the gospel. Many people in order to make room for an egalitarian position have to do something with the way we read Scripture. It loosens our understanding of Scripture."[59] Only those who agree with biblical womanhood, Keller suggests, have a right understanding of the gospel.

Biblical womanhood as we know it today had thus become fully formed: Not only does history show that women have always been subordinate to men (patriarchy), not only does the New Testament confirm that women should be subordinate to men (Paul), not only did the Reformation restore the importance and dignity of the role of wife and mother, but now we can state with assurance that female subordination is gospel truth. Women are created as distinct from men and, by the design of our female bodies, intended for domesticity and subordination. Women's subordination even reflects the design of the Godhead itself. Just as Jesus is subordinate to God the Father, wives should be subordinate to their husbands. The Bible clearly preaches female submission, and if we disbelieve the Bible on this account, then we call into question the entire veracity of the Bible.

The definition of heresy had shifted.

The heretics were now those who resisted the gospel truth of women's subordination to men. The heretics were me and my husband, as we dared ask permission for a woman to teach a high school Sunday school class. We had become the slippery slope. No wonder we were fired. We were dangerous to the gospel of Christ.

IT WAS OCTOBER 15, 2017. I was standing in my kitchen holding the back door open for my dog. She was taking her time wandering around in our backyard, so I picked up my phone and started scrolling through Twitter. I immediately saw the tweet. It was from Alyssa Milano, retweeted by one of my friends. This is what it said: "If you've been sexually harassed or assaulted write 'me too' as a reply to this tweet."[1]

I stared at it for a long minute. I wanted to reply "me too," and I did, four days later. But I buried it in a tweet about Kristin Kobes Du Mez's Anxious Bench post, "Me Too. And Why This Is a Christian Problem." "#MeToo," I wrote. "Thanks @kkdumez; It IS a Christian problem."[2] Most people probably missed that my #MeToo literally meant *Me Too*. I wasn't brave enough yet.

I have told you my second darkest story about my experiences inside complementarianism. I have told you how my husband was fired after questioning the role of women in our church. I have let you glimpse the pain and trauma that that experience caused my family. I have told you how it pushed me to stop being silent, to speak the historical truth about complementarianism.

But I haven't told you my darkest story.

I haven't told you how I was once invited to a series of evening seminars led by a popular conservative speaker named Bill Gothard; I went. I didn't know that Gothard's Institute in Basic Life Principles had already been plagued by scandal and accusations of abuse. I didn't consider that Gothard's teachings—that God's perfect design was best expressed "in the authoritarian rule of men"—could become dangerous.[3] I didn't consider how the young man who had invited me might internalize Gothard's teachings about how a wife owed total submission to her husband or how he might apply them to our dating relationship. According to Gothard, we weren't dating. We were courting, which meant marriage was our future. I didn't consider that as he listened to Gothard's teachings about God's ordained "chain of command," this young man might become an abuser.

As a young woman growing up in the Southern Baptist Church, I internalized many teachings about biblical womanhood. "In my experience," writes Kate Bowler, "evangelical girls learn about the limits of their own spiritual authority as an accounting of small details, little moments of encouragement or discouragement that nudge them toward a sense of being acceptable."[4] This was my experience too. Like the impressionable young person I was, I believed James Dobson's perspective in *Love for a Lifetime*—that women are weak while men are strong. So I stayed with my boyfriend, hoping what I experienced as anger would mature into strength and that all would become right with my world.

It didn't. I became broken, exhausted, and tired of God. I didn't care that much about church anymore. The preacher's words at the conservative church I attended rang with what I thought was the authority of the Word of God. These words were writing for me a future I no longer wanted but one I felt powerless to escape. I was supposed to be like Sarah, a woman commended in the Old Testament for deferring to her husband as lord and embracing her role as wife and mother. But I felt more like Hagar, rejected and afraid. Years later, when Rachael Denhollander spoke at the 2019 Southern Baptist Convention, her words captured my experience: "I think it is very telling that I have heard hundreds, literally hundreds, of sermons directed on the quiet and submissive sphere that a woman should have," she said. "I have heard not one on how to value a woman's voice. I have heard not one on the issue of sexual assault."[5] Not one time during those years did I hear a preacher speak out against abusive relationships; not one time did a pastor speak about the dangers inherent in patriarchal power hierarchies. What I did hear was what Rachael Denhollander heard—women are called to be wives and mothers, submissive and silent.

All my mental energy focused on keeping my life together. I still remember trying to watch *Sleeping with the Enemy* one night with a friend. The 1991 movie features Julia Roberts as a physically abused wife. I had to leave the room. It felt too close to home. I had become so good at checking out mentally, pretending that what was happening to me wasn't really happening. But watching Julia Roberts' fictional character straighten the canned food in her kitchen cabinet, trying to stave off the violent temper of her husband, made me see the harsh reality of my own relationship.

One night, after an encounter that felt particularly scary, I escaped into the safety of my home. When my hands started shaking too hard to open the door to my room, I just sank to the ground in the hallway. I knew the relationship was wrong. Horribly wrong. I had known it for a long time. I knew it because of the radically different example set by my own family. I knew it because of the radically different example I saw in the Bible. I knew how Jesus treated women. I knew how God always fought for the oppressed, for those who couldn't fight for themselves. I knew that what God said about women was quite different from what men like Bill Gothard preached.

Eventually my hands stopped shaking, and I stood back up. I opened my door, pausing for a minute in the liminal space of the doorframe, shadowed by the light from the hall. "Help me," I prayed. "Help me get out."

The next day, a miracle happened. He didn't call. He didn't come. For over two weeks, he stayed gone. To this day, I don't know why. All I know is that time and distance gave me strength. With his voice gone, I could hear God again. Over and over, I read 1 Corinthians, marveling at how it said so much more than "women should be silent" (1 Corinthians 14:34–35). So much more, in fact, that those two verses—once overpowering to me—were dwarfed. I realized the dialogical nature of the letter and Paul's overarching plea for the congregants to follow him as he followed Christ (10:31–11:1). Chapter 13 became my solace as Paul showed the Corinthians a more excellent way than division and strife—the never-ending love of Christ. At the end of those two weeks, I realized how dimly I had been viewing God's calling on my life. Emboldened by the Word of God and the care of my friends and family, I walked away. I never looked back.

This is my #MeToo story. My #ChurchToo story.

This experience, along with my husband's firing, frames how I think about complementarianism today.

From both of these traumatic experiences, one much more recent and one fading farther and farther into the past, I am scarred. I will always carry the scars. I have experienced the worst of what complementarianism has to offer. But it wasn't until I began to pull on the historical threads that weave complementarianism together that I really began to doubt it. You see, I had fallen for the biggest lie of all: that adhering to complementarianism is the only option for those who believe the Bible is the authoritative Word of God.

After all, Paul says clearly that the man is the head and the wife is to submit. Except now I know that when Paul's words are contextualized both theologically and historically, they read rather differently. So while experience shapes my perspective of complementarian teachings, evidence from my research as a scholar, my teaching as a college professor, and my professional and personal study of the Bible has led me to abandon these teachings. Evidence shows me how Christian patriarchy was built, stone by stone, throughout the centuries. Evidence shows me how, century after century, arguments for women's subordination reflect historical circumstances more than the face of God. Evidence shows me that just because complementarianism uses biblical texts doesn't mean it reflects biblical truth. Evidence shows me the trail of sin and destruction left in the wake of teachings that place women under the power of men. Evidence shows me, throughout history, the women who have always known the truth about patriarchy and who have always believed that Jesus sets women free. So let me give you my final pitch. Because isn't it time for all of us to be free?

Because It Is Time to Stop It

One of my friends, shortly after seeing a draft of my table of contents for this book, asked if the final chapter would contain a new vision for a theological approach to women in the church. Her words panicked me. I am a historian; not a theologian— and a very practical historian at that. In fact, my first thought when I read her words reveals a great deal about me. My thought was about a Mad TV comedy sketch in which Bob Newhart plays the psychiatrist Dr. Switzer. Dr. Switzer's novel advice to clients, regardless of their problem, is two words: "Stop it!"

"There you go," says Dr. Switzer. "I mean, you don't want to go through life being scared of being buried alive in a box, do you? I mean, that sounds frightening. . . . Stop it!"[6]

For those who still believe that biblical womanhood is God-ordained, my advice is Dr. Switzer's: Stop it! We have become so embroiled in arguments about Greek grammar and whose Bible translation is better that we have forgotten what Jesus told us was most important: "Love the Lord your God with all your heart, and with all your soul, and with all your mind. . . . [And] love your neighbor as yourself" (Matthew 22:37–39). We have forgotten that the harshest words Jesus utters in the Bible are not to the ordinary people and sinners around him—the tax collectors and prostitutes and gentiles and women, whom the disciples kept trying to push away. The harshest words Jesus utters in the Bible are to the strict male religious leaders functioning as self-appointed border guards of orthodoxy. "Woe to you, scribes and Pharisees, hypocrites! For you are like white-washed tombs, which on the outside look beautiful, but inside they are full of the bones of the dead and of all kinds of filth" (Matthew 23:27). Doesn't it sound like Jesus told the Pharisees "Stop it!" because what they were doing led to death instead of life?

I only skirted the fringes of the Bill Gothard movement. But I can tell you from experience that it was a whitewashed tomb. It almost buried my young self. I remember once, years later, as I sat in my first faculty office, a newly minted PhD, a friend dropped by. He was part of both my academic and evangelical world, and we had been talking about the (most recent) evangelical sex scandal exploding the news. "I think there's a link between complementarianism and abuse," I told him. He shook his head, frowning a bit. "There's no proof of that," he said.

But there is. We can no longer deny a link between complementarianism and abuse. So much evidence now exists that John Piper, Al Mohler, and Russell Moore have gone on the defensive, trying to proclaim how their "Christian patriarchy" is different (see my first chapter).[7] Du Mez eviscerates their claim, providing the proof my friend could not see—that the conservative church model of authoritarian leadership combined with rigid gender roles fosters a culture of abuse (decade after decade, church after church, leader after leader). Does this model hurt everyone? Of course not. It just hurt the thirty or more women who made allegations against Bill Gothard.[8] It just hurt the victims who filed a class-action suit against Sovereign Grace Ministries for creating an environment in which, they alleged, the sexual abuse of children flourished.[9] It just hurt the seven hundred victims of sexual abuse linked to Southern Baptist churches over a period of twenty years.[10]

It just hurt women like me.

Conservative evangelicals preach "a mutually reinforcing vision of Christian masculinity—of patriarchy and submission, sex and power," Du Mez writes. "It was a vision that promised protection for women but left women without defense, one that worshiped power and turned a blind eye to justice, and one that transformed the Jesus of the Gospels into an image of their own making."[11] Not only do legal cases and newspaper reports and victim allegations tell us that Du Mez is right, but my own life bears witness. Hierarchy gives birth to patriarchy, and patriarchy gives birth to the abuse of both sex and power. I will never forget the words of Gwen Casados, who lost her daughter Heather to a drug overdose fourteen years and one suicide attempt after she was sexually molested as a teenager in her church choir room. "I never got her back," her mother said.[12]

The historical reality is that social systems that invest some people with power over the lives of other people result in the destruction of people. Ed Stetzer recently observed that "the Venn diagram of reformed, complementarian, and misogynist has a pretty significant overlap."[13] This sounds like what Gerda Lerner described in 1986—only her Venn diagram was the significant overlap of patriarchy with militarism, hierarchy, and racism.[14]

Isn't it time we take Dr. Switzer's advice? Isn't it time we stop an "appeal to the Bible that has awful consequences for millions of women"?[15] Isn't it time that white Christians realize that the roots of biblical womanhood extend from white supremacy? In order for early modern Europeans to biblically justify their white superiority, they had to champion the subservience of both women and Black people. As Katie Cannon explains, "Ideas and practices that favored equal rights of all people were classified as invalid and sinful because they conflicted with the divinely ordained structure that posited inequality between Whites and Blacks. . . . The institutional framework that required Black men, women and children to be treated as chattel, as possessions rather than as human beings, was understood as being consistent with the spirit, genius and precepts of the Christian faith."[16] Patriarchy walks hand in hand with racism, and it always has. The same biblical passages used to declare Black people unequal are used to declare women unfit for leadership. Patriarchy and racism are "interlocking structures of oppression."[17] Isn't it time we get rid of both?

Once again, I propose that we stop fighting to make Christianity look like the world around us and start fighting to make it look like the world God inspired Paul to show us was possible: "There is no longer Jew or Greek; there is no longer slave or free, there is no longer male and female; for all of you are one in Christ Jesus" (Galatians 3:28).

Because It Is Time to Fight Back

In July 1948, a medieval scholar and writer of detective fiction fought for women's ordination. You have already met her. Her name is Dorothy L. Sayers, and she penned a response in 1948 to her friend C. S. Lewis. Lewis, the beloved author of the Narnia books and (my personal favorite) *Surprised by Joy*, was concerned about the Church of England's movement toward ordaining women. He wrote to Sayers, asking to use her influence as a respected Christian intellectual to stand with him against female ordination. "The defence against the innovation must if possible be done by a woman," he wrote. Lewis was certain Sayers agreed with him. After all, Lewis supported women as teachers and preachers. He just drew the line at the sacramental role of the priest, and he thought a woman's voice advocating for this position would be especially useful.[18]

Sayers wouldn't do it. "I fear you would find me rather an uneasy ally," she wrote to him. "I can never find any logical or strictly theological reason against [women's ordination]. In so far as the Priest represents Christ, it is obviously more dramatically appropriate that a man should be, so to speak, cast for the part. But if I were cornered and asked point-blank whether Christ Himself is the representative of male humanity or of all humanity, I should be obliged to answer 'of all humanity'; and to cite the authority of St. Augustine for saying that woman is also made in the image of God."[19] No logical or theological reason exists to prohibit female priests (much less preachers and teachers), wrote Sayers. And so she refused Lewis's request. She refused to remain silent about her views on women, and she fought for female ordination based on the *imago Dei*.

A few hundred years before, another female writer did something similar. You have also met her already. Her name is Christine de Pizan, and she used her pen to fight against misogyny during the fifteenth century. Through an unfortunate series of events, Christine de Pizan found herself a young widow with a family to support and no money. She was a well-educated woman, thanks to her father (as women were barred from university education at this time), and she had a web of connections with the French royal court. She soon began to write professionally, first as a manuscript copyist and later as an author. She began with poetry (love ballads) and devotional religious texts. Then, in 1404, she got her big break. Philip of Burgundy commissioned her to write a biography of his brother, Charles V. The rest, as they say, is history.

Of all she has written, she is perhaps most famous for her defense of women. One of the "bestsellers" in Christine's world was a thirteenth-century text called *The Romance of the Rose* (yes, medieval people read trashy romance novels). It was an allegory about a young man questing after a rosebud (the symbolism should be clear). Although the text's original author, Guillaume de Lorris, was less hostile toward women, another author—Jean de Meun—wrote rather differently about women in the lengthy conclusion he added to the text. Indeed, Christine de Pizan regarded the poem (especially as revised by Meun) as crude, immoral, slanderous, and misogynistic. The popularity of the text made it even more appalling (sort of like how I feel about *Fifty Shades of Gray*). As Christine wrote about Jean de Meun, "He has dared to defame and blame without exception an entire sex."[20]

So Christine de Pizan fought back. She wrote a series of letters attacking the misogyny of *The Romance of the Rose.* She staked out an explicitly pro-woman position defending and empowering the female sex. She accused men of maligning and mistreating women for no good reason. She advocated for women to exercise more authority in their lives, instructing women on how to be strong and capable and even work in the world of men. She also confronted misogyny directly (such as in her later *The Book of the City of Ladies*), using her writings to try to change the prevailing negative ideas about women. While scholars disagree about how progressive (feminist) Christine actually was, they agree that Christine championed education as a path forward for women. She worked for not only better education for women themselves but also better education about the significant and often overlooked roles women have played throughout history.[21]

But why did she do this? *The Romance of the Rose* did not directly affect her. She had built a productive career, and her family was doing well. Why did she bother? Christine de Pizan realized that the battle against misogyny was bigger than her own life. The attitudes conveyed in *The Romance of the Rose* affected real women—women who might not be able to fight for themselves. Christine showed this in one of her letters against *The Romance of the Rose*, which told the story of a woman who suffered directly from the misogynistic text. She wrote,

A married man . . . believed in the *Roman de la Rose* as in the gospel. This was an extremely jealous man, who, whenever in the grip of passion, would go and find the book and read it to his wife; then he would become violent and strike her and say such horrible things as, "These are the kinds of tricks you pull

211

on me. This good, wise man Master Jean de Meun knew well what women are capable of." And at every word he finds appropriate, he gives her a couple of kicks or slaps. Thus it seems clear to me that whatever other people think of this book, this poor woman pays too high a price for it.[22]

Ideas matter. Ideas that depict women as less than men influence men to treat women as less than men. Ideas that objectify women result in women being treated like objects (sex objects, mostly). So it's not any surprise that Paige Patterson, who commented on the body of a sixteen-year-old girl to a crowd of Christians (resulting in their laughs and applause), shares the same understanding of women's roles as the Baptist churches involved in the sexual abuse of hundreds of women.[23] Christine de Pizan understood that ideas matter. She understood so well that she connected the ideas presented in a popular book to the abuse of an unnamed woman who was trapped in an abusive marriage. She fought for this woman by fighting against damaging ideas about women.

As a Christian woman who grew up in the Southern Baptist world, I agree with Christine de Pizan. She realized that at the root of abusive behavior toward women—physical, emotional, psychological, economic—lay misogynistic ideas about women. She realized that misogyny hurts all of us, whether we recognize it or not, and it especially hurts those already marginalized by economics, education, race, and even religion. Christine used what she had to fight against that misogyny; to love those whom God loves; to help make the lives of women better, even the life of that "poor woman [who] pays too high a price." Christine realized that to change the lives of women, she first had to change ideas about women.

As a pastor's wife silenced in complementarian churches for many years, I also agree with Sayers. Although her response was not quite as dramatic as Christine's attack on *The Romance of the Rose*, Sayers was just as bold. She refused to be silent. In her letter to Lewis, she refused to capitulate her convictions about women as equally made and gifted in the image of God. She actively spoke out on women's behalf, clearly stating that there was no logical or theological reason to prohibit women's ordination. She said this even when it meant challenging and possibly alienating her friend. I wish that I had had Sayers's courage earlier in my life. Both Christine and Sayers exemplify a continuity I have found in my years researching and teaching women's history: women never stop fighting to do what they believe God has called them to do.

Because It Is Time to Remember That We Do Not Stand Alone

In 1998 I bought a book I couldn't afford on my graduate stipend. But my husband had just spent $50 on a new U2 CD, so I bought my book. Edited by Beverly Mayne Kienzle and Pamela J. Walker, it is titled *Women Preachers and Prophets through Two Millennia of Christianity*. Kienzle and Walker argue that a narrow definition of preaching has obscured preaching women throughout Christian history. Yet regardless of whether the ecclesiastical establishment recognized their work, women persisted in preaching the gospel and ministering in the service of God. "The recurring presence of women's preaching attests to both the continuing struggle within Christianity over problems of authority and the indomitable spirit of women's voices," write Kienzle and Walker.[24] From Mary Magdalene to Waldensian women, Ursuline nuns, Moravian wives, Quaker sisters, Black women preachers, and suffragette activists, history shows us that women do not wait on the approval of men to do the work of God. We can hear women's voices in our Christian past, and despite all the obstacles in their way, nevertheless, "they are preaching."[25]

I have a mug in my office that bears the slogan "Write Women Back into History." My goal isn't just to change the stories I teach in my history classes, to let women know that they are just as much part of the human story as men are. My goal is also to change the future by more accurately understanding our past. What if evangelicals remembered women like Christine de Pizan and Dorothy L. Sayers? What if we remembered that women have always been leaders, teachers, and preachers, even in evangelical history? What if our seminaries used textbooks that included women? What if our Sunday school and Bible study curriculum correctly reflected Junia as an apostle, Priscilla as a coworker, and women like Hildegard of Bingen as preachers? What if we recognized women's leadership the same way Paul did throughout his letters—even entrusting the Letter to the Romans to the deacon Phoebe? What if we listened to women in our evangelical churches the way Jesus listened to women?

Women stand with a great cloud of witnesses. We always have. It is time, far past time, for us to remember.

Because It Is Time for Us to Stand Together

It was late July 2017. I stood, with my map of London, right behind Royal Albert Hall. I was looking for suffragette historical sites that I could walk to that day when I suddenly realized where I was: Royal Albert Hall is one of the most important suffrage sites in London.

Between 1908 and 1913, the hall hosted around thirty different suffrage events, including the Women's Social and Political
Union meeting in spring 1908, headed by Emmeline Pankhurst
and her daughters, Christabel, Sylvia, and Adela. As Sylvia
described the moment, "Every seat in the great Albert Hall was
sold long before the day of the event, and hundreds of people
were turned away at the doors. The vast audience was composed
almost entirely of women, and there were 200 women stewards
in white dresses."[26] Royal Albert Hall became known as the
"Temple of Liberty" for women fighting for suffrage in Britain.
Their goal was universal suffrage—for all women to have the
right to vote. Eventually, they achieved this victory, and (despite
British imperialism and imperialist attitudes among suffrage
leaders) the vote for women in Britain would include women
of color and working-class women.[27] But suffrage came slowly,
in stages. In 1918, only a limited group of women received suffrage, and it would take another ten years of fighting before
women received equal voting rights with men.[28]

In 1917, one year before women's first (partial) suffrage victory in England, the women of the Royal Albert Hall choir
performed a concert for the National Service Mass Meeting for
Women. The meeting honored women who worked in support
of the Great War (ambulance drivers, nurses, Land Army, etc.),
and it was attended by Queen Mary.[29] The choir sang a song that
would become emblematic of women's perseverance in their
fight for the vote. Indeed, the next year it was sung for the first
time (but not the last) at a suffrage demonstration.

The song was William Blake's poem "And Did Those Feet in
Ancient Time," put to music by Sir Hubert Parry and reborn
as the hymn "Jerusalem."[30] I stood on the steps of the Royal
Albert Hall in the hazy morning light. I could imagine the

words echoing throughout the curved building, filtering beyond its walls and into the streets of London.

> I will not cease from Mental Fight,
> Nor shall my Sword sleep in my hand:
> Till we have built Jerusalem,
> In Englands green & pleasant Land.[31]

I looked up at the rounded red and gold dome, rising in the still gray sky above. I knew my fight wasn't over. We still didn't know what the future held and the trauma of the past hurt every day. But my family was free. The oppressive atmosphere we had lived under was gone. I could write and teach without fear of retribution; my husband could teach and preach without fear of losing his job; our children were no longer being taught dangerous heresies about the eternal subordination of Jesus or damaging patriarchal ideas about women and men.

My daughter was free, but other women's daughters were not.

Like the suffragists still fighting in 1918 for universal women's suffrage in England, I could not cease from my Mental Fight either. I had already decided to stop being silent. Now it was time to speak loud enough for the evangelical world to hear.

Biblical womanhood is Christian patriarchy. The only reason it continues to flourish is because women and men—just like you and me—continue to support it. What if we all stopped supporting it? What if, instead of letting denominational divides and peripheral theological beliefs continue to separate us, we stood together as people of faith who believe that God has called us to change this world? Historically, one of the greatest problems for women is that we do not remember our past and we do not work together to change our future. We do not stand together. But what if we did?

What if we heeded Beth Moore's plea to grapple with the entire texts of how women are portrayed throughout the Bible—not just in a few selected Pauline texts. "Above all else," Moore writes, "we must search the attitudes & practices of Christ Jesus himself toward women. HE is our Lord. He had women followers!"[32] What if we actually did this, and refused to let 1 Corinthians 14 and 1 Timothy 2 drown out every other scriptural voice?

What if we stopped forgetting our past and remembered that women—just like us—preached their way through the landscape of Christian history? What if we remembered that we are surrounded by a cloud of female witnesses and that we will never stand alone?

What if we listened to Dorothy L. Sayers's argument that she "can never find any logical or strictly theological reason against [women's ordination]"?[33] What if we realized that God has never stopped calling women to do his work—as preachers, teachers, missionaries, evangelists, and authors? What if we realized that when we look at the whole of the global world, it simply doesn't make sense to define occupations by gender? What does make sense is Paul's reminder that all of our work is important and that by doing what we are called to do, we build up the Body of Christ together. What if we finally stood together, united by our belief in Jesus instead of divided by arguments over power and authority?

What if we followed the example of Jesus, who let Mary of Bethany sit at his feet like a male disciple and who overruled his disciples to make sure he heard the words of the woman of Canaan? What if we realized that, even when the male disciples pushed women away, Jesus always listened to women speak? Complementarianism is patriarchy, and patriarchy is about power. Neither have ever been about Jesus.

I don't remember when I started it, but for a long time now, I have been dismissing my students from class with this phrase: Go, be free! I think that is a fitting way to end this book as well.

Jesus set women free a long time ago.

Isn't it finally time for evangelical Christians to do the same? Go, be free!

Notes

Introduction

1. James Dobson, *Love for a Lifetime: Building a Marriage That Will Go the Distance* (1987; repr., Colorado Springs: Multnomah, 1998), 63. See also Kristin Kobes Du Mez, *Jesus and John Wayne: How White Evangelicals Corrupted a Faith and Fractured a Nation* (New York: Liveright, 2020), 83.

2. Elisabeth Elliot, *Let Me Be a Woman: Notes to My Daughter on the Meaning of Womanhood* (1976; repr., Carol Stream, IL: Tyndale, 2013), 50.

3. Ben Witherington stated this in a lecture he delivered at Baylor University during a symposium I helped organize with the Institute for the Study of Religion (ISR) in September 2013. It stuck with me. The symposium was titled "Women and the Bible," and it also featured Kristin Kobes Du Mez. Witherington has made this statement several times, including on his blog: Ben Witherington, "The Eternal Subordination of Christ and of Women," *Ben Witherington* (blog), March 22, 2006, http://benwitherington.blogspot .com/2006/03/eternal-subordination-of-christ-and-of.html.

4. Sarah Pulliam Bailey, "Southern Baptist Leader Paige Patterson Encouraged a Woman Not to Report Alleged Rape to Police and Told Her to Forgive Assailant, She Says," *Washington Post*, May 22, 2018, https://www.washing tonpost.com/news/acts-of-faith/wp/2018/05/22/southern-baptist-leader-enc ouraged-a-woman-not-to-report-alleged-rape-to-police-and-told-her-to-for give-assailant-she-says. Ken Camp, "Southern Baptists Deal with Fallout over Paige Patterson," *Baptist Standard*, May 25, 2018, https://www.baptiststan dard.com/news/baptists/southern-baptists-deal-fallout-paige-patterson.

5. "Read Rachael Denhollander's Full Victim Impact Statement about Larry Nassar," CNN.com, January 30, 2018, https://www.cnn.com/2018/01/24 /us/rachael-denhollander-full-statement/index.html. See also Morgan Lee's interview with Denhollander: "My Larry Nassar Testimony Went Viral. But

There's More to the Gospel Than Forgiveness," *Christianity Today*, January 31, 2018, https://www.christianitytoday.com/ct/2018/january-web-only/rach ael-denhollander-larry-nassar-forgiveness-gospel.html.

6. Ed Stetzer, "Andy Savage's Standing Ovation Was Heard Round the World. Because It Was Wrong," *Christianity Today*, January 11, 2018, https:// www.christianitytoday.com/edstetzer/2018/january/andy-savages-standing -ovation-was-heard-round-world-because.html.

7. Ruth Graham, "How a Megachurch Melts Down," *The Atlantic*, November 7, 2014, https://www.theatlantic.com/national/archive/2014/11/hous ton-mark-driscoll-megachurch-meltdown/382487.

8. Jen Pollock Michel, "God's Message to #MeToo Victims and Perpetrators," *Christianity Today*, January 18, 2018, https://www.christianity today.com/women/2018/january/gods-message-to-metoo-victims-and-perpe trators.html.

9. *Evangelical* is a contested term. While I would like to argue that *evangelical* refers primarily to shared theological beliefs—our focus on the Bible and the resurrection of Jesus as well as our emphasis on conversion and evangelism—I can't. *Evangelical* has become an identity (and mostly a white conservative identity), not just a shared set of theological beliefs. As Kristin Kobes Du Mez writes, "For conservative white evangelicals, the 'good news' of the Christian gospel has become inextricably linked to a staunch commitment to patriarchal authority, gender difference, and Christian nationalism, and all of these are intertwined with white racial identity." Du Mez, *Jesus and John Wayne*, 7. See also Thomas S. Kidd, *Who Is An Evangelical?* (New Haven: Yale University Press, 2019).

Chapter 1 The Beginning of Patriarchy

1. Owen Strachan, "Divine Order in a Chaotic Age: On Women Preaching," *Thought Life* (blog), May 7, 2019, https://www.patheos.com/blogs /thoughtlife/2019/05/divine-order-in-a-chaotic-age-on-women-preaching. The translation of Genesis 1:1 is Strachan's.

2. Russell Moore, "Feminism in Your Church and Home with Russell Moore, Randy Stinson, and C. J. Mahaney," interview by Mark Dever, 9Marks Leadership Interviews, April 30, 2007, audio, 01:05:01, quote at 30:07, https://www.9marks.org/interview/feminism-your-church-and-home -russell-moore-randy-stinson-and-cj-mahaney.

3. Russell Moore, "After Patriarchy, What? Why Egalitarians Are Winning the Gender Debate," *Journal of the Evangelical Theological Society* 49, no. 3 (September 2006): 574, https://www.etsjets.org/files/JETS-PDFs/49/49-3/JE TS_49-3_569-576_Moore.pdf.

4. Rachel Held Evans, *A Year of Biblical Womanhood* (Nashville: Nelson, 2012). I am grateful to Evans. Her voice, through her blogs and her books, was one of the first I heard that shared my growing concerns about biblical

womanhood. She passed away unexpectedly and tragically in 2019 at the age of 37.

5. Rachel Held Evans, "It's Not Complementarianism; it's Patriarchy," *Rachel Held Evans* (blog), May 3, 2012, https://rachelheldevans.com/blog/complementarians-patriarchy.

6. Owen Strachan, "Of 'Dad Moms' and 'Man Fails': An Essay on Men and Awesomeness," *Journal for Biblical Manhood and Womanhood* 17, no. 1 (Spring 2012): 25, https://cbmw.org/wp-content/uploads/2013/03/JBMW -Spring-12-Complete.pdf.

7. Judith Bennett, *History Matters: Patriarchy and the Challenge of Feminism* (Philadelphia: University of Pennsylvania Press, 2006), 55. See her full discussion of patriarchy on pp. 55–60.

8. "What Americans Think about Women in Power," Barna Group, March 8, 2017, https://www.barna.com/research/americans-think-women-power. The Barna researchers also describe "nine specific theological criteria" they used to classify respondents as evangelical.

9. Katelyn Beaty addresses how evangelical ideas about gender roles impact women's work in *A Woman's Place: A Christian Vision for Your Calling in the Office, the Home, and the World* (New York: Howard, 2016). For example, she relates how Karen Dabaghian, a computer software professional in San Francisco experiences disconnect between her work and her church: "In high-tech, nobody cares [about your gender]. . . . Then I go into this broader Christian environment, and all of a sudden, I feel gendered, in a way that is not something I am excited about" (236).

10. "Waco, TX," Data USA, accessed February 18, 2020, https://datausa .io/profile/geo/waco-tx-metro-area#economy.

11. Moore, "After Patriarchy, What?," 576; Russell Moore, "Women, Stop Submitting to Men," *Journal for Biblical Manhood and Womanhood* 17, no. 1 (Spring 2012): 9, https://cbmw.org/wp-content/uploads/2013/03/JBMW -Spring-12-Complete.pdf.

12. Russell Moore, "Is Your Marriage Baal Worship?," RussellMoore. com, September 26, 2018, https://www.russellmoore.com/2018/09/26/is-your -marriage-baal-worship. See also Russell Moore, *The Storm-Tossed Family: How the Cross Reshapes the Home* (Nashville: B&H, 2018), 82–90.

13. Moore, "Women, Stop Submitting to Men," 8–9.

14. Moore, *Storm-Tossed Family*, 84–89.

15. See Sarah Pulliam Bailey's article about Russell Moore's perspective on Beth Moore teaching and preaching: "Russell Moore, the president of the SBC's policy arm (and no relation to Beth Moore), called the recent debate over the popular Bible teacher's speaking a 'social media dustup,' not reflected in churches on Sunday mornings. He and Mohler do not advocate for women preaching in front of men, but they say there is room for disagreement among churches." Sarah Pulliam Bailey, "Southern Baptists Are Supposed to

Talk about Sexual Abuse. But Right Now They're Discussing Whether One Woman Can Preach," *Washington Post*, June 9, 2019, https://www.washing tonpost.com/religion/2019/06/09/southern-baptists-are-supposed-talk-about -sex-abuse-right-now-theyre-discussing-whether-one-woman-can-preach.

16. You can find the entire 1998 addition here: "Report of Committee on Baptist Faith and Message," Utm.edu, https://www.utm.edu/staff/caldwell /bfm/1963-1998/report1998.html. See also "Baptist Faith and Message 2000," Southern Baptist Convention, June 14, 2000, http://www.sbc.net/bfm2000 /bfm2000.asp, under the heading "XVIII. The Family."

17. Barry Hankins, *Uneasy in Babylon: Southern Baptist Conservatives and American Culture* (Tuscaloosa: University of Alabama Press, 2002), 214–15.

18. Bennett, *History Matters*, 82–107.

19. Danny P. Jackson, introduction to *The Epic of Gilgamesh*, trans. Danny P. Jackson, 2nd ed. (Wauconda, IL: Bolchazy-Carducci, 1997), xi–xii.

20. Jackson, introduction to *Epic of Gilgamesh*, xii–xvi.

21. Jackson, *Epic of Gilgamesh*, 53–54.

22. Jackson, *Epic of Gilgamesh*, 17.

23. Rivkah Harris, "Images of Women in the Gilgamesh Epic," in *Lingering over Words: Studies in Ancient Near Eastern Literature in Honor of William L. Moran*, ed. Tzvi Abusch, John Huehnergard, and Piotr Steinkeller (Atlanta: Scholars Press, 1990), 219–30.

24. Harris, "Images of Women in the Gilgamesh Epic," 220.

25. Jackson, *Epic of Gilgamesh*, 68.

26. Albert Mohler, "A Call for Courage on Biblical Manhood and Womanhood," *Albert Mohler* (blog), June 19, 2006, https://albertmohler.com/2006 /06/19/a-call-for-courage-on-biblical-manhood-and-womanhood.

27. Denny Burk (@DennyBurk), "I've noticed that in Star Wars," Twitter, December 30, 2017, 11:39 a.m., https://twitter.com/DennyBurk/status/9471 45180913729537.

28. Marten Stol, *Women in the Ancient Near East*, trans. Helen Richardson and Mervyn Richardson (Boston: de Gruyter, 2016), 691.

29. "The National Intimate Partner and Sexual Violence Survey," Centers for Disease Control and Prevention, last modified June 19, 2019, https://www .cdc.gov/violenceprevention/datasources/nisvs/index.html.

30. Hankins, *Uneasy in Babylon*, 213–15, 225. See also "Baptist Faith and Message 2000," under the heading "XVIII. The Family."

31. Hankins, *Uneasy in Babylon*, 215–16.

32. Kate Narveson, *Bible Readers and Lay Writers in Early Modern England: Gender and Self-Definition* (London: Routledge, 2016), 51–77.

33. Douay-Rheims 1899 American Edition. The Douay-Rheims is an English translation of the Latin Vulgate, first produced in 1582.

34. Alice Mathews, *Gender Roles and the People of God: Rethinking What We Were Taught about Men and Women in the Church* (Grand Rapids: Zondervan, 2017), 43–47.

35. Stanley Gundry, "From *Bobbed Hair, Bossy Wives, and Women Preachers* to *Woman Be Free*: My Story," in *How I Changed My Mind about Women in Leadership: Compelling Stories from Prominent Evangelicals*, ed. Alan F. Johnson (Grand Rapids: Zondervan, 2010), 102.

36. Quoted in Kristin Kobes Du Mez, *A New Gospel for Women: Katharine Bushnell and the Challenge of Christian Feminism* (Oxford: Oxford University Press, 2015), 120–22.

37. Du Mez, *New Gospel for Women*, 120–22.

38. Hedy Red Dexter and J. M. Lagrander, "Bible Devotionals Justify Traditional Gender Roles: A Political Agenda That Affects Social Policy," *Social Justice* 26, no. 1 (Spring 1999): 99–114.

39. James Dobson, "A New Look at Masculinity and Femininity" (brochure published by Focus on the Family, 1994), quoted in Dexter and Lagrander, "Bible Devotionals Justify Traditional Gender Roles," 107.

40. James Dobson, *Love Must Be Tough* (Waco: Word, 1983), 148. This woman wrote to Dobson for advice. A description of the woman's letter and Dobson's response is also found in the 1999 and 2007 editions of his book: *Love Must Be Tough* (Dallas: Word, 1999), 160–62; and *Love Must Be Tough* (Carol Stream, IL: Tyndale, 2007), 160–62. Kristin Kobes Du Mez writes that Dobson "recommended a healthy skepticism toward certain allegations of domestic violence." Kristin Kobes Du Mez, *Jesus and John Wayne: How White Evangelicals Corrupted a Faith and Fractured a Nation* (New York: Liveright, 2020), 144.

41. Du Mez, *Jesus and John Wayne*, 167.

42. John Piper and Wayne Grudem, eds., *Recovering Biblical Manhood and Womanhood* (1991; repr., Wheaton: Crossway, 2006), 409–10. See also Du Mez, *Jesus and John Wayne*, 167.

43. Wayne Grudem, *Systematic Theology: An Introduction to Biblical Doctrine* (Grand Rapids: Zondervan, 1994), 464.

44. Mary Stewart Van Leeuwen, a psychology and philosophy professor, provides an insightful overview of the "complementarity anxiety" of both complementarians and egalitarians in *A Sword between the Sexes? C. S. Lewis and the Gender Debates* (Grand Rapids: Brazos, 2010), 168–70.

45. Gerda Lerner, *The Creation of Patriarchy* (New York: Oxford University Press, 1986), 228–29.

46. Clarice J. Martin, "Womanist Interpretations of the New Testament: The Quest for Holistic and Inclusive Translation and Interpretation," in *I Found God in Me: A Womanist Biblical Hermeneutics Reader*, ed. Mitzi J. Smith (Eugene, OR: Cascade Books, 2015), 32.

47. Clarice J. Martin, "The *Haustafeln* (Household Codes) in Afro-American Biblical Interpretation: 'Free Slaves' and 'Subordinate Women,'" in *Stony the Road We Trod: African American Biblical Interpretation*, ed. Cain Hope Felder (Minneapolis: Fortress, 1991), 226.

48. Martin, "*Haustafeln* (Household Codes)," in Felder, *Stony the Road We Trod*, 228.

49. Merry E. Wiesner-Hanks, *Gender in History: Global Perspectives*, 2nd ed. (Malden, MA: Wiley-Blackwell, 2011), 18.

50. Mathews, *Gender Roles and the People of God*, 33.

51. Febbie C. Dickerson, "Acts 9:36–43: The Many Faces of Tabitha, a Womanist Reading," in Smith, *I Found God in Me*, 302.

52. Beth Moore (@BethMooreLPM), "What I plead for," Twitter, May 11, 2019, 9:44 a.m., https://twitter.com/bethmoorelpm/status/11272079379 09325824; Beth Moore (@BethMooreLPM), "Is to grapple with the entire text," Twitter, May 11, 2019, 9:51 a.m., https://twitter.com/bethmoorelpm /status/1127209694500671489.

53. John Piper, "Headship and Harmony," Desiring God, May 1, 1984, https://www.desiringgod.org/articles/headship-and-harmony.

54. Sarah Bessey, *Jesus Feminist: An Invitation to Revisit the Bible's View of Women* (New York: Howard, 2013), 14.

Chapter 2 What If Biblical Womanhood Doesn't Come from Paul?

1. "What Americans Think about Women in Power," Barna Group, March 8, 2017, https://www.barna.com/research/americans-think-women-power.

2. Beth Allison Barr, "No Room in Wayne Grudem's World for a Female President," *The Anxious Bench* (blog), July 31, 2016, https://www.patheos .com/blogs/anxiousbench/2016/07/wayne-grudem-donald-trump-and-the -female-elephant-in-the-room.

3. "What Americans Think about Women in Power."

4. Bruce Ware, "Summaries of the Egalitarian and Complementarian Positions," The Council on Biblical Manhood and Womanhood, June 26, 2007, https://cbmw.org/2007/06/26/summaries-of-the-egalitarian-and-com plementarian-positions.

5. Beverly Roberts Gaventa, "Gendered Bodies and the Body of Christ," in *Practicing with Paul: Reflections on Paul and the Practices of Ministry in Honor of Susan G. Eastman*, ed. Presian R. Burroughs (Eugene, OR: Cascade Books, 2018), 55.

6. Boykin Sanders, "1 Corinthians," in *True to Our Native Land: African American Biblical Interpretation*, ed. Brian K. Blount (Minneapolis: Fortress, 2007), 296.

7. I adapted this phrase from a line from Dorothy L. Sayers, who writes that "surely it is not the business of the Church to adapt Christ to men, but to adapt men to Christ." Dorothy L. Sayers, *Letters to a Diminished Church:*

Passionate Arguments for the Relevance of the Christian Doctrine (Nashville: Nelson, 2004), 20.

8. For more about *Festial*, see Beth Allison Barr, *The Pastoral Care of Women in Late Medieval England* (Woodbridge, UK: Boydell, 2008); and Beth Allison Barr and Lynneth J. Miller, "John Mirk," in *Oxford Bibliographies in Medieval Studies*, ed. Paul E. Szarmach (New York: Oxford University Press, 2018), https://www.oxfordbibliographies.com/view/document/obo-97 80195396584/obo-9780195396584-0259.xml. I also discuss this sermon in Beth Allison Barr, "Paul, Medieval Women, and Fifty Years of the CFH: New Perspectives," *Fides et Historia* 51, no. 1 (Winter/Spring 2019): 1–17.

9. All references are taken from BL MS Cotton Claudius A II. For printed editions, see John Mirk, *John Mirk's "Festial,"* ed. Susan Powell (Oxford: Oxford University Press, 2009), 2:252–56.

10. Mirk, *John Mirk's "Festial,"* 2:253–54.

11. "Baptist Faith and Message 2000," Southern Baptist Convention, June 14, 2000, http://www.sbc.net/bfm2000/bfm2000.asp, under the heading "XVIII. The Family."

12. Christine Peters, "Gender, Sacrament and Ritual: The Making and Meaning of Marriage in Late Medieval and Early Modern England," *Past & Present* 169 (November 2000). 78.

13. The marriage ceremony dictates that the groom should say, "In the name of the Father, the Son, and the Holy Ghost, with this ring I thee wed," indicating the emphasis on God first. Perhaps it is not surprising that medieval women often left their wedding rings to churches at their deaths. See Sue Niebrzydowski, *Bonoure and Buxum: A Study of Wives in Late Medieval English Literature*, vol. 2 of *Somerset Medieval Wills, Transcripts of Sussex Wills* (Oxford: Peter Lang, 2006), 87.

14. Barr, "Paul, Medieval Women," 1–17.

15. Daniel Mark Cere, "Marriage, Subordination and the Development of Christian Doctrine," in *Does Christianity Teach Male Headship? The Equal-Regard Marriage and Its Critics*, ed. David Blankenhorn, Don Browning, and Mary Stewart Van Leeuwen (Grand Rapids: Eerdmans, 2004), 110.

16. Alcuin Blamires, "Paradox in the Medieval Gender Doctrine of Head and Body," in *Medieval Theology and the Natural Body*, ed. Peter Biller and A. J. Minnis (Woodbridge, UK: York Medieval Press, 1997), 29.

17. Blamires, "Paradox in the Medieval Gender Doctrine of Head and Body," 22–23.

18. Pope John Paul II, *Mulieris Dignitatem*, 24, quoted in Cere, "Marriage, Subordination and the Development of Christian Doctrine," 110.

19. Phyllis Trible coined the phrase "texts of terror." See Phyllis Trible, *Texts of Terror: Literary-Feminist Readings of Biblical Narratives* (Philadelphia: Fortress, 1984).

20. For more in general about women in the Greco-Roman world, I recommend Sarah B. Pomeroy's books *Goddesses, Whores, Wives, and Slaves: Women in Classical Antiquity* (1975; repr., New York: Schocken, 1995) and *The Murder of Regilla: A Case of Domestic Violence in Antiquity* (Cambridge, MA: Harvard University Press, 2007). Additionally, Mary Beard's *SPQR: A History of Ancient Rome* (New York: Liveright, 2016) provides an engaging introduction to Roman history.

21. Rachel Held Evans, "Aristotle vs. Jesus: What Makes the New Testament Household Codes Different," *Rachel Held Evans* (blog), August 28, 2013, https://rachelheldevans.com/blog/aristotle-vs-jesus-what-makes-the-new-testament-household-codes-different.

22. Carolyn Osiek and Margaret MacDonald, *A Woman's Place: House Churches in Earliest Christianity* (Minneapolis: Fortress, 2006), 122–23. Osiek and MacDonald locate women's "leadership roles in early church groups" as part of a growing cultural pattern in which women were gaining more social freedoms and visibility (249).

23. Shi-Min Lu, "Woman's Role in New Testament Household Codes: Transforming First-Century Roman Culture," *Priscilla Papers* 30, no. 1 (Winter 2016): 11, https://www.cbeinternational.org/resource/article/priscilla-papers-academic-journal/womans-role-new-testament-household-codes.

24. Aristotle, *Politics*, 1259a37, in *Women's Life in Greece and Rome*, ed. Mary R. Lefkowitz and Maureen B. Fant, 4th ed. (London: Bloomsbury, 2016), 64.

25. Lucy Peppiatt, *Rediscovering Scripture's Vision for Women: Fresh Perspectives on Disputed Texts* (Downers Grove, IL: IVP Academic, 2019), 92.

26. Scot McKnight, *The Letter to the Colossians* (Grand Rapids: Eerdmans, 2018), 346.

27. Beverly Roberts Gaventa makes the same observation in her discussion of the body of Christ in 1 Corinthians 12:17–21. Gaventa, "Gendered Bodies," in Burroughs, *Practicing with Paul*, 53–54.

28. Osiek and MacDonald, *Woman's Place*, 122.

29. Ian Morris, "Remaining Invisible: The Archeology of the Excluded in Classical Athens," in *Women and Slaves in Greco-Roman Culture*, ed. Sandra R. Joshel and Sheila Murnaghan (London: Routledge, 1998), 217–20.

30. Aristotle, *Generation of Animals*, 737a, 775a, in *Woman Defamed and Woman Defended: An Anthology of Medieval Texts*, ed. Alcuin Blamires, Karen Pratt, and C. W. Marx (Oxford: Clarendon, 1992), 40–41.

31. Galen, *On the Usefulness of the Parts of the Body* II.299, in Blamires, Pratt, and Marx, *Woman Defamed and Woman Defended*, 41–42.

32. John Piper, "'The Frank and Manly Mr. Ryle'—The Value of a Masculine Ministry" (lecture, Desiring God 2012 Conference for Pastors). The entire presentation can be accessed at https://www.desiringgod.org/messages/the-frank-and-manly-mr-ryle-the-value-of-a-masculine-ministry.

33. Beverly Roberts Gaventa, *Our Mother Saint Paul* (Louisville: Westminster John Knox, 2007), 7.

34. Gaventa, *Our Mother Saint Paul*, 13–14.

35. Gaventa, *Our Mother Saint Paul*, 14.

36. Caroline Walker Bynum, *Jesus as Mother: Studies in the Spirituality of the High Middle Ages* (Berkeley: University of California Press, 1982), 112–13.

37. Quoted in Bynum, *Jesus as Mother*, 113–14.

38. Pliny, "Pliny and Trajan: Correspondence, c. 112 CE," *Ancient History Sourcebook*, last modified January 21, 2020, https://sourcebooks.fordham.edu/ancient/pliny-trajan1.asp.

39. Osiek and MacDonald, *Woman's Place*, 135.

40. John Piper and Wayne Grudem, eds., *Recovering Biblical Manhood and Womanhood* (1991; repr., Wheaton: Crossway, 2006), xv.

41. Peppiatt, *Rediscovering Scripture's Vision for Women*, 93.

42. Gaventa, "Gendered Bodies," in Burroughs, *Practicing with Paul*, 48.

43. See Evan Andrews, "Ancient Rome's Darkest Day," September 1, 2018, http://www.history.com/news/ancient-romes-darkest-day-the-battle-of-cannae. See also Titus Livy, *History of Rome*, book 34.

44. Pomeroy, *Goddesses, Whores, Wives, and Slaves*, 177–80.

45. Livy, *History of Rome*, in Lefkowitz and Fant, *Women's Life in Greece and Rome*, 171.

46. Juvenal, *Satires* 6. See Charles H. Talbert, "Biblical Criticism's Role: The Pauline View of Women as a Case in Point," in *The Unfettered Word*, ed. Robinson B. James (Waco: Word, 1987), 66.

47. Carolyn Osiek and David L. Balch, *Families in the New Testament World* (Louisville: Westminster John Knox, 1997), 103–55. See also Margaret Y. MacDonald, "Reading 1 Corinthians 7 through the Eyes of Families," in *Text, Image, and Christians in the Graeco-Roman World: A Festschrift in Honor of David Lee Balch*, ed. Aliou Niang and Carolyn Osiek, Princeton Theological Monograph Series 176 (Eugene, OR: Pickwick, 2012), 38–52.

48. Osiek and Balch, *Families in the New Testament World*, 112.

49. Lucy Peppiatt, *Women and Worship at Corinth: Paul's Rhetorical Arguments in 1 Corinthians* (Eugene, OR: Wipf & Stock, 2015), 4, 67–68.

50. Peppiatt, *Rediscovering Scripture's Vision for Women*, 142.

51. D. W. Odell-Scott, "Let the Women Speak in Church: An Egalitarian Interpretation of 1 Cor 14:33b–36," *Biblical Theology Bulletin* 13 (August 1, 1983): 90–93; Talbert, "Biblical Criticism's Role," in James, *Unfettered Word*, 62–71; see also Linda Belleville, "Women in Ministry," in *Two Views on Women in Ministry*, ed. James R. Beck and Craig L. Blomberg (Grand Rapids: Zondervan, 2001), 77–154. A plethora of scholars have supported this theory, primarily because Paul's words are so similar to Roman sources and because they do not fit with his other teachings. Other scholars point out that there is no clear indication in the text that this is a Corinthian quotation.

52. Marg Mowczko provides an accessible and well-cited scholarly overview on 1 Corinthians 14:34–35. See her blog post and bibliography: Marg Mowczko, "Interpretations and Applications of 1 Corinthians 14:34–35," *Marg Mowczko* (blog), July 9, 2011, https://margmowczko.com/interpretat ions-applications-1-cor-14_34-35.

53. Scholarship outside of complementarian circles overwhelmingly agrees that Paul is not telling all women to be silent; he is only addressing a particular problem. See Craig S. Keener, "Learning in the Assemblies: 1 Corinthians 14:34–35," in *Discovering Biblical Equality: Complementarity without Hierarchy*, ed. Ronald W. Pierce and Rebecca Merrill Groothius (Downers Grove, IL: InterVarsity, 2005), 161–71; Ben Witherington III, *Conflict and Community in Corinth: A Socio-Rhetorical Commentary on 1 and 2 Corinthians* (Grand Rapids: Eerdmans, 1995); see also Cynthia Long Westfall, *Paul and Gender: Reclaiming the Apostle's Vision for Men and Women in Christ* (Grand Rapids: Baker Academic, 2016).

54. Gaventa, "Gendered Bodies," in Burroughs, *Practicing with Paul*, 54.

55. "The good news is we can ditch Aristotle and keep Jesus," Evans wrote in her August 28, 2013, blog post, "Aristotle vs. Jesus."

56. Kevin Madigan and Carolyn Osiek, eds., *Ordained Women in the Early Church: A Documentary History* (Baltimore: Johns Hopkins University Press, 2011), 13–19.

57. *The Ryrie Study Bible* (Chicago: Moody, 1986), 1564.

58. Eldon Jay Epp, *Junia: The First Woman Apostle* (Minneapolis: Fortress, 2005), 60–65.

59. Beverly Roberts Gaventa, foreword to Epp, *Junia*, xi–xii.

60. Origen, "*Commentary on Romans* 10.17 on Romans 16:1–2," in Madigan and Osiek, *Ordained Women in the Early Church*, 14.

61. John Chrysostom, "*Homily 30* on Romans 16:1–2," in Madigan and Osiek, *Ordained Women in the Early Church*, 14–15.

62. John Chrysostom, "*Homily 11* on 1 Timothy 3:11," in Madigan and Osiek, *Ordained Women in the Early Church*, 19.

63. Madigan and Osiek, *Ordained Women in the Early Church*, 19.

64. Madigan and Osiek, *Ordained Women in the Early Church*, 205.

Chapter 3 Our Selective Medieval Memory

1. Margery Kempe, *The Book of Margery Kempe*, ed. B. A. Windeatt (New York: Penguin, 1985), 163. I discuss this incident briefly in Beth Allison Barr, "'She Hungered Right So after God's Word': Female Piety and the Legacy of the Pastoral Program in the Late Medieval English Sermons of Bodleian Library MS Greaves 54," *Journal of Religious History* 39, no. 1 (March 2015): 31–50.

2. Kempe, *Book of Margery Kempe*, 163.

3. Kempe, *Book of Margery Kempe*, 164 (italics added).

4. Kempe, *Book of Margery Kempe*, 164.

5. Kempe, *Book of Margery Kempe*, 164.

6. Kempe, *Book of Margery Kempe*, 167.

7. For more about the conjugal debt, see James Brundage, *Law, Sex, and Christian Society in Medieval Europe* (1987; repr., Chicago: University of Chicago Press, 2009), 198.

8. Kempe, *Book of Margery Kempe*, 58.

9. Isabel Davis, "Men and Margery: Negotiating Medieval Patriarchy," in *A Companion to "The Book of Margery Kempe,"* ed. John Arnold and Katherine Lewis (Cambridge: Brewer, 2004), 52.

10. Kempe, *Book of Margery Kempe*, 86–87.

11. Christine de Pizan, *The Book of the City of Ladies*, trans. Earl Jeffrey Richards (New York: Persea, 1982), 27.

12. In their introduction to *The Oxford Handbook of Women and Gender in Medieval Europe* (New York: Oxford University Press, 2013), Judith Bennett and Ruth Mazos Karras write that there was "far more flexibility and space for women within medieval Christianity than historians once imagined. In this research area, perhaps more than any other, feminist histories today speak more of opportunity and less of constraint" (13). I recommend this book in its entirety for those interested in medieval women's history.

13. Jacobus de Voragine, "The Life of Saint Paula," quoted in Larissa Tracy, *Women of the* Gilte Legende*: A Selection of Middle English Saints Lives* (Woodbridge, UK: Boydell & Brewer, 2014), 47.

14. John Mirk, *John Mirk's "Festial,"* ed. Susan Powell (Oxford: Oxford University Press, 2009), 2:181–83. Margaret's story is also told in Tracy, *Women of the* Gilte Legende, 40–44.

15. Mirk, *John Mirk's "Festial,"* 2:181–83.

16. Mirk, *John Mirk's "Festial,"* 2:182. I have modernized the text from the Middle English.

17. Mirk, *John Mirk's "Festial,"* 2:181–83.

18. Katie M. Reid, *Made Like Martha: Good News for the Woman Who Gets Things Done* (New York: WaterBrook, 2018), 5.

19. Sarah Mae, *Having a Martha Home the Mary Way: 31 Days to a Clean House and a Satisfied Soul* (Carol Stream, IL: Tyndale Momentum, 2016), 12.

20. Pope Gregory the Great preached a sermon on September 21, 591, conflating Mary Magdalene as the woman in Luke 7:36–50, John 11:1–45, and Mark 16:9. Katherine Ludwig Jansen, "Maria Magdalena: *Apostolorum Apostola*," in *Women Preachers and Prophets through Two Millennia of Christianity*, ed. Beverly Mayne Kienzle and Pamela J. Walker (Berkeley: University of California Press, 1998), 60.

21. Jansen, "Maria Magdalena," in Kienzle and Walker, *Women Preachers and Prophets*, 66.

22. Jacobus de Voragine, *The Golden Legend: Readings on the Saints*, trans. William Granger Ryan (Princeton: Princeton University Press, 2012), 409–11.

23. Tracy, *Women of the* Gilte Legende, 102.

24. Carolyn A. Muessig, "Prophecy and Song: Teaching and Preaching by Medieval Women," in Kienzle and Walker, *Women Preachers and Prophets*, 146–47.

25. Muessig, "Prophecy and Song," in Kienzle and Walker, *Women Preachers and Prophets*, 146.

26. Ben Witherington III, "Why Arguments against Women in Ministry Aren't Biblical," *The Bible & Culture* (blog), June 2, 2015, https://www.patheos.com/blogs/bibleandculture/2015/06/02/why-arguments-against-women-in-ministry-arent-biblical.

27. Jane Tibbetts Schulenburg, *Forgetful of Their Sex: Female Sanctity and Society, ca. 500–1100* (Chicago: University of Chicago Press, 2018), 186.

28. Lisa M. Bitel, *Landscape with Two Saints: How Genovefa of Paris and Brigit of Kildare Built Christianity in Barbarian Europe* (Oxford: Oxford University Press, 2009), 71.

29. Bitel, *Landscape with Two Saints*, 184.

30. Bitel, *Landscape with Two Saints*, 184.

31. Barbara Newman, *Voice of the Living Light: Hildegard of Bingen and Her World* (Berkeley: University of California Press, 1998), 20–21. Medieval clergy did invoke Paul's prohibitions, but they do not do so in the late medieval English sermons I study. Mostly, Pauline prohibitions appear in discussions of canon law and among theologians. See Jansen, "Maria Magdalena," in Kienzle and Walker, *Women Preachers and Prophets*, 67–69.

32. Elaine J. Lawless, "Introduction: The Issue of Blood—Reinstating Women into the Tradition," in Kienzle and Walker, *Women Preachers and Prophets*, 2.

33. Jacqueline Murray, "One Flesh, Two Sexes, Three Genders?," in *Gender and Christianity in Medieval Europe: New Perspectives*, ed. Lisa M. Bitel and Felice Lifshitz (Philadelphia: University of Pennsylvania Press, 2013), 40.

34. Jerome, "*Commentarius in Epistolam ad Ephesios* 3.5," quoted in Dyan Elliott, "Gender and the Christian Traditions," in Bennett and Karras, *Oxford Handbook of Women and Gender*, 24.

35. The best book on this topic is Jennifer Thibodeaux, *The Manly Priest: Clerical Celibacy, Masculinity, and Reform in England and Normandy, 1066–1300* (Philadelphia: University of Pennsylvania Press, 2015).

36. Thibodeaux, *Manly Priest*, 39.

37. Quoted in Gary Macy, *The Hidden History of Women's Ordination: Female Clergy in the Medieval West* (Oxford: Oxford University Press, 2012), 93–95. See also Alcuin Blamires, Karen Pratt, and C. W. Marx, eds., *Woman*

Defamed and Woman Defended: An Anthology of Medieval Texts (Oxford: Clarendon, 1992), 232–35.

38. Ian Forrest, "Continuity and Change in the Institutional Church," in *The Oxford Handbook of Medieval Christianity*, ed. John H. Arnold (Oxford: Oxford University Press, 2014), 192.

39. Women were not allowed to enter the cathedral or the cemetery at Durham. Dominic Marner, *St. Cuthbert: His Life and Cult in Medieval Durham* (Toronto: University of Toronto Press, 2000), 33.

40. Simeon of Durham, "A History of the Church of Durham," quoted in *Women's Lives in Medieval Europe: A Sourcebook*, ed. Emilie Amt, 2nd ed. (New York: Routledge, 2010), 191.

41. Jane Tibbetts Schulenburg, "Gender, Celibacy, and Proscriptions of Sacred Space: Symbol and Practice," in *Women's Space: Patronage, Place, and Gender in the Medieval Church*, ed. Virginia Chieffo Raguin and Sarah Stanbury (New York: SUNY Press, 2005), 189.

42. Simeon of Durham, "History of the Church of Durham," quoted in Amt, *Women's Lives in Medieval Europe*, 191.

43. De Pizan, *Book of the City of Ladies*, 219.

44. De Pizan, *Book of the City of Ladies*, 252.

45. Timothy Paul Jones, *Christian History Made Easy* (Torrance, CA: Rose, 2009), 61, 85.

46. Justo L. González, *The Story of Christianity*, vol. 1, *The Early Church to the Dawn of the Reformation* (San Francisco: HarperOne, 2010), 4.

47. González, *Story of Christianity*, 1:328.

48. Carolyn Muessig, introduction to *A Companion to Catherine of Siena*, ed. George Ferzoco, Beverly Kienzle, and Carolyn Muessig (Leiden: Brill, 2011), 18.

49. González, *Story of Christianity*, 1:399.

50. Bruce Shelley, *Church History in Plain Language*, 4th ed. (Grand Rapids: Zondervan Academic, 2013), 535–38.

Chapter 4 The Cost of the Reformation for Evangelical Women

1. Elizabeth H. Flowers, *Into the Pulpit: Southern Baptist Women and Power since World War II* (Chapel Hill: University of North Carolina Press, 2014), 130.

2. Flowers, *Into the Pulpit*, 131.

3. Quoted in Flowers, *Into the Pulpit*, 132.

4. Flowers, *Into the Pulpit*, 132–33.

5. Flowers, *Into the Pulpit*, 133.

6. Marilyn J. Westerkamp, *Women and Religion in Early America, 1600–1850: The Puritan and Evangelical Traditions* (London: Routledge, 1999), 5.

7. I recommend Jane Tibbetts Schulenburg, *Forgetful of Their Sex: Female Sanctity and Society, ca. 500–1100* (Chicago: University of Chicago Press, 2018).

8. Lyndal Roper, *The Holy Household: Women and Morals in Reformation Augsburg* (Oxford: Oxford University Press, 1991), 1–2.

9. Merry E. Wiesner-Hanks, *Gender in History: Global Perspectives*, 2nd ed. (Malden, MA: Wiley-Blackwell, 2011), 123–24.

10. Katherine L. French and Allyson M. Poska, *Women and Gender in the Western Past* (Boston: Houghton Mifflin, 2007), 1:219.

11. Susan C. Karant-Nunn and Merry E. Wiesner-Hanks, *Luther on Women: A Sourcebook* (Cambridge: Cambridge University Press, 2003), 177.

12. Kirsi Stjerna, *Women and the Reformation* (Malden, MA: Blackwell, 2009), 51–70.

13. Judith M. Bennett, *Ale, Beer, and Brewsters in England: Women's Work in a Changing World, 1300–1600* (New York: Oxford University Press, 1996), 146.

14. Bennett, *Ale, Beer, and Brewsters in England*, 149.

15. Wayne Watson, "Somewhere in the World," Spotify, track 6 on *Giants in the Land*, World Entertainment, 1985.

16. Yusufu Turaki, "Marriage and Sexual Morality," ESV.org, https://www.esv.org/resources/esv-global-study-bible/marriage-and-sexual-morality.

17. Katelyn Beaty, *A Woman's Place: A Christian Vision for Your Calling in the Office, the Home, and the World* (New York: Howard, 2016), 109.

18. Andrea L. Turpin, "All the Single Ladies in the Church," *The Anxious Bench* (blog), January 8, 2020, https://www.patheos.com/blogs/anxiousbench/2020/01/all-the-single-ladies-in-the-church.

19. Virginia Woolf, *A Room of One's Own* (New York: Harcourt, Brace, 1929).

20. Margaret Bendroth, *Fundamentalism and Gender, 1875 to the Present* (New Haven: Yale University Press, 1993), 88–89.

21. Merry E. Wiesner-Hanks, *Women and Gender in Early Modern Europe*, 3rd ed. (Cambridge: Cambridge University Press, 2008), 216.

22. Argula von Grumbach, *A Woman's Voice in the Reformation*, ed. Peter Matheson (Edinburgh: T&T Clark, 1995), 90.

23. Wiesner-Hanks, *Women and Gender in Early Modern Europe*, 216.

24. *Writings of Edward the Sixth: William Hugh, Queen Catherine Parr, Anne Askew, Lady Zane Grey, Hamilton, and Balnaves* (London: Religions Tract Society, 1836), 12.

25. Wiesner-Hanks, *Women and Gender in Early Modern Europe*, 217.

26. Quoted in Wiesner-Hanks, *Women and Gender in Early Modern Europe*, 281.

27. Nicole Beriou, "The Right of Women to Give Religious Instruction in the Thirteenth Century," in *Women Preachers and Prophets through Two*

Millennia of Christianity, ed. Beverly Mayne Kienzle and Pamela J. Walker (Berkeley: University of California Press, 1998), 138–39.

28. R. N. Swanson, *Religion and Devotion in Europe* (Cambridge: Cambridge University Press, 1995), 304.

29. I expand on this argument here: Beth Allison Barr, "Paul, Medieval Women, and Fifty Years of the CFH: New Perspectives," *Fides et Historia* 51, no. 1 (Winter/Spring 2019): 1–17.

30. Lancelot Andrewes, *Apospasmatia Sacra; or, A Collection of Posthumous and Orphan Lectures Delivered at St. Paul's and St. Giles His Church by the Right Honourable Reverend Father in God, Lancelot Andrewes* (London: R. Hodgkinsonne, 1657), 235 (italics added).

31. Isaac Marlow, *A Brief Discourse concerning Singing in the Public Worship of God in the Gospel-Church* (London: n.p., 1690), 21, quoted in Beth Allison Barr, "Women in Early Baptist Sermons: A Late Medieval Perspective," *Perspectives in Religious Studies* 41, no. 1 (2014), 13–29. I expand on my Pauline argument in this article too.

32. Benjamin Keach, *An Answer to Mr. Marlow's Appendix* (London: n.p., 1691), 34–35. Fellow minister Hanserd Knollys also rejected Marlow's interpretation. As Knollys responded, "Women have the Essence of Singing (*as well as Men*) both in their Souls, and with their Voices; and are allowed to speak by all the Churches of Saints." Hanserd Knollys, *An Answer to a Brief Discourse concerning Singing in the Publick Worship of God in the Gospel-Church by I. M. 1690* (London: n.p., 1691), 11–12.

33. Quoted in Wiesner-Hanks, *Women and Gender in Early Modern Europe*, 281.

34. Beth Allison Barr, "'She Hungered Right So after God's Word': Female Piety and the Legacy of the Pastoral Program in the Late Medieval English Sermons of Bodleian Library MS Greaves 54," *Journal of Religious History* 39, no 1 (March 2015): 31–50.

35. Roper, *Holy Household*, 2.

36. Ann Eljenholm Nichols, *Seeable Signs: The Iconography of the Seven Sacraments, 1350–1544* (Woodbridge, UK: Boydell & Brewer, 1997).

37. Groups existed for all women, not just wives, though wives are the subject of French's observation here. Katherine L. French, *The Good Women of the Parish: Gender and Religion after the Black Death* (Philadelphia: University of Pennsylvania Press, 2008), 156.

38. French, *Good Women of the Parish*, 221.

39. Beth Allison Barr, "'He Is Bothyn Modyr, Broþyr, & Syster vn-to Me': Women and the Bible in Late Medieval and Early Modern English Sermons," *Church History and Religious Culture* 94, no 3 (Summer 2014): 297–315.

40. French, *Good Women of the Parish*, 226–27, 230.

41. French, *Good Women of the Parish*, 230.

Chapter 5 Writing Women Out of the English Bible

1. Aimee Byrd has an excellent chapter discussing the impact of gendering Bible translations in her book *Recovering from Biblical Manhood and Womanhood: How the Church Needs to Rediscover Her Purpose* (Grand Rapids: Zondervan Reflective, 2020), 31–48.

2. Susan Olasky, "Femme Fatale: The Feminist Seduction of the Evangelical Church," *World* 12, no. 2 (March 29, 1997): 12–15, https://world.wng .org/1997/03/femme_fatale.

3. Susan Olasky, "The Battle for the Bible," *World* 12, no. 5 (April 19, 1997): 14–18, https://world.wng.org/1997/04/the_battle_for_the_bible.

4. Wayne Grudem, "What's Wrong with 'Gender-Neutral' Bible Translations?" (pamphlet, The Council on Biblical Manhood and Womanhood, Libertyville, IL, 1997), 27, http://www.waynegrudem.com/wp-content/up loads/2012/03/What-s-Wrong-with-Gender-Neutral-Bible-Translations.pdf.

5. "Colorado Springs Guidelines for Translation of Gender-Related Language in Scripture," Bible Research, September 9, 1997, http://www.bible -researcher.com/csguidelines.html.

6. "Resolution on Bible Translation," Southern Baptist Convention, Dallas, TX, 1997, http://www.sbc.net/resolutions/284/resolution-on-bible-trans lation.

7. Wayne Grudem, "The 'Gender-Neutral' NIV: What Is the Controversy About?," *Journal of Biblical Manhood and Womanhood* 7, no. 1 (Spring 2002): 37.

8. Art Toalston, "James Dobson Joins Critics of Gender-Neutral NIV Revision," *Baptist Press*, February 6, 2002, http://www.bpnews.net/12684/ja mes-dobson-joins-critics-of-genderneutral-niv-revision.

9. David Bayly, "Decline of the NIV?," *World* 14, no. 22 (June 5, 1999), https://world.wng.org/1999/06/decline_of_the_niv.

10. The ESV website gives a sampling of these endorsements, including from John Piper, R. C. Sproul, Joni Eareckson Tada, and Steve Green. See "Endorsements," ESV.org, https://www.esv.org/translation/endorsements.

11. Taken directly from the inscription inside the church of St. Magnus the Martyr.

12. Beryl Smalley, *The Study of the Bible in the Middle Ages* (1964; repr., Notre Dame, IN: University of Notre Dame Press, 1978), xxvii.

13. Frans van Liere, *An Introduction to the Medieval Bible* (Cambridge: Cambridge University Press, 2014), 189.

14. Henry Ansgar Kelly, *The Middle English Bible: A Reassessment* (Philadelphia: University of Pennsylvania Press, 2016), 67.

15. Kelly, *Middle English Bible*, 130.

16. Stephen Morrison, ed., *A Late Fifteenth-Century Dominical Sermon Cycle*, 2 vols. (Oxford: Oxford University Press, 2012), 1:xxi–liii.

17. Kelly, *Middle English Bible*, 63.

18. James H. Morey, *Book and Verse: A Guide to Middle English Biblical Literature* (Champaign: University of Illinois Press), 2000.

19. "Class 5: The High Middle Ages," Capitol Hill Baptist Church, June 24, 2016, https://www.capitolhillbaptist.org/sermon/class-5-the-high-middle -ages.

20. See Class 6 and Class 7, which focus on Martin Luther, John Calvin, and Huldrych Zwingli, https://www.capitolhillbaptist.org/resources/core -seminars/series/church-history.

21. Van Liere, *Introduction to the Medieval Bible*, 178.

22. Larissa Taylor, *Soldiers of Christ: Preaching in Late Medieval and Reformation France* (New York: Oxford University Press, 1992), 4; Beverly Kienzle, *The Sermon* (Turnhout, Belgium: Brepols, 2000), 143.

23. Beth Allison Barr, "Medieval Sermons and Audience Appeal after the Black Death," *History Compass* 16, no 9 (2018): 2–3, https://doi.org/10.1111 /hic3.12478.

24. Grudem, "'Gender-Neutral' NIV," 37.

25. Vern S. Poythress, "Small Changes in Meaning Can Matter: The Un- acceptability of the TNIV," *Journal of Biblical Manhood and Womanhood* 10, no. 2 (Fall 2005): 28–34.

26. Poythress, "Small Changes in Meaning Can Matter," 28.

27. Richard S. Hess, "Splitting the Adam: The Usage of *'adam* in Gen- esis i-v," in *Studies in the Pentateuch*, ed. J. A. Emerton (Leiden: Brill, 1991), 1–15. Beth Allison Barr, "Words That Matter: The Significance of 'Good Men and Women,'" in *The Pastoral Care of Women in Late Medieval England* (Woodbridge, UK: Boydell, 2008), 36–42.

28. Salisbury Cathedral MS 3, folio 54v.

29. Bodleian Library MS Greaves 54, folio 35v. See further discussion and examples in Beth Allison Barr, "'He Is Bothyn Modyr, Broþyr, & Syster vn-to Me': Women and the Bible in Late Medieval and Early Modern English Ser- mons," *Church History and Religious Culture* 94, no. 3 (Summer 2014): 306.

30. Morrison, *Late Fifteenth-Century Dominical Sermon Cycle*, 1:348–54. Barr, "'He Is Bothyn Modyr, Broþyr, & Syster vn-to Me,'" 306–7.

31. Bart Ehrman, *Whose Word Is It? The Story behind Who Changed the New Testament and Why* (New York: Continuum, 2006), 55.

32. Linda Woodbridge quotes this gloss in her *English Revenge Drama: Money, Resistance, Equality* (Cambridge: Cambridge University Press, 2010), 149.

33. Maurice S. Betteridge, "The Bitter Notes: The Geneva Bible and Its Annotations," *The Sixteenth Century Journal* 14, no. 1 (Spring 1983): 41–62.

34. Femke Molekamp, "Genevan Legacies: The Making of the English Geneva Bible," in *The Oxford Handbook of the Bible in Early Modern En- gland, 1350–1700*, ed. Kevin Killeen, Helen Smith, and Rachel Willie (Oxford: Oxford University Press, 2015), 52.

35. For more on this topic, see my annotated bibliography on KJV scholarship: Beth Allison Barr, "The Word That Endureth Forever: A Century of Scholarship on the King James Version," in *The King James Bible and the World It Made*, ed. David Lyle Jeffrey (Waco: Baylor University Press, 2011), 149–76.

36. David Crystal, *Begat: The King James Bible and the English Language* (Oxford: Oxford University Press, 2010), 110–11, 237, 32, 86, 258 (page numbers refer to each quotation respectively).

37. Dorothy L. Sayers, *Are Women Human? Penetrating, Sensible, and Witty Essays on the Role of Women in Society* (1971; repr., Grand Rapids: Eerdmans, 2005), 53–54.

38. Hilda L. Smith, *All Men and Both Sexes: Gender, Politics, and the False Universal in England, 1640–1832* (University Park: Pennsylvania State University Press, 2002), 198–200.

39. William Gouge, "VIII. Duties of Masters," in *Of Domesticall Duties: Eight Treatises* (1622; repr., Ann Arbor: Text Creation Partnership, 2011), A2r–A5r, http://name.umdl.umich.edu/A68107.0001.001. He explains his choice at the end of the introduction. I discuss Gouge in my article "'He Is Bothyn Modyr, Broþyr, & Syster vn-to Me,'" 307–8.

40. Gouge, *Of Domesticall Duties*, A2r–A5r.

41. Lucy Peppiatt, *Rediscovering Scripture's Vision for Women: Fresh Perspectives on Disputed Texts* (Downers Grove, IL: IVP Academic, 2019), 132–34.

42. Peppiatt, *Rediscovering Scripture's Vision for Women*, 139.

43. Rodney Stark, "Reconstructing the Rise of Christianity: The Role of Women," *Sociology of Religion* 56, no. 3 (1995): 238, quoted in Peppiatt, *Rediscovering Scripture's Vision for Women*, 134.

44. Naomi Tadmor, *The Social Universe of the English Bible: Scripture, Society, and Culture in Early Modern England* (Cambridge: Cambridge University Press, 2010), 58–67. I also discuss this in my 2014 article "'He Is Bothyn Modyr, Broþyr, & Syster vn-to Me,'" 304, 313.

45. Tadmor, *Social Universe of the English Bible*, 67.

46. Tadmor, *Social Universe of the English Bible*, 67–68.

47. Tadmor, *Social Universe of the English Bible*, 58–59.

Chapter 6 Sanctifying Subordination

1. *Speculum Sacerdotale: Edited from British Museum MS. Additional 36791*, ed. E. H. Weatherly (London: Oxford University Press, 1936), 128.

2. James Brundage, *Law, Sex, and Christian Society in Medieval Europe* (1987; repr., Chicago: University of Chicago Press, 2009), 198, 241–42.

3. Marilyn J. Westerkamp, *Women and Religion in Early America, 1600–1850: The Puritan and Evangelical Traditions* (New York: Routledge, 1999), 131–33.

4. Westerkamp, *Women and Religion in Early America*, 4–5.

5. Merry E. Wiesner-Hanks, *Gender in History: Global Perspectives*, 2nd ed. (Malden, MA: Wiley-Blackwell, 2011), 123.

6. Lynn Abrams, *The Making of Modern Woman: Europe, 1789–1918* (New York: Longman, 2002), 43.

7. Margaret Bendroth, *Fundamentalism and Gender, 1875 to the Present* (New Haven: Yale University Press, 1993), 69.

8. Abrams, *Making of Modern Woman*, 157.

9. Catherine A. Brekus, *Strangers and Pilgrims: Female Preaching in America, 1740–1845* (Chapel Hill: University of North Carolina Press, 2000), 153.

10. Abrams, *Making of Modern Woman*, 48.

11. Abrams, *Making of Modern Woman*, 48.

12. John MacArthur said this to Beth Moore when speaking at a Truth Matters conference in 2019. The podcast highlighting this can be found here: "John MacArthur's Truth Matters Conference: SBC Meltdown," October 20, 2019, in *The Reformed Rant* podcast, Stitcher, 51:08, https://www.stitcher.com/podcast/the-reformed-rant/e/64717094?autoplay=true.

13. Katherine L. French and Allyson M. Poska, *Women and Gender in the Western Past* (Boston: Houghton Mifflin, 2007), 2:262.

14. French and Poska, *Women and Gender in the Western Past*, 2:263.

15. Jean-Jacques Rousseau, *Emile* (London: Dent, 1948), 349. See also Abrams, *Making of Modern Woman*, 45–46.

16. Quoted in French and Poska, *Women and Gender in the Western Past*, 2:314. See also 262–63.

17. French and Poska, *Women and Gender in the Western Past*, 2:297.

18. Quoted in Joyce Burnette, *Gender, Work and Wages in Industrial Revolution Britain* (Cambridge: Cambridge University Press, 2008), 134.

19. Quoted in French and Poska, *Women and Gender in the Western Past*, 2:309–10.

20. Quoted in Barbara Welter, "The Cult of True Womanhood," *American Quarterly* 18, no. 2 (1966): 151–74.

21. French and Poska, *Women and Gender in the Western Past*, 2:313–14.

22. Judith Bennett, *History Matters: Patriarchy and the Challenge of Feminism* (Philadelphia: University of Pennsylvania Press, 2006), 54.

23. Kate Bowler, *The Preacher's Wife: The Precarious Power of Evangelical Women Celebrities* (Princeton: Princeton University Press, 2019), 172–73.

24. Bowler, *Preacher's Wife*, 14.

25. Brekus, *Strangers and Pilgrims*, 152.

26. Brekus, *Strangers and Pilgrims*, 341.

27. Brekus, *Strangers and Pilgrims*, 340.

28. Randall Balmer, "American Fundamentalism: The Ideal of Femininity," in *Fundamentalism and Gender*, ed. John Stratton Hawley (New York: Oxford University Press, 1994), 55.

29. P. J. Tibayan, "Seeing Jesus on the Stage of Marriage," in *Happily Ever After: Finding Grace in the Messes of Marriage* (Minneapolis: Cruciform, 2016), 5.

30. Quoted in Abrams, *Making of Modern Woman*, 29.

31. Shari Puterman, "Meet the Transformed Wife, Whose 'Working Mom' Chart Rocked the World," *Daily Advertiser*, December 23, 2018, https://www.theadvertiser.com/story/life/allthemoms/2018/12/17/story-behind-transformed-wifes-working-moms-chart/2317019002. See also *The Transformed Wife* blog at https://thetransformedwife.com.

32. "What Americans Think about Women in Power," Barna Group, March 8, 2017, https://www.barna.com/research/americans-think-women-power.

Chapter 7 Making Biblical Womanhood Gospel Truth

1. Russell D. Moore, "After Patriarchy, What? Why Egalitarians Are Winning the Gender Debate," *Journal of the Evangelical Theological Society* 49, no. 3 (September 2006): 572, https://www.etsjets.org/files/JETS-PDFs/49/49-3/JETS_49-3_569-576_Moore.pdf.

2. Moore, "After Patriarchy, What?," 571.

3. Moore, "After Patriarchy, What?," 569, 576.

4. The collection for First Baptist Church Elm Mott is still unprocessed, but the documents can be found in the Texas Collection Archives at Baylor University. Some of the historical notes of the church have been preserved in Hay Battaile's "A History of First Baptist Church of Elm Mott, Elm Mott, Texas, 1879–1979," 1979, Elm Mott First Baptist Church Records, The Texas Collection, Baylor University. The records pertaining to Mrs. Lewis Ball can be found on pages 10–11, although the handwritten secretary notes contain much more detail. The following quotations are from these records.

5. Elm Mott First Baptist Church Records, The Texas Collection, Baylor University.

6. Carol Ann Vaughn, "Baptist Women: Ordination within the Historical SBC," God, Faith, Media, September 12, 2000, https://goodfaithmedia.org/baptist-women-ordination-within-the-historical-sbc-cms-414; Harry N. Hollis Jr., *Christian Freedom for Women and Other Human Beings* (Nashville: Broadman, 1974).

7. Charles Deweese, *Women Deacons and Deaconesses: 400 Years of Baptist Service* (Macon, GA: Mercer University Press, 2005), 11.

8. *The Broadman Bible Commentary*, vol. 10, *Acts–1 Corinthians* (London: Marshall, Morgan & Scott, 1971). See the discussion of Romans 16.

9. Timothy Larsen, "Evangelicalism's Strong History of Women in Ministry," *Reformed Journal* 5, no. 32 (September/October 2017), https://reformedjournal.com/evangelicalisms-strong-history-women-ministry.

10. Larsen, "Evangelicalism's Strong History."

11. Larsen, "Evangelicalism's Strong History."

12. Wayne Grudem, "Women Pastors: Not the 'Path to Blessing,'" interview by Laura Sheahen, Beliefnet, October 2006, https://www.beliefnet.com/faiths/christianity/2006/10/women-pastors-not-the-path-to-blessing.aspx.

13. Grudem, "Women Pastors."

14. Larsen, "Evangelicalism's Strong History."

15. Bettye Collier-Thomas, *Daughters of Thunder: Black Women Preachers and Their Sermons, 1850–1979* (San Francisco: Jossey-Bass, 1998).

16. Collier-Thomas, *Daughters of Thunder*, 91.

17. Collier-Thomas, *Daughters of Thunder*, 153–54.

18. Florence Spearing Randolph, "If I Were White," in Collier-Thomas, *Daughters of Thunder*, 128–29; John Piper, "Can a Woman Preach if Elders Affirm It?," February 6, 2015, in *Ask Pastor John* podcast, Desiring God, https://www.desiringgod.org/interviews/can-a-woman-preach-if-elders-affirm-it; Mary A. Kassian, "Women Teaching Men—How Far Is Too Far?," Desiring God, May 21, 2016, https://www.desiringgod.org/articles/women-teaching-men-how-far-is-too-far.

19. Quoted in Curtis Freeman, *A Company of Women Preachers: Baptist Prophetesses in Seventeenth-Century England* (Waco: Baylor University Press, 2011), 608, 610.

20. Hanserd Knollys, introduction to *A Christian Woman's Experiences of the Glorious Working of God's Free Grace*, by Katherine Sutton (Rotterdam: Henry Goddæus, 1663; Rochester, NY: American Baptist Historical Society, 1981), quoted in Freeman, *Company of Women Preachers*, 592. I also discuss Sutton in my article "Women in Early Baptist Sermons: A Late Medieval Perspective," *Perspectives in Religious Studies* 41, no. 1 (2014): 13–29.

21. Jacqueline Murray, "One Flesh, Two Sexes, Three Genders?," in *Gender and Christianity in Medieval Europe: New Perspectives*, ed. Lisa M. Bitel and Felice Lifshitz (Philadelphia: University of Pennsylvania Press, 2013), 49.

22. Kathleen Blumreich, ed., *The Middle English "Mirror": An Edition Based on Bodleian Library MS Holkham Misc. 40* (Tempe, AZ: Arizona Center for Medieval and Renaissance Studies, 2002), 86 (see also 82–87). I have modernized the Middle English in this and following quotations.

23. Kathleen Blumreich, "'I Ne Sey Noght Is in Despyt of Women'": Antifeminism in Robert de Gretham's *Mirror*," *Medieval Feminist Forum: A Journal of Gender and Sexuality* 38, no. 1 (2004): 42.

24. Geoffrey Chaucer, *The Riverside Chaucer*, ed. Larry D. Benson, 3rd ed. (Boston: Houghton Mifflin, 1987), 262–69.

25. Karen Winstead, *Chaste Passions: Medieval English Virgin Martyr Legends* (Ithaca, NY: Cornell University Press, 2000). As she writes, "Some readers may be offended at the glib tone and coarse language that characterize so many of the texts; few will expect saints—especially female saints—to swear like sailors. One of the principal lessons that those who consider the

sacred and the profane dichotomous can learn from these stories is how integral the profane was to medieval sacred culture" (5).

26. Blumreich, *Middle English "Mirror,"* 87.

27. Winstead, *Chaste Passions*, 53–54.

28. Winstead, *Chaste Passions*, 49–60.

29. Marilyn J. Westerkamp, *Women and Religion in Early America, 1600–1850: The Puritan and Evangelical Traditions* (New York: Routledge, 1999), 180.

30. Jemar Tisby, *The Color of Compromise: The Truth about the American Church's Complicity in Racism* (Grand Rapids: Zondervan Reflective, 2019), 19.

31. Coventry Patmore, *The Angel in the House* (London: Cassell & Company, 1887). The phrase "angel in the house" describes the ideal Victorian woman: a loving (and submissive) wife and mother who was dedicated to her home.

32. Dorothy L. Sayers, "Are Women Human?," in *Are Women Human? Penetrating, Sensible, and Witty Essays on the Role of Women in Society* (1971; repr., Grand Rapids: Eerdmans, 2005), 49.

33. See Margaret Bendroth, *Fundamentalism and Gender, 1875 to the Present* (New Haven: Yale University Press, 1993), and George Marsden, *Fundamentalism and American Culture*, 2nd ed. (New York: Oxford University Press, 2006).

34. Bendroth, *Fundamentalism and Gender*, 33.

35. Inerrancy is not quite this simple. There are different types of inerrantists, as Barry Hankins explains in *Uneasy in Babylon: Southern Baptist Conservatives and American Culture* (Tuscaloosa: University of Alabama Press, 2002), 4–5. But in my Southern Baptist world, inerrancy was a zero-sum game. Hankins writes, "Used in populist fashion, as it was during the SBC controversy, it simply means that the Bible is without error in all matters on which it touches, including science and history" (4).

36. Hankins, *Uneasy in Babylon*, 5.

37. Bendroth, *Fundamentalism and Gender*, 36.

38. See, for example, John R. Rice, *Bobbed Hair, Bossy Wives, and Women Preachers: Significant Questions for Honest Christian Women Settled by the Word of God* (Murfreesboro, TN: Sword of the Lord, 1941), 14–15. For more on the connection between inerrancy and gender, see Bendroth, *Fundamentalism and Gender*, 34–36, and Kristin Kobes Du Mez, *Jesus and John Wayne: How White Evangelicals Corrupted a Faith and Fractured a Nation* (New York: Liveright, 2020), 108–9.

39. Quoted in Bendroth, *Fundamentalism and Gender*, 36.

40. Du Mez, *Jesus and John Wayne*, 108–9.

41. As Kevin Giles writes, "This is the center of Athanasius's argument in the opening chapter in *Four Orations Against the Arians*." Kevin Giles, *The*

Trinity and Subordinationism: The Doctrine of God and the Contemporary Gender Debate (Downers Grove, IL: InterVarsity, 2002), 41n37.

42. Katherine L. French and Allyson M. Poska, *Women and Gender in the Western Past* (Boston: Houghton Mifflin, 2007), 2:519.

43. Mary Stewart Van Leeuwen, *A Sword between the Sexes? C. S. Lewis and the Gender Debates* (Grand Rapids: Brazos, 2010), 70–87.

44. Giles, *Trinity and Subordinationism*, 21–28.

45. Bruce Ware, *Big Truths for Young Hearts: Teaching and Learning the Greatness of God* (Wheaton, IL: Crossway, 2009), 55–56.

46. Aimee Byrd, *Recovering from Biblical Manhood and Womanhood: How the Church Needs to Rediscover Her Purpose* (Grand Rapids: Zondervan Reflective, 2020), 100.

47. Byrd, *Recovering from Biblical Manhood and Womanhood*, 101.

48. Phillip Cary, "The New Evangelical Subordinationism: Reading Inequality into the Trinity," in *The New Evangelical Subordinationism? Perspectives on the Equality of God the Father and God the Son*, ed. Dennis W. Jowers and H. Wayne House (Eugene, OR: Pickwick, 2012), 1, quoted in Van Leeuwen, *Sword between the Sexes?*, 80.

49. Giles, *Trinity and Subordinationism*, 41.

50. Giles, *Trinity and Subordinationism*, 43–52.

51. Giles, *Trinity and Subordinationism*, 15.

52. Giles, *Trinity and Subordinationism*, 109–12. Giles contends that evangelicals have done exactly what Karl Barth argued is the most common cause of theological error—moved analogically from "fallen human relations to divine relations" instead of the other way around (110).

53. Judith M. Bennett and Sandy Bardsley, *Medieval Europe: A Short History*, 12th ed. (New York: Oxford University Press, 2020), 47.

54. R. P. C. Hanson, *The Search for the Christian Doctrine of God: The Arian Controversy, 318–381* (London: T&T Clark, 2005), 122.

55. Byrd, *Recovering from Biblical Manhood and Womanhood*, 101.

56. Lynne Hybels, *Nice Girls Don't Change the World* (Grand Rapids: Zondervan, 2005), 24.

57. "Baptist Faith and Message 2000," Southern Baptist Convention, June 14, 2000, http://www.sbc.net/bfm2000/bfm2000.asp, under the heading "XVIII. The Family."

58. "Foundational Documents: Confessional Statement," The Gospel Coalition, https://www.thegospelcoalition.org/about/foundation-docume nts/#confessional-statement.

59. Denny Burk, "How Complementarianism Is a Gospel Issue," *Denny Burk* (blog), August 16, 2012, https://www.dennyburk.com/why-complemen tarianism-is-a-gospel-issue.

Chapter 8 Isn't It Time to Set Women Free?

1. Alyssa Milano (@Alyssa_Milano), "If you've been sexually harassed or assaulted," Twitter, October 15, 2017, 4:21 p.m., https://twitter.com/Alyssa_Milano/status/919659438700670976.

2. Beth Allison Barr (@bethallisonbarr), "#Me Too: Thanks @kkdumez," Twitter, October 19, 2017, 10:04 a.m., https://twitter.com/bethallisonbarr/status/921014090197291008.

3. Kristin Kobes Du Mez, *Jesus and John Wayne: How White Evangelicals Corrupted a Faith and Fractured a Nation* (New York: Liveright, 2020), 76. Du Mez explains the rise of Bill Gothard, including the early scandals in his ministry, on pp. 74–78.

4. Kate Bowler, *The Preacher's Wife: The Precarious Power of Evangelical Women Celebrities* (Princeton: Princeton University Press, 2019), ix.

5. Matt Mencarini, "The Sacrifice," *Courier Journal*, September 4, 2019, https://www.courier-journal.com/in-depth/news/2019/09/04/rachael-den hollander-sacrifice-continues-after-accusing-usa-gymnastics-larry-nassar/19 19109001.

6. Bob Newhart, "Stop It!," Mad TV, season 6, episode 24, aired May 12, 2001, YouTube video, 6:04 at 3:07, https://www.youtube.com/watch?v=4BjKS1-vjPs.

7. Du Mez, *Jesus and John Wayne*, 292–94.

8. Du Mez, *Jesus and John Wayne*, 282–83.

9. Du Mez, *Jesus and John Wayne*, 279–80.

10. Robert Downen, Lise Olsen, and John Tedesco, "Abuse of Faith," *Houston Chronicle*, February 10, 2019, https://www.houstonchronicle.com/news/investigations/article/Southern-Baptist-sexual-abuse-spreads-as-lead ers-13588038.php.

11. Du Mez, *Jesus and John Wayne*, 294.

12. Downen, Olsen, and Tedesco, "Abuse of Faith."

13. Ed Stetzer, "Complementarians in Closed Rooms," The Exchange, *Christianity Today*, June 19, 2020, https://www.christianitytoday.com/edstet zer/2020/june/complementarians-closed-rooms-aimee-byrd-beth-moore.html.

14. Gerda Lerner, *The Creation of Patriarchy* (New York: Oxford University Press, 1986), 229.

15. Kevin Giles, "Complementarian Theology in Crisis," in *Eyes to See and Ears to Hear Women: Sexual Assault as a Crisis of Evangelical Theology*, ed. Tim Krueger (Minneapolis: CBE International, 2018), 60, https://www.cbeinternational.org/resource/article/complementarian-theology-crisis.

16. Katie Geneva Cannon, "Slave Ideology and Biblical Interpretation," in *Katie's Canon: Womanism and the Soul of the Black Community* (New York: Continuum, 1995), 41.

17. Mitzi J. Smith, "'This Little Light of Mine': The Womanist Biblical Scholar as Prophetess, Iconoclast, and Activist," in *I Found God in Me: A*

Womanist Biblical Hermeneutics Reader, ed. Mitzi J. Smith (Eugene, OR: Cascade Books, 2015), 111.

18. Mary Stewart Van Leeuwen, *A Sword between the Sexes? C. S. Lewis and the Gender Debates* (Grand Rapids: Brazos, 2010), 80–81.

19. Van Leeuwen, *Sword between the Sexes?*, 80–81.

20. Christine de Pizan, *The Book of the City of Ladies*, trans. Earl Jeffrey Richards (New York: Persea, 1982), 3–5. See also Roberta Krueger, "Towards Feminism: Christine de Pizan, Female Advocacy, and Women's Textual Communities in the Late Middle Ages and Beyond," in Judith Bennett and Ruth Mazos Karras, *The Oxford Handbook of Women and Gender in Medieval Europe* (New York: Oxford University Press, 2013), 590–606.

21. Krueger, "Towards Feminism," in Bennett and Karras, *Oxford Handbook of Women and Gender*, 598–601.

22. Quoted in Carolyn Dinshaw, *Chaucer's Sexual Poetics* (Madison: University of Wisconsin Press, 1989), 130.

23. Du Mez, *Jesus and John Wayne*, 289–90. See also Jesse Carey, "Paige Patterson Made Some Really Creepy Comments about a 16-Year-Old Girl When He Was President of the SBC," *Relevant Magazine*, May 2, 2018, https://relevantmagazine.com/god/church/paige-patterson-made-really-creepy-comments-16-year-old-girl-president-sbc.

24. Beverly Mayne Kienzle and Pamela J. Walker, eds., *Women Preachers and Prophets through Two Millennia of Christianity* (Berkeley: University of California Press, 1998), xiv.

25. Darleen Pryds, "Proclaiming Sanctity through Proscribed Acts: The Case of Rose of Viterbo," in Kienzle and Walker, *Women Preachers and Prophets*, 166.

26. E. Sylvia Pankhurst, *The Suffragette: The History of the Women's Militant Suffrage Movement, 1905–1910* (New York: Sturgis & Walton, 1911), 209. See also Laura E. Nym Mayhall, *The Militant Suffrage Movement: Citizenship and Resistance in Britain, 1860–1930* (New York: Oxford University Press, 2003). See also the Royal Albert Hall website: https://www.royalalberthall.com.

27. For more about suffrage and race in Britain, see Ian Christopher Fletcher, Laura E. Nym Mayhall, and Philippa Levine, eds., *Women's Suffrage in the British Empire: Citizenship, Nation and Race* (New York: Routledge, 2000).

28. Timothy Larsen reminds us that "the provisions of the bill deliberately made the qualifications for women more restrictive than those for men to ensure that women did not become the majority of voters." Timothy Larsen, *Christabel Pankhurst: Fundamentalism and Feminism in Coalition* (Woodbridge, UK: Boydell, 2002), 9n20.

29. "Her Majesty and the Women's National Service Movement," *The Illustrated London News*, March 24, 1917, https://babel.hathitrust.org/cgi/pt?id=njp.32101059281764&view=1up&seq=359.

30. Martin Clayton and Bennett Zon, eds., *Music and Orientalism in the British Empire, 1780s–1940s: Portrayal of the East* (New York: Routledge, 2016), 99–100. "Jerusalem" is still sung the last night of the Proms at Royal Albert Hall.

31. William Blake, "And Did Those Feet in Ancient Time," in *English Romantic Poetry: An Anthology*, ed. Stanley Appelbaum (Mineola, NY: Dover, 1996), 22.

32. Beth Moore (@BethMooreLPM), "Is to grapple with the entire text," Twitter, May 11, 2019, 9:51 a.m., https://twitter.com/bethmoorelpm/status/1127209694500671489; Beth Moore (@bethmoorelpm), "Above all else," Twitter, May 11, 2019, 9:57 a.m., https://twitter.com/bethmoorelpm/status/1127211070811197440.

33. Van Leeuwen, *Sword between the Sexes?*, 80.

Author Bio

BETH ALLISON BARR (PhD, University of North Carolina at Chapel Hill) is associate professor of history and associate dean of the Graduate School at Baylor University. Her academic specialties include European women, medieval and early modern England, and church history. She has previously served as president of the Texas Medieval Association and the Conference on Faith and History. She is a pastor's wife and mother of two and lives in Waco, Texas.

Previous Books by Beth Allison Barr

The Pastoral Care of Women in Late Medieval England
The Acts of the Apostles: Four Centuries of Baptist Interpretation (co-editor)
Faith and History: A Devotional (co-editor)